D1600905

Don Quijote
Across Four Centuries

Don Quijote Across Four Centuries

Papers from the Seventeenth
Southern California Cervantes Symposium,
UCLA, 7-9 April 2005

Edited by

CARROLL B. JOHNSON

Juan de la Cuesta

Newark, Delaware

The text of Ilan Stavans' Spanglish translation of *Don Quijote* I,1 accompanying the article by James Iffland is reprinted from *Spanglish: The Making of a New American Language*. New York: Rayo/HarperCollins, 2003. Used by permission of the publisher.

Copyright © 2006 by Juan de la Cuesta — Hispanic Monographs
270 Indian Road
Newark, Delaware 19711
(302) 453-8695
Fax: (302) 453-8601
www.JuandelaCuesta.com

MANUFACTURED IN THE UNITED STATES OF AMERICA

ISBN: 1-58871-088-2

Table of Contents

The Symposium and the Cervantes Society of America

JAMES A. PARR

I THINK IT IS fair to say that there is considerable linkage between our symposium and the Cervantes Society of America. Allow me to elaborate on that statement.

Obviously, several of us are active on both fronts, and occasionally the two entities overlap and even coalesce, as happened when Carroll Johnson hosted both groups simultaneously a few years ago on this same campus. Although the CSA was launched first, our symposium is by no means a spin-off of the larger group. The symposium is autonomous and ordinarily does not coordinate its activities with the Society.

The Cervantes Society of America finds its origins in sessions held in 1977 at Fordham, in the northeast, and in 1978 at Pomona College, in the southwest. So, in a very real sense, the CSA is a spin-off of our little band of Cervantistas in tandem with like-minded folk on the east coast. Let me quote from Patricia Kenworthy's "The Cervantes Society of America: A Brief History":

> At the Fordham Cervantes Conference in December 1977, the gathered scholars proposed the creation of a society for those interested in the life of Miguel de Cervantes. On the West Coast, Professor Michael McGaha discussed the idea with the participants at the Pomona Conference on 'Cervantes and the Renaissance.' It was agreed that Professor Leo J. Hoar would call the first organizational meeting at Fordham and that these deliberations would provide a model for further development at Pomona. (*Cervantes* 1 [Fall 1981]: 7-8)

Very much involved in the formative phase of the Cervantes Society

7

were Michael McGaha, John J. Allen, and Leo Hoar, who constituted the committee to draft the constitution. These three were ably assisted by Luis Murillo and Elias Rivers, according to Kenworthy's brief history. Professor Murillo, more than anyone, has been, in addition, the prime mover behind our symposium, initiated in 1989. It is doubtful that we would be experiencing now the 17th edition were it not for Luis Murillo's efforts, always outside the limelight but focused and essential to our success and continuity.

Our group has provided the CSA with three presidents and one editor of the journal *Cervantes*. Juan Bautista Avalle-Arce was the first president of the organization, and Carroll B. Johnson has served recently in that same capacity. Michael McGaha performed admirably as editor for an extended period.

To conclude, the histories of the symposium and the society have been inextricably intertwined from the beginnings of both. This is so, largely because of the personalities involved, who have for many years worn two hats, while pledging allegiance to both groups—a situation analogous, perhaps, to enjoying dual citizenship. The symposium is largely an accident of geography and serendipity. The Cervantes Society, however, is a more carefully conceived and organized entity, with a much wider reach and scope. Like several here present, I am privileged to have played a supporting role in both. It was my pleasure to organize the first of these symposia in 1989, at the University of Southern California, to honor a distinguished alumnus of that institution, Luis Murillo. There was no awareness on my part then that the symposium might take on a life of its own, but it is gratifying to see that things have developed in that way.

PRESIDENT, CERVANTES SOCIETY OF AMERICA

En pos de la creación cervantina: el *Quijote*, "libro de entretenimiento"

AUGUSTIN REDONDO

DESDE UN PRINCIPIO HEMOS de advertir que, como se está celebrando el cuarto centenario de la publicación del *Quijote* de 1605, centraremos nuestras observaciones en este libro, aunque también podamos referirnos, de paso, al de 1615. De todas formas, es en el texto de 1605 en que Cervantes encuentra la fórmula de una nueva creación literaria que ha de perfeccionar en la segunda parte.

Por razones que ignoramos, *El ingenioso hidalgo don Quixote de la Mancha* sale sin las acostumbradas aprobaciones (a diferencia de lo que ha de pasar con la obra de 1615). Esta ausencia es de lamentar pues dichos textos nos proporcionan con frecuencia una serie de informaciones sobre la lectura hecha por los censores acerca del libro de que se trata.

Sin embargo, las aprobaciones del segundo *Quijote* permiten aclarar varios aspectos de esa lectura.

Pero, antes de ir más allá, es necesario dejar sentado que es el propio Cervantes el que reivindica la unidad profunda que existe entre el texto de 1605 y el de 1615, pues en el "prólogo al lector" que encabeza este último, indica de manera significativa: "...quiero [...] advertirte que consideres que esta segunda parte de *Don Quijote* es cortada del mismo artífice y del mismo paño que la primera" (II, p. 37).[1]

Es de observar que los censores de 1615 caracterizan la segunda parte de la obra como "libro de mucho entretenimiento" (Doctor Gutierre de Cetina) y "de honesta recreación y apacible divertimiento" (Maestro Joseph de Valdivielso).

---

[1] Como en nuestros trabajos anteriores, seguiremos utilizando la ed. del *Quijote* hecha por Luis Andrés Murillo.

9

Dicho de otra manera, el *Quijote* es un "libro de entretenimiento."
Si no olvidamos que el término *novela* para designar a un relato de
ficción largo es una creación muy posterior, ya que este término, a principios
del siglo XVII, no se emplea sino para caracterizar las narraciones cortas al
itálico modo y luego, a partir de las cervantinas *Novelas ejemplares* publica-
das en 1613, para referirse a su versión castellana, según el modelo ideado
por el manco de Lepanto, bien se comprenderá que estamos frente a un tipo
específico de relato.

Efectivamente, el vocablo "libro" es un vocablo abierto, que sirve para
referirse a diversos tipos de narración caracterizados por el determinativo
que los acompaña: "libros de pastores," "libros de caballerías," "libros de
entretenimiento," etc.

Por lo que hace a esta última expresión, corresponde a un concepto
nuevo, que no aparece en ninguno de los tratados de los preceptistas, por
ejemplo en la *Philosophía antigua poética* del aristotélico López Pinciano,
publicada en 1596.[2]

El término "entretenimiento" es muy revelador. Como lo dice Covarrubias, en su *Tesoro* de 1611, "entretenimiento [es] cualquier cosa que divierta
y entretenga al hombre."[3] La red semántica salta a la vista y remite a lo que
decía el Maestro Valdivieldo cuando hablaba de *recreación* y de *divertimiento*
(o diversión). Se trata pues de un *pasatiempo agradable* y es de notar que en
el *Quijote* la palabra *pasatiempo* va generalmente unida a un vocabulario
significativo: *gusto, burla, risa, contento.*[4]

Así pues la orientación festiva de los libros de entretenimiento se halla
subrayada.

Esto ha de relacionarse con el cambio de atmósfera que corresponde a
los primeros años del siglo XVII, después de la muerte del severo Felipe II.
La Corte vuelve a descubrir entonces el poder de la risa liberadora y los
cortesanos se sumen en una serie de fiestas y mascaradas en que reinan el
gozo y la alegría. Es como si los cortesanos quisieran olvidar la grave crisis
que corroe los reinos de España y, paralelamente, como si desearan alejarse
del Escorial y de todo lo que había representado. La Corte se instala pues en

---

[2] Hemos empleado la ed. del texto realizada en 1953 por Alfredo Carballo
Picazo.

[3] Véase Sebastián de Covarrubias, *Tesoro...*, entrada "entretener," p. 526a.

[4] Véanse las diversas referencias a *pasatiempo* en las concordancias del *Quijote*
que acompañan la ed. coordinada por Francisco Rico.

Valladolid donde permanece entre 1601 y 1606 y se "carnavaliza."[5] Es entonces cuando, en consonancia con esta atmósfera de diversión, tan bien evocada por el portugués Tomé Pinheiro da Veiga en su *Fastiginia*[6] redactada por estos años, salen varios libros de entretenimiento, apareciendo directamente la expresión en algunos de ellos, como el *Libro de entretenimiento de La Pícara Justina*, publicado en 1605, o los *Diálogos de apacible entretenimiento* de Gaspar Lucas Hidalgo, del mismo año. Esta orientación es también la que tiene *El Buscón* de Quevedo (1ª redacción: 1604-1605) y sobre todo el *Quijote*.

El narrador bien subraya todo lo dicho, al empezar el capítulo 28 de la primera parte de la obra:

> ...*gozamos* ahora, en nuestra edad, *necesitada de alegres entretenimientos,* no sólo de la dulzura de su *verdadera historia* [de don Quijote], sino de los *cuentos* y *episodios* della, que, en parte, no son menos *agradables* y *verdaderos* que la misma historia..." (I, 28, p. 344)

De tal modo se pone de relieve la adecuación del texto al festivo momento histórico en que sale. Además se insiste sobre la orientación jocosa del libro y sobre el gozo provocado por su lectura, así como sobre los diversos elementos de que se compone y también sobre el juego que existe entre la verdad de la narración y el arte/artificio que da la posibilidad de agradar al lector, en conformidad con el horizonte de expectativas (para decirlo con las palabras de Hans Robert Jauss) y ello, gracias a la capacidad de invención de quien se definiría como "raro inventor."

Por otra parte, lo que llama la atención en todos estos libros de entretenimiento es que, con relación a la época precedente, se invierten las perspectivas: lo que se afirma como la finalidad primera ahora es el gozo, la diversión. Esto no quiere decir que la doctrina esté ausente, sino que viene a tener una menor importancia que el deleite y la risa. Bien lo dice Cervantes al final del prólogo al lector del *Quijote* de 1605 cuando subraya que lo que desea es que al leer la historia, "el melancólico se mueva a risa, el risueño la acreciente" (I, p. 58).

"Libro de entretetenimiento" y pues libro divertido, alegre, eso es el *Quijote* en primer lugar, y así lo recibieron sus lectores del siglo XVII, lo que

---

[5] Véase nuestro libro, *Otra manera de leer el "Quijote,"* pp. 60-61, 205-206, etc.
[6] Véase Tomé Pinheiro da Veiga, *Fastiginia*, pp. 19 y sigs.

no impide otros niveles de lectura ni la profunda meditación que "el que ahondare más," según la expresión del autor del *Lazarillo*, pueda llevar a cabo acerca del texto.

Pero, a pesar de que la noción de "libro" remite a una estructura abierta, que suscita el *experimento*, fuera de los cánones de los clásicos, ¿cuál es la orientación tomada por las narraciones de entretetenimiento o las reflexiones que éstas han podido suscitar en los que han escrito sobre el tema, entre los contemporáneos de Cervantes?

Desde este punto de vista, quisiéramos llamar la atención sobre dos textos que nos parecen muy significativos.[7]

El primero se titula *Honesto y agradable entretenimiento de Damas y Galanes*, y es una traducción/adaptación al castellano por Francisco Truchado de los célebres relatos de Gian Francesco Straparola di Caravaggio (*Le Piacevoli Notti*). La primera parte de este texto se publica en 1580 y la segunda en 1581, pero la obra goza de varias ediciones, en particular de una que encierra las dos partes, en 1598, y luego de otra similar, en 1612. Los dos volúmenes, de manera independiente o reunidos, tuvieron buena aceptación y se publicaron con un parecer muy favorable de Juan López de Hoyos, el maestro que fue de Cervantes.[8] Y precisamente, al evocar las condiciones en que se han de elaborar las narraciones ante un círculo de oyentes (damas y galanes)—lo que no deja de hacer pensar en el *Decamerón*—se evoca el tiempo predilecto de estas reuniones, el de *Carnaval*, en que abundan los juegos, las invenciones y bailes "y otros entretenimientos alegres," como la dulce conversación, el narrar cuentos, o por mejor decir fábulas, y también enigmas.[9] El ambiente jocoso de esos días de Carnestolendas, con sus diversas actividades, se halla de tal modo integrado al texto y corre a lo largo de la obra. Esta orientación del relato de entretenimiento, vinculado

---

[7] Sobre el particular, véase también nuestro estudio, "El *Persiles*, 'libro de entretenimiento' peregrino."

[8] Por lo que hace a la primera parte del libro, hemos utilizado la ed. de Granada, 1582 y, por lo que atañe a la segunda, la ed. princeps de Baeza, 1581. El parecer de Juan López de Hoyos, de Madrid, 9 de julio de 1581, figura al final de la *Segunda parte del honesto y agradable entretenimiento*, fol. 270 r°-271r°. Escribe por ejemplo: "Él corresponde con su título: porque es un jardín de honestas fictiones ejemplares y de buen discurso [...]. No hallo en él cosa que no sea muy gustosa e de buen ingenio..."

[9] Véase *Honesto y agradable entretenimiento de Damas y Galanes*, [1ᵃparte], fol. 11v°-12v°.

a la tradición carnavalesca, en particular por lo que hace al juego con el mundo al revés y a la utilización de la parodia, han de recuperarla los libros a los cuales nos hemos referido, que salen en ese año 1605, o que se idean entonces. Entre ellos está el *Quijote*.

El otro texto que deseamos alegar es el del mercedario Alonso Remón, publicado en 1623, bajo el título de *Entretenimientos y juegos honestos y recreaciones cristianas*.

El autor delinea el campo que corresponde al entretenimiento, al evocar los pasatiempos correspondientes: conversar, referir cuentos o casos sucedidos, decir donaires y jugar. Esto está en consonancia con lo indicado en el texto precedente y asimismo con las orientaciones del *Quijote*, lo que corresponde a esa exaltación que se hace en el texto cervantino de la "sabrosa conversación," del placer de decir y de escuchar cuentos, fábulas o ficciones o también del manejo del donaire muchas veces unido al brío y al gozo, todo ello en una atmósfera lúdica, lo que proporciona "mucho gusto y pasatiempo."[10] De ahí, paralelamente, la importancia que cobran palabras reveladoras: *alegría, contento, regocijo, fiesta, burla.*

Fray Alonso Remón caracteriza también las particularidades de esas manifestaciones de la recreación, insistiendo en unas cuantas modalidades de la manera de narrar, valorando *la invención, la novedad, la variedad, el ingenio.*[11]

Esta línea es, del mismo modo, la que sigue Cervantes en la historia del hidalgo manchego.

Ya se comprenderá mejor por qué se puede calificar al libro cervantino de "libro de entretenimiento."

Quisiéramos volver ahora sobre algunas de las peculiaridades señaladas, poniendo de relieve cómo la parodia permite una descodificación de la literatura contemporánea de la obra, en particular de la caballeresca, ya que el *Quijote*, como se ha escrito, es el "libro de los libros," para permitir luego una recodificación del conjunto y la emergencia de una nueva poética.

No obstante, no tenemos que olvidar que, para que la parodia — imitación degradada, burlesca, de un texto noble o serio — pueda surtir efecto, el receptor ha de tener presente al referente de que se trata. Dicho de otra manera, y ya que el *Quijote* es primero una "invectiva contra los libros de caballerías," según dice el autor en el prólogo de 1605, no hay que perder

---

[10] Véase *Entretenimientos y juegos honestos...*, fol. 498b.
[11] *Ibid.*, fol. 16 r°.

de vista que el *Quijote* es, a su modo, un "libro de caballerías" y que el conocimiento de la literatura caballeresca corre a lo largo de la obra. En especial es lo que ocurre con el *Amadís* y su continuación el *Esplandián*, a pesar de que, en el famoso escrutinio del capítulo 6, a éste último se le rechaza, si bien se acepta al primero (I, 6, pp. 110-112). Pero este conocimiento es mucho más extenso y abarca a las diversas modalidades literarias.

* * *

El *Quijote* de 1605 aparece, de buenas a primeras, como un libro insólito. Todo deja pensar que se trata de materia caballeresca, pero los "libros de caballerías" se presentan como volúmenes en folio generalmente e impresos a dos columnas, en letra gótica. Además la portada integra en una viñeta a un caballero joven, brioso, con un casco muy emplumado, empuñando una espada y montado en un caballo tan brioso como él. Aquí, nada de eso. El libro es un impreso en cuarto sin columnas y con tipos más modernos. Además, no aparece ninguna representación heróica, sino la marca tipográfica del impresor. Es necesario añadir que si los héroes de la materia caballeresca llevan nombres rimbonbantes, que remiten también a países más o menos lejanos que huelen a exotismo (Amadís de Gaula, Lisuarte de Grecia, Palmerín de Inglaterra, etc.), aquí el nombre del personaje no puede ser más zafio y degradado, unido además a la zona más rústica de España, con una alusión tal vez a la mácula, relacionada con una posible falta de limpieza de sangre del protagonista.[12] Por otra parte, al personaje que da su nombre al libro, se le califica de *zote* es decir de "muy torpe," mientras que se dice que es un "*ingenioso* hidalgo," lo que constituye una doble paradoja, tanto por lo que hace al apelativo como a esa extraña unión y a lo que implica entonces el estatus del hidalgo, quien puede no ser noble, porque además, su "don" es postizo a todas luces.[13]

La orientación festiva de la obra aparece pues desde la portada del libro y el lector ya sabe que está en plena parodia con relación a los "libros de caballerías."

Paralelamente, la estructura misma del *Quijote* de 1605 evoca la del *Amadís*, dado que, como éste, se compone de cuatro partes o libros (recuérdese que en el célebre escrutinio de la biblioteca del protagonista se

---

[12] Véase nuestro estudio "Acerca de la portada de la primera parte del *Quijote*."
[13] *Ibid.*, pp. 528-531.

habla de *Los cuatro [libros] de Amadís de Gaula)*. Las aventuras de Amadís, ha de proseguirlas su hijo, Esplandián. Se trata de *Las sergas de Esplandián*, viniendo a ser éstas la quinta parte de *Amadís de Gaula*. En efecto, del *Esplandián* se dice en el *Quijote* que es "hijo legítimo de Amadís de Gaula" (I, 6, p. 111) como si se asistiera a un verdadero engendramiento de los "libros de caballerías" a partir del primer progenitor, del fundador del linaje. En el caso de la obra cervantina, las cosas no pueden sino ir por otro camino. En efecto, el *Quijote* de 1615 hubiera tenido que ser, remedando lo que había pasado con el *Amadís* y el *Esplandián*, el quinto libro o la quinta parte de *Don Quijote de la Mancha*, pero ello resulta imposible ya que el hidalgo no podía engendrar a ningún hijo que prosiguiera sus aventuras. Es que, como se indica en el prólogo de 1605, el protagonista fue "el más casto enamorado [...] que de muchos años a esta parte se vio en aquellos contornos" (I, p. 58). El autor hablará pues de "segunda parte" y el héroe de esta segunda parte será otra vez el caballero manchego, especie de engendramiento, de duplicación de sí mismo, pero una duplicación más elaborada, capaz de contemplar no al padre de la parte anterior sino a otro personaje, semejante a lo que él es y también diferente de él. La cosa llega a tanto que, como en un verdadero juego de espejos, se manifiesta asimismo en la segunda parte otro don Quijote —el apócrifo— parecido en algo al auténtico y profundamente diferente de él al mismo tiempo (II, 52 y II, 72).

La dimensión paródica se confirma cuando el lector se da cuenta de que el paratexto encierra diversas poesías tanto de cabo roto como sonetos, por ejemplo, que proyectan una mirada burlona sobre el hidalgo y sus aventuras, así como sobre los otros protagonistas (incluyendo a Dulcinea) y sobre sus monturas. Se trata de un juego intertextual tanto con los "libros de caballerías" como con la literatura contemporánea, en particular con otro "libro de entretenimiento" que acaba de salir, el de *La Pícara Justina* .[14]

Esa corriente se halla ampliada cuando el receptor llega al prólogo. Éste empieza de una manera también insólita, que invierte todas las perspectivas. Bien sabido es que, según el canon de los prólogos, el lector al cual se dirige el autor y cuya benevolencia desea captar aparece como "lector prudente," "lector discreto," etc., lo que pone de realce la inteligente capacidad lectora del receptor. En el *Quijote* de 1605, nada de eso, sino un "desocupado lector" y "desocupado" es sinónimo de "ocioso" como el mismo texto cervantino

---

[14] Sobre este aspecto de la relación entre *La Pícara Justina* y el *Quijote*, véase Marcel Bataillon, *Pícaros y picaresca*, pp. 80-86.

lo subraya al hablar de los "ratos ociosos y desocupados" (II, 40, p. 343).[15] Toda la ideología de la Contrarreforma embiste contra la ociosidad (el ocio)[16] que es madre de todos los vicios y contraria a la vida de la república. No por nada salen en época de Felipe II y Felipe III varias pragmáticas y cédulas que embisten contra los "ociosos, vagabundos y mal entretenidos,"[17] lo que no deja de unir en la misma reprobación la ociosidad y el entretenimiento, aun cuando se hable del mal entretenimiento. Resulta muy significativo el que en 1600 Gaspar Gutiérrez de los Ríos, en un libro sobre la estimación de las artes, dedique varias páginas a embestir "Contra los ociosos." No vacila en escribir que:

"la ociosidad es el mismo vicio e injusticia, escuela e oficina de maldades con que se pierde el alma, el cuerpo, los Reynos y la República."[18]

Dando un paso más, afirma: "El ocioso imposible es que sea prudente [...]. Con la ociosidad se entorpece la memoria, el ingenio y la parte superior

---

[15] Véase también: "...para honesto pasatiempo, no solamente de los *ociosos*, sino también de los más *ocupados*" (I, 48, p. 572). Para Covarrubias, las cosas están tan claras como para Cervantes, ya que indica: "*desocupado*, el que no tiene que entender" (*Tesoro...*, p. 461a) y acerca de *entender*, afirma: "entender en algo es trabajar" (*ibid.*, p. 523a). Paralelamente, dice que "el *ocioso* [es] el que no se ocupa en cosa alguna" (p. 835a). De ahí que escriba en la entrada "ocupar": "*desocupado, el ocioso*" (p. 835a).

[16] Covarrubias señala: "*Ocio*: no es tan usado vocablo como ociosidad" (*Tesoro...*, p. 835a).

[17] Por lo que hace a las decisiones del poder, en 1566 y 1601, por ejemplo, véase Faustino Gil Ayuso, *Noticia bibliográfica de textos y disposiciones legales...*, nᵒˢ 270 y 531. El 9 de mayo de 1609, Luis Cabrera de Córdoba apunta significativamente lo siguiente: "Para el buen gobierno y policía de la Corte, se ha despachado cédula de S. M. [...] para limpiar la Corte de los mal entretenidos y vagamundos y gente de mal vivir..." (*Relaciones...*, pp. 368-369). Posteriormente, ya en 1745, se publicará una "Ordenanza de S. M. contra los ociosos, vagabundos y mal entretenidos" (Antonio Palau y Dulcet, *Manual del librero hispanoamericano*, t. XI, nᵒ 203269). El problema de la ociosidad unida al vagabundeo está relacionado con el gran debate qui tiene vigencia en el Siglo de Oro sobre la pobreza, la mendicidad y el trabajo, valiéndose de la distinción fundamental entre "pobres legítimos" y "pobres fingidos". Para una visión de conjunto sobre el particular, véase la introducción de Michel Cavillac a su ed. de Cristóbal Pérez de Herrera, *Amparo de pobres*.

[18] Véase Gaspar Gutiérrez de los Ríos, *Noticia general para la estimación de las artes...*, p. 273. Recuérdese que, poco después, en 1603, Francisco de Luque Fajardo publica su *Fiel desengaño contra la ociosidad y los juegos*.

de la razón, con las demás potencias y sentidos."[19]

Lo que en tiempos anteriores fue una de las características indispensables de la creación, ese *otium*, exaltado en particular por los humanistas del Renacimiento (por un Ángel Policiano, un Marsilio Ficino o un Pico de la Mirándola, por ejemplo)[20] se pone ahora en tela de juicio.

Esa "ociosa lectura de los libros de caballerías" tan censurada en el texto ,[21] y asimismo en los versos de cabo roto preliminares, los que se atribuyen a Urganda la Desconocida, en que se afirma que "ociosas letu- / trastornaron la cabe-" (I, p. 60) del hidalgo manchego, vienen a valorarse con cierta ironía en este principio de prólogo, el cual implica también al lector. Nótese que la palabra *ocioso* aparece bajo la pluma de Cervantes para caracterizar, en efecto, a la inactividad del protagonista: "los ratos que estaba *ocioso* que eran los más del año se daba a leer libros de caballerías " (I, 1, p. 71). No es pues extraño que, como lo indicaba Gutiérrez de los Ríos, a don Quijote se le entorpeciera la parte superior de la razón, es decir se volviera loco.

No obstante, ese "desocupado lector" bien es simétrico de don Quijote. Éste es un melancólico, según la teoría de los humores, y ocupa sus continuos ocios no sólo en leer y en soñar su vida, a partir de los "libros de caballerías," sino también en hacer acto creador, en conformidad con esa tradición, respaldada por la autoridad de Aristóteles, que hacía de los creadores unos melancólicos.[22] El hidalgo manchego tiene la tentación de terminar la historia de *Belianís de Grecia* (I, 1, p. 73) y asimismo, en dos ocasiones, escribe unas brillantes páginas de "libros de caballerías," después del episodio del yelmo de Mambrino (I, 21, pp. 258-261) y cuando está conversando con el canónigo (I, 50, pp. 584-586), sin dejar de imaginar el principio de la crónica de sus aventuras (I, 1, p. 80).[23]

Ese ocioso lector a quien Cervantes otorga una suprema autonomía, al dejarle libre de opinar como lo desea sobre la historia, implicándole directamente en el relato (I, p. 51), se transforma en cierto modo en otro

---

[19] Véase G. Gutiérrez de los Ríos, *Noticia general para la estimación de las artes...*, pp. 273-274.

[20] Véase Raymond Klibansky, Erwin Panofsky y Fritz Saxl, *Saturne et la Mélancolie*, pp. 392 y sigs.

[21] Véase, por ejemplo: I, 49, p. 577.

[22] Véase nuestro libro, *Otra manera de leer el "Quijote,"* I, 4: "La melancolía y el *Quijote* de 1605," pp. 121-146.

[23] *Ibid.*, pp. 136-137 y 140.

creador.

Por fin el propio autor, aparece en ese prólogo como otro ocioso melancólico, que está esperando la inspiración creadora, en la actitud misma que corresponde a la representación de la Melancolía, en el conocido grabado de Durero.[24]

De tal modo se establecen vínculos privilegiados entre el lector, el autor y el protagonista. Es como si ese juego de espejos al cual hemos aludido ya multiplicara la misma figura básica, la de Cervantes, por una parte como lector, por otra como personaje. Gracias a la parodia inicial, el célebre manco está reconstruyendo de otra manera, a nivel del prólogo, el problema de la narración y de sus características, está echando las bases de otro discurso poético.

Por otra parte, esa duplicación del autor en el prólogo bajo la forma del melancólico (él mismo) y del gracioso (el amigo) nos adentra también en otra de las dimensiones del texto, la que corresponde a la aparición de los dos personajes clave: el melancólico y cuaresmal don Quijote, el Caballero de la Triste Figura, y el risueño y carnavalesco Sancho. Es decir que ya está presente toda la construcción de la obra alrededor de los dos protagonistas. Además, tal tipo de duplicación y de proyección nos sume en las profundidades de la elaboración cervantina de los protagonistas, como si gracias al espejo deformante de la parodia, el Cervantes que se mira en él se difractara bajo la forma del flaco y del gordo, lo que enlaza también con diversas tradiciones sobre las cuales volveremos.

Burla burlando, estamos así en el centro mismo de la creación cervantina.

Basta con empezar la lectura del libro de 1605 para darse cuenta hasta qué punto se están invirtiendo de nuevo todas las perspectivas.

Conocidas son las características del hidalgo, de ese hombre ya entrado en años, seco de carnes, enjuto de rostro y, como se nos dirá posteriormente, largo, flaco, tendido, amarillo, lo que dibuja ya esa silueta alargada e insólita del personaje que ha de quedar en la retina de los lectores hasta llegar a la bella evocación de Ortega y Gasset, quien lo representa como un punto interrogativo sobre la llanura manchega.[25] Además, sin nombre averiguado,

---

[24] *Ibid.*, pp. 133-134. Véase también Javier García Gibert, *Cervantes y la Melancolía.* Sobre el tema de la Melancolía, de manera general, y sobre sus representaciones, cfr. R. Klibansky, E. Panofsky y F. SAXL, *Saturne et la Mélancolie.*

[25] Véase José Ortega y Gasset, *Meditaciones del "Quijote,"* p. 58.

sin raíces, con un estatus incierto, viene a ser una verdadera parodia de los jóvenes y briosos héroes de los "libros de caballerías," hijos de reyes y príncipes, unidos a un linaje y a un espacio precisos.

Sin embargo, al negarle la pertenencia a un solar, al situarlo en un lugar de cuyo nombre no quiere acordarse, el autor le libera de los vínculos acostumbrados de los personajes, le confiere una libertad de destino que ha de transformar profundamente su recorrido vital. Paralelamente, esa negación del espacio, desliga en cierto modo al protagonista del encuadre tópico de las narraciones caballerescas pero asimismo del de otro tipo de relato, muy en boga en el momento en que sale el *Quijote*, el de la picaresca, y más directamente del *Guzmán de Alfarache*, obra que el creador considera de manera crítica como puede percibirse en diversos trozos del texto y especialmente en el episodio de Ginés de Pasamonte (I, 22, pp. 271-273).[26]

El espacio de la obra cervantina no es pues el de las olorosas florestas ni el de los castillos de los "libros de caballerías," sino el del campo manchego, de la Sierra Morena y de las ventas. Tampoco es el espacio ampliamente urbano de los libros picarescos.

El espacio del *Quijote* se abre a la libertad de los protagonistas. El lector vislumbra entonces esos caminos manchegos quemados por el sol que, sin embargo, como lo apuntará Gustave Flaubert posteriormente, no se hallan descritos en el texto.[27] También se empapa del frescor de esas umbrías tan garcilasianas donde corre el agua, evocadas en unos cuantos pasajes de la obra. A partir de un detalle y de manera indirecta, Cervantes le comunica así al texto un poder de evocación, de sugerencia de sensaciones íntimas asimiladas por el lector (en particular visuales y olfativas) que es uno de los encantos de la creación cervantina.

De la misma manera, con los protagonistas penetra en esas ventas, paródicas de los castillos caballerescos, pero tan llenas de vida que no ha sido necesario describirlas. Son al mismo tiempo un sitio de paso, fuera de las constricciones sociales, en que la imaginación y los actos se liberan, en que todo puede ocurrir, en que la libertad creadora puede expandirse.

El *Quijote* viene a ser de tal modo el espacio, el "lugar" de todos los encuentros, tanto de los hombres y mujeres de la España circundante que se

---

[26] Baste con remitir a Claudio Guillén, "Luis Sánchez, Ginés de Pasamonte y los inventores del género picaresco."

[27] Véase Gustave Flaubert, *Correspondance*, II, p. 417 (Lettre à Louise Colet): "Comme on voit ces routes d'Espagne qui ne sont nulle part décrites."

introduce en el texto, como, metafóricamente, de la literatura anterior ("libros de caballerías" y de pastores, romancero, narraciones amorosas, teatro, etc.). Por otra parte, el juego ya evocado se amplía cuando el lector se entera de que el melancólico y desocupado hidalgo, enfrascado en la lectura de los "ociosos libros de caballerías," se ha vuelto loco, siendo la locura uno de los puntos de llegada de la melancolía. El protagonista loco proyecta entonces la literatura en la vida y no puede sino comportarse de una manera demente provocando una serie de catástrofes, mientras que, derrotado en todos sus encuentros llevados a cabo, como caballero andante que pretende ser, yace por el suelo, maltrecho. Estamos muy lejos del recorrido triunfante de los héroes de los libros de caballerías ya que la gesta de don Quijote no es sino la de un fracaso continuamente repetido. Éste le conduce, al final de la primera parte, a la jaula en que solían encerrar a los locos en los manicomios, como por ejemplo en la toledana Casa del Nuncio. El mundo al revés se manifiesta a lo largo de las ridículas aventuras del hidalgo y su comportamiento no puede sino provocar la risa del lector.

Sin embargo, ese mundo de la locura que se apodera del protagonista y traduce el desasosiego de un ser en crisis, en busca de identidad, está en consonancia con los trastornos de una época en crisis, la que conoce la España de las últimas décadas del siglo XVI y de las primeras del siglo XVII, crisis que se apodera asimismo de la Europa de esos años. No es pues de extrañar que el tema de la locura haya preocupado a los hombres de esa época (piénsese en los libros de Tommaso Garzoni, de André du Laurens o de Alonso de Santa Cruz y también en *El licienciado Vidriera* del propio Cervantes).[28]

La locura del protagonista, que cobra una dimensión festiva, aparece gráficamente ante los ojos de todos, a partir del momento en que don Quijote lleva puesta en la cabeza, a modo de casco, la bacía del barbero, vuelta al revés — instrumento e inversión vinculados al universo de la alegre *moria*[29] —. Esta imagen ha sido tan significativa que se ha inmiscuido en las representaciones del héroe, sin que ya nos demos cuenta siempre de su valor emblemático que, sin embargo, bien percibían los hombres del siglo XVII.

---

[28] Véase, por ejemplo, Augustin Redondo y André Rochon (eds.), *Visages de la la folie* (1500-1650).

[29] Véase nuestro libro, *Otra manera de leer el "Quijote,"* pp. 225, 478-479.

Por lo demás, la literatura caballeresca no ve enloquecer a sus héroes, excepto si se trata de melancolía erótica, lo que les ocurre a Orlando y a Amadís cuando éste se retrae a la Peña Pobre. Es lo que les pasa asimismo en nuestro libro a ese pastor que parece salir de los libros pastoriles, a ese Grisóstomo (que llega a suicidarse) y a Cardenio. Pero don Quijote, recluido en la Sierra Morena, tiene que *fingir* el enajenamiento amoroso para imitar a sus modelos. Estamos en plena inversión burlesca dado que se ve a un loco fingir la locura y, para manifestarla, rasgar sus vestiduras hasta quedarse en camisa y dar dos zapatetas en el aire, enseñando lo que debiera haber escondido (I, 25, p. 318).

Paralelamente, el loco Caballero de la Triste Figura se halla enfrentado a otro loco, en el episodio de la Sierra Morena. Se trata de Cardenio, loco de amor, transformado en "El Roto de la Mala Figura" ya que, como loco, tiene rotos los vestidos y muy mal aspecto físico. Dos locos están cara a cara y cada uno puede contemplar en el otro las manifestaciones de su extraña alteridad, de su enajenamiento (I, 23, p. 290). La locura — esa otra cara de la razón — enseña su faz a cada uno de ellos que son tan semejantes (hasta por el nombre) y al mismo tiempo tan diferentes. Pero cuando Cardenio se halla preso de un acceso de demencia erótica, es don Quijote, el loco emblemático, el que recibe un guijarrazo y luego razona con mucha prudencia (I, 24, pp. 297-299). Estamos frente a la paradoja del protagonista, ese "loco cuerdo," como ha de decir el Caballero del Verde Gabán, frente a las "discretas locuras" del personaje, como ha de escribir Cervantes en el prólogo de la segunda parte del libro (II, p. 37).

Es que don Quijote es un ser paradójico por ese juego constante entre la razón y la locura. Además, si por un lado se ha liberado del mundo circundante, por otro está profundamente inserto en él. Si llega a ignorar las realidades que le rodean, también es un observador muy perspicaz de ellas. Asimismo si por una parte trasciende las verdades establecidas, por otra también las conoce y las respeta parcialmente. Si bien se transforma en demiurgo y se crea a sí mismo, determinando las características de su gesta, también necesita la ayuda de otros creadores que determinen las condiciones y la trayectoria de esa gesta, lo que le incumbe por ejemplo al gracioso ventero quien, tan paródica y burlescamente, le arma caballero en la venta (I, 3). Como padrino, en efecto, le da una serie de consejos, siendo el primero de ellos el de ir acompañado de un escudero, de modo que es dicho ventero el que da vida a Sancho Panza.

A partir del capítulo 7 está constituida la célebre pareja, siendo el cuaresmal don Quijote y el carnavalesco Sancho dos personajes opuestos y complementarios, la cara y cruz de la misma realidad vital y asimismo dos proyecciones en el texto de la larga tradición popular carnavalesca, tradición que se compagina con la atmósfera festiva de los primeros años del siglo XVII.[30]

Al mismo tiempo, irrumpe en la obra la *Commedia dell'Arte*, tan penetrada de atmósfera carnavalesca y de elementos de los "libros de caballerías" parodiados. Estamos aludiendo especialmente a los dos cómicos tan populares en la España de finales del siglo XVI y hasta 1603, Ganassa (o sea "quijada larga"), alargado y delgado, y Bottarga, panzudo, que representaban juntos más de una vez, constituyendo una pareja cómica y carnavalesca, con cruces, inversión de situaciones, actuaciones burlescas, desempeñando muchas veces Ganassa el papel de Arlequín, el eterno loco de dichos espectáculos. Asimismo Cervantes construye su obra de tal manera que todo gira rápidamente alrededor de ese duo célebre en la *Commedia dell'Arte*, el señor y su servidor.[31]

La influencia del arte escénico en el *Quijote* aparece a las claras además, en situaciones teatrales parodiadas como por ejemplo la de la armazón de caballero del protagonista en la primera venta (I, 3), o la de aquella burla que se le hace al otro barbero en la segunda, en que los personajes reunidos le convencen de que la bacía no es tal sino el yelmo de Mambrino y la albarda del asno no es sino un jaez de caballo, como si se tratara de otro retablo de las maravillas (I, 44-45). Este último lance pone de relieve al mismo tiempo esa búsqueda constante del texto sobre el ser y el parecer, sobre la verdad del lenguaje, gracias a la aventura de la palabra, lo que ha de conducir a dar otro valor al signo lingüístico gracias a la solución ideada por Sancho Panza, al crear su célebre "baciyelmo."

También resulta muy espectacular y reveladora la escena en que, al final de la primera salida, el héroe yace por el suelo, después de haber sido apaleado por uno de los mozos de mulas de los mercaderes toledanos (I, 4). El Manchego empieza entonces a desvariar y, enajenado, cree que es Valdovinos, el protagonista del célebre romance del marqués de Mantua, lo que provoca de nuevo la irrupción del romancero en la obra. Luego piensa que es el moro Abindarráez de *El Abencerraje y la hermosa Jarifa* (I, 5, pp. 102-

---

[30] Véase nuestro libro, *Otra manera de leer el Quijote*"
[31] *Ibid.*, pp. 209-213. Véase además Manuel Sito Alba, "La Commedia dell'Arte, clave esencial de la gestación del *Quijote*."

106).

Tal tipo de enajenación abre a la imaginación creadora del poeta a partir de referentes muy conocidos y parodiados un sinfín de posibilidades de construcción del texto, aun cuando no se utilicen posteriormente. El *Quijote* es incuestionablemente una obra abierta, en que los experimentos y las vías narrativas son múltiples y se elaboran dentro de un sistema de intertextualidad algunas veces directamente perceptible y otras sólo después de una atenta indagación. El lector tiene que implicarse cada vez más en el relato, establecer con él un diálogo constante para llegar a alcanzar lo que Rabelais había llamado la "sustanciosa médula."

De paso, como en el trozo aludido, van emergiendo diversos problemas unidos a los que vive la España contemporánea. Recuérdese que, por los años en que Cervantes escribe su libro, se desarrolla un poderoso sentimiento antimorisco entre la mayoría de la población castellana. Al respecto, nótese que, cuando don Quijote está velando las armas en el patio de la venta, tiene que defender la pila (palabra que puede cobrar un sentido religioso) contra los arrieros, que pasaban por ser moriscos. En efecto éstos querían quitar las armas puestas sobre dicha pila para sacar agua. Bien se comprenderá entonces el valor simbólico que puede cobrar tal episodio.[32] En el pasaje al cual nos hemos referido anteriormente, la amada de Abindarráez / don Quijote es la hermosa Jarifa, una mora. ¿No se perfilará, por detrás de esta dama, la de los pensamientos del protagonista, Dulcinea/Aldonza Lorenzo? En efecto, ésta vive en el Toboso, lugar donde menudeaban los moriscos campesinos, sobre todo después del destierro a Castilla, en 1570-1571, de los del reino de Granada, como lo revelan las *Relaciones topográficas* de los años 1575-1580.[33] ¿Se pondrá en tela de juicio, en son festivo, la "raza" de dicha Aldonza? ¿Y qué es de don Quijote/Abindarráez? Entre burlas y veras afloran de tal modo en el texto los problemas candentes de esa España en crisis. El asunto se hallará también evocado de otra manera con la llegada a España del capitán cristiano, cautivo en los baños de Argel, que ha podido

---

[32] Véase nuestro libro, *Otra manera de leer el "Quijote,"* p. 298-299.

[33] Véase lo que indican los informantes de la villa de El Toboso, el 1 de enero de 1576: "Habrá en dicho pueblo setecientas casas y novecientos vecinos, al presente, con los moriscos que de las Alpujarras del reino de Granada se truxeron" (*Relaciones de pueblos del obispado de Cuenca,* p. 520). Sobre las características de los moriscos del lugar, cfr. Bernard Loupias, "En marge d'un recensement des morisques de la 'Villa del Toboso' (1594)."

fugarse con la hija de un rico moro enamorada de él, la cual quiere convertirse a la religión cristiana—transformándose pues en morisca—y casarse con él. Este tipo de unión mixta existía muy poco en la España de Felipe II y Felipe III.[34]

Detrás de la narración agradable que enlaza con un caso histórico y es una muestra de esa variedad introducida en la historia de Don Quijote, utilizando para ello un cuento folklórico y el conocido esquema del relato de cautivo,[35] ¿no se estará suscitando la reflexión del lector sobre el gran problema de la alteridad y de la convivencia que tienen que resolver los reinos hispanos, mientras se barajan soluciones diversas, algunas muy radicales, que han de adoptarse unos años después y han de resultar tan dañinas para la república y sus hombres?

Pero ya están lanzados por los caminos los dos protagonistas, el señor y su servidor. El texto cervantino, penetrado de ironía, de una ironía inversora de perspectivas, hace participar al lector en esos diálogos tan sabrosos y divertidos entre el caballero y su escudero que utilizan una lengua coloquial sin problemas de comprensión (a la diferencia de la que aparece en más de una ocasión en los "libros de caballerías," en particular la que adopta Feliciano de Silva con su "razón de la sin razón"). Se adentra paulatinamente en la visión que cada personaje tiene del otro, revelándose al mismo tiempo cómo se ve cada uno de ellos en el espejo que el otro constituye para él y cómo llegan a un aprecio recíproco. De tal modo se constituye progresivamente el relato gracias al diálogo o sea gracias a ese dialogismo sobre el cual, tras Bajtin, se ha insistido tanto como elemento fundamental de la llamada "novela moderna."

De manera natural, se van insertando en el relato historias tan gustosas como la de los amores de Cardenio y Luscinda, de Dorotea y don Fernando o como esos cuentos de nunca acabar que Sancho le dice a su amo en el episodio de los batanes, siendo la *Novela del Curioso Impertinente*, un

---

[34] Sobre el problema morisco, y para ahorrar bibliografía, baste remitir a Antonio Domínguez Ortiz y Bernard Vincent, *Historia de los moriscos*.

[35] Sobre este episodio se ha escrito mucho. Véanse por ejemplo Maxime Chevalier, "El cautivo entre cuento y novela"; Jaime Oliver Asín, "La hija de Agi Morato...," Francisco Márquez Villanueva, *Personajes y temas del "Quijote,"* pp. 92-146; etc. Véase, por fin, uno de los últimos trabajos sobre el particular: Diego Vila, "Tráfico de higos, regalados garzones y contracultura..."

llamativo ejemplo de esa mezcla de escritura y oralidad[36] ya que es el cura quien, con voz adecuada, lee o mejor dicho interpreta, a modo de actor, el texto para sus oyentes. Pero, a pesar de lo que se ha podido escribir, el episodio del *Curioso Impertinente* relata otro caso de locura, la que, por parte de Anselmo, consiste en tentar a Dios, con la fidelidad de su esposa. Desde ese punto de vista, no hay ninguna ruptura con la historia principal y los tres protagonistas, como Grisóstomo, mueren de melancolía erótica.

Cervantes juega así con la teatralidad y la puesta en abismo, elaborando en ocasiones un sistema de cajas chinas para el mayor deleite del lector.

Es que, además, el texto no deja de ser alegre, divirtiendo al receptor con los desvaríos del caballero, las simplezas, sandeces fingidas o sartas de refranes del escudero, amén de la comicidad de las situaciones. Es el caso, por ejemplo, de don Quijote que bebe con una paja en la primera venta — parodia de un trozo del *Lazarillo* — por mantener puesta la celada y sostener la visera con las manos, o se transforma en loco de amor, parodiando a Orlando y a Amadís. Algo parecido pasa con Sancho manteado, volando por los aires, como perro o pelele de Carnaval, por no decir nada de las burlas ideadas por el cura, el barbero y Dorotea (*alias* la princesa Micomicona). El mismo caballero puede ser también muy gracioso, a sabiendas o no, como cuando relata el cuento del pintor de Úbeda, Orbaneja, quien, cuando le preguntaban lo que pintaba, decía "lo que saliere" o el de la viuda "hermosa libre y rica" que se había prendado de un joven fraile lego y como el superior se extrañara de que hubiera escogido a un hombre tan bajo y soez, ella le había contestado con mucho donaire: "para lo que yo le quiero, tanta filosofía y más sabe que Aristóteles."[37]

No por nada es el *Quijote* un "libro de entretenimiento" y está en consonancia con lo indicado en los dos libros citados al principio. El placer de contar, de multiplicar las intervenciones de los personajes con visiones y opiniones diferentes, de transformarlos en autores da un nuevo giro a la creación cervantina.

Por otra parte, bien sabidas son las vacilaciones encerradas en el texto acerca del autor o de los autores de la historia de don Quijote. Desde este punto de vista hay un momento fundamental en el texto. Recuérdese que en

---

[36] Sobre la tradición de oralidad y escritura y su dialéctica, véanse Michel Moner, *Cervantès conteur...*; José Manuel Martín Morán, "Don Quijote en la encrucijada oralidad/literatura," etc.

[37] Sobre el particular, véase nuestro trabajo, "Don Quijote, gracioso".

el capítulo 8, el texto deja a don Quijote y al Vizcaíno con las espadas alzadas, procedimiento narrativo utilizado con frecuencia en el arte de contar para encandilar el interés del lector o del oyente.[38] Se dice entonces que el autor/narrador de la historia "no halló más escrito" (I, 8, p. 137).

Es de notar que Cervantes está utilizando lo ocurrido en el capítulo 98 del *Esplandián* en que Rodríguez de Montalvo declara que está cansado y que su pluma no puede continuar la historia. Urganda, la maga, le dice entonces que ha de interrumpir el relato porque está trabajando mal y sólo reanudará su tarea cuando ella se lo indique.[39]

Como puede verse, Cervantes parodia lo indicado en el texto de Rodríguez de Montalvo, pero reconstruye de otra manera la indicación primera ya que la transforma en uno de los procedimientos empleados en el arte de narrar para recrudecer el interés del receptor.

Pero hay más. Recuérdese que el segundo autor va a encontrar el auténtico manuscrito de las aventuras de don Quijote en el alcaná de Toledo, en la tienda de un sedero.[40] Como el texto está escrito en árabe, tiene que valerse de la ayuda de un morisco aljamiado, para traducirlo.

En el *Esplandián*, en el capítulo 99, Rodríguez de Montalvo cae en una cueva y, guiado por Urganda, inicia un viaje subterráneo, antecedente del episodio de la cueva de Montesinos. Va a ver en particular a Amadís, a Galaor, a Esplandián, todos encantados, que han de resucitar con el Rey Artús. Sobre todo da con el maestro Elisabat, el sabio, quien tiene entre las manos el libro de la historia de los grandes hechos de Esplandián, redactada por él, como testigo de vista en la mayoría de los casos.[41] Se trata pues de una auténtica *crónica*. Pero como está escrita en letra griega, Urganda le pide a su sobrina Julianda que la traduzca. Rodríguez de Montalvo escucha atentamente la traducción y cuando regresa a su morada, guiado ahora por

---

[38] Acerca de este tipo de recurso, véase, por ejemplo, M. Moner, *Cervantès conteur...*, pp. 47-48.

[39] Véase Garci Rodríguez de Montalvo, *Las sergas de Esplandián*, cap. 98, pp. 495b-496b.

[40] Acerca del escrito perdido y oculto, que hay que relacionar en particular con la tradición de los libros de caballerías y con lo que se dice al final de la primera parte del *Quijote* (I, 52, p. 604), pero asimismo con el tema de los famosos "plomos" de Granada, se ha escrito mucho. No obstante, véase François Delpech, "El hallazgo del escrito oculto...."

[41] G. Rodríguez de Montalvo, *Las sergas de Esplandián*, cap. 99, pp. 497b-501a

Julianda, se retrae a su casa: "apartado de todos, tomando tinta y papel, comencé a escribir aquello que en la memoria traía como agora oiréis."[42]

Tenemos aquí la afirmación del valor histórico de la crónica de Esplandián que va a llegar a los lectores por un sistema de mediaciones, en que se mezclan escritura y oralidad. Ello permite pasar del primer autor al segundo, gracias a un traductor.

Cervantes parodia sistemáticamente y con ironía los elementos que le suministra el "libro de caballerías."

El autor de la historia auténtica de Esplandián es Elisabat. La primera parte de este nombre evoca al profeta hebreo Elí(as), sabio y mago, y la segunda, el reposo observado los sábados por los judíos para consagrarlo al culto divino. O sea que ese apelativo huele a judío. Si no olvidamos la importancia desempeñada por la onomástica en el *Quijote*,[43] así como el interés por la paronomasia, tan común entre los españoles de esa época (según lo indica Correas[44]), no sería de extrañar que, puesto a parodiar el texto de Montalvo, Cervantes hubiera jugado con la otra minoría que abundaba en Toledo, como la judía en tiempos anteriores. Así hubiera creado un equivalente de ese Elisabat, transformado ahora en el autor moro, el historiador árabe Cide Hamete Benengeli,[45] el de las toledanas berenjenas

---

[42] *Ibid.*, pp. 501b.

[43] Véase nuestro libro, *Otra manera de leer el "Quijote,"* pp. 155-156, 196-198, 213-220, 231-235, etc. Cfr. asimismo Dominique Reyre, *Dictionnaire des noms des personnages du "Don Quichotte."*

[44] Véase Gustavo Correas, *Vocabulario de refranes...*, p. 41b: "...en la lengua española, usamos mucho la figura "paranomasia," ke es semejanza de un nombre a otro porke para dar grazia kon la alusión i ambigüedad a lo ke dezimos, nos kontentamos i nos basta parezerse en algo un nombre a otro para usarle por él."

[45] Nótese que el *Eli—* del principio de Elisabat figura ahora al final de *Benengeli*. Así como Elías, el nombre del profeta hebreo, está formado sobre la raíz *Eli*=Dios, de la misma manera Benengeli significaría "el hijo del Evangelio." —Sobre el nombre del cervantino historiador árabe se ha escrito mucho. Véase, en particular, el artículo de S. Bencheneb y Charles Marcilly, "Qui était Cide Hamete Benengeli?." Para las diversas teorías interpretativas acerca del nombre del cronista, cfr. por ejemplo, Helena Percas de Ponseti, *Cervantes y su concepto del arte*, I, pp. 117-118. Sobre este contexto, véase también ahora lo que escribe Carroll B. Johnson, "Phantom Pretexts: *Don Quijote* and the Metafictional Conventions of Chivalric Romance."

(berenjenas que, según Sebastián de Horozco, eran también alimento típico de los judeoconversos de la imperial ciudad[46]).

El juego se prosigue ya que la letra griega del *Esplandián* se cambia aquí en letra árabe, rebajando humorísticamente el valor antiguo cobrado por todo lo griego, pues se trata ahora de la desprestigiada escritura árabe.[47] Obsérvese de paso cómo el escritor le está guiñando el ojo al lector pues todo texto escrito en árabe era sospechoso y sólo podía circular disimuladamente, por ser caso de Inquisición. Paralelamente, Julianda que, en otro contexto, bien pudiera haber sido hija de ese conde don Julián, que abrió las puertas de la Península a los moros, viene a transmutarse en el morisco aljamiado y bien sabido es que moros y moriscos, como se ha de decir en el texto, tenían fama de ser mentirosos. A diferencia de Julianda, y a pesar de prometer "traducir bien y fielmente" (I, 9, p. 143), ¡cuántas modificaciones habrá introducido dicho morisco en su versión de lo escrito por ese "verídico" (en realidad embustero) historiador árabe!

Estamos en plena parodia pero, entre burlas, se está planteando un problema fundamental que dará lugar al gran debate de los capítulos 47-48 entre el cura y el canónigo sobre la concepción de la obra literaria, las relaciones entre oralidad y escritura, la diferencia entre historia/crónica e historia/ficción, sobre el problema de la mímesis y de la verosimilitud.[48] Paralelamente, también van multiplicándose los autores del texto, lo que pone de realce la importancia de las mediaciones y de los diversos puntos

---

[46] Sebastián de Horozco, en *El libro de los proverbios glosados*, al comentar el refrán "Toledo, aho berengena/yo no las como que soy de LLerena" indica lo siguiente: "... en Toledo son pocas las [berengenas] que hay y éssas de muy buenas simientes medianas y de buen mantenimiento de las quales no solamente los confesos por quien por ventura se dixo el refrán mas aún los xpianos viejos, hijosdalgo y caballeros, clérigos y legos y de todas suertes comen de diversas maneras. *Así que la berengena de Toledo no se tiene por manjar de judíos* ni por razón de ellas pueden ser *motejados de confessos los toledanos* como los neçios lo entienden" (II, p. 483).

[47] Recuérdese, no obstante, que el *Lepolemo* (*El caballero de la Cruz*, citado en el escrutino, I, 6, p. 113) es un libro de caballerías que se supone escrito en lengua árabe, por el sabio Xartón, quien viene a ser una especie de anticipo de Cide Hamete Benengeli. Es lo que ya había subrayado Diego Clemencín: cfr. su ed. del *Quijote*, reproducida en 1980 (por ejemplo, nota 20 del cap. I, 9, p. 1105b).

[48] Son éstos temas muy trillados por los críticos desde las atinadas observaciones de Edward C. Riley, en su *Teoría de la novela en Cervantes*, de manera que, de momento, no iremos más allá de lo que acabamos de apuntar.

de vista, de las diversas voces, o sea de ese perspectivismo tan frecuente en el libro.

Nótese asimismo que la parodia se prosigue a otro nivel: el segundo autor no hace sino remedar a Montalvo con una acentuación del fenómeno de reescritura, dado que durante mes y medio se encierra en su casa con el traductor y parece notar por escrito, directa y fielmente, la versión enunciada oralmente por el trujamán (mentiroso), mientras que en el *Esplandián*, el segundo autor confía a su memoria la traducción (verídica) de Julianda antes de dar forma escrita al relato, en su morada. Por lo demás, este tipo de proceso en que el autor necesita de un traductor para que su texto alcance a los receptores, o sea el sistema de los libros de caballerías, el de un relato que implica varias voces, tiene otra modalidad en la segunda parte, la que corresponde a Maese Pedro, el titiritero, quien tiene que servirse de un trujamán, el cual comenta para el público lo que el maestro trasmite con otro lenguaje, el lenguaje de los títeres (II, 26).

De todas formas, el texto cervantino encierra una profunda ironía que permite poner en tela de juicio la noción misma de verdad del primer autor, en favor o en detrimento del segundo autor quien redacta el texto. Sobresale en realidad una verdad múltiple tanto más evidente cuanto que dicho texto se halla completado por otro sistema de representación y de interpretación que no se sabe a quien se debe. Es lo que revelan los famosos cartapacios.

En efecto, en el margen de uno de ellos, figura una alusión escrita a Dulcinea del Toboso. Cervantes está parodiando la técnica de la *lectio* universitaria con las famosas acotaciones marginales. Señala dicha inscripción: "dicen que [Dulcinea] tuvo la mejor mano para salar puercos que otra mujer de toda la Mancha" (I, 9, p. 143). La dama se halla rebajada a nivel de una campesina que participa en la matanza del cochino y en su conservación (estamos en la Mancha, tierra de bellotas y pues de piaras de cerdos). Además, uno de los atributos tópicos de la dama, la "blanca mano" de la cual hablan la poesía cortés, la petrarquista, Garcilaso, etc. y el propio texto cervantino con referencia a Dorotea (I, 28, p. 346), se halla invertido de modo burlesco.

Paralelamente, aparecen tres personajes en el primer cartapacio. Sancho de Azpetia, el Vizcaíno, se halla caracterizado por su mula de alquiler, el Caballero de la Mancha desaparece detrás de su caballo hasta el extremo de que, a los pies de Rocinante, el título dice: "Don Quijote." La montura viene a ser el doble paródico del protagonista, de manera que la evocación que se hace del rocín le convendría perfectamente al de la Triste Figura: "Tan largo y tendido, tan atenuado y flaco, con tanto espinazo, tan ético confirmado" (I, 9, p. 144). Lo mismo le pasa a Sancho con su asno. Ésta es la primera representación "gráfica" de los dos personajes y de sus monturas, antes de que el grabado se apodere de ellos.

Pero esta manera de comparar un ser humano a un animal del cual tiene las características es una técnica utilizada con frecuencia por los bufones, la del *motejar*, como lo había ilustrado Francesillo de Zúñiga, el truhán de Carlos V, en su crónica burlesca del Emperador.[49] La misma técnica se emplea también en *La Pícara Justina*, libro en el cual hay varios cruces con el *Quijote*. Ya se puede notar la orientación festiva que se le da al texto encontrado y, de manera general, a la narración.

El texto, como se acaba de ver, va precedido de las pinturas de tres personajes, especialmente de la de los dos protagonistas. Se trata de una estructura típica de las portadas de los libros impresos, en particular de los "libros de caballerías." Pero aquí, los personajes son paródicos y además, están al lado de sus monturas, las cuales no son sino monturas degradadas con referencia a aquéllas tan briosas que cabalgaban los héroes caballerescos. Aquí se habla de un caballo que ni siquiera es rocín (fue rocín antes), de un asno y de una mula. De tal modo, la orientación burlesca se encuentra acentuada.

Por otra parte, resulta muy revelador que a la obra se la titule de dos modos diferentes en este trozo. Cuando el narrador está buscando el texto de las aventuras del Caballero de la Mancha, el título aparece bajo la forma: *Vida y milagros de nuestro famoso español don Quijote de la Mancha, luz y espejo de la caballería manchega* (I, 9, p. 141). Éste es un título típico de una relación de santo, especialmente de una de esas que iban impresas en los pliegos de dos o cuatro hojas, tan populares y difundidas,[50] como si, en son de burla, el hidalgo se hubiera transformado en uno de aquellos santos caballeros, citados por él en la segunda parte, que bien pudieran haberle servido de modelo. En el cartapacio, figura únicamente: *Historia de don Quijote de la Mancha*. En este segundo caso, se trata de un título ambiguo que sólo insiste

---

[49] Véase Francesillo de Zúñiga, *Crónica burlesca del Emperador Carlos V*, por ejemplo pp. 72-74. Así, a don Juan de Acuña, el bufón le compara con un "rocín de albarda" (p. 74).

[50] Sobre las "relaciones de santos," en particular acerca de las que estaban vinculadas a fray Diego de Alcalá, véase nuestro libro, *Otra manera de leer el "Quijote,"* pp. 285-287.

sobre la noción de narración (*historia*) en detrimento de la de verdad (lo que subrayaba la *crónica* de Esplandián). No es pues una historia *verdadera* porque, a pesar de calificar a Cide Hamete de *verídico*, éste es un historiador árabe o sea mentiroso.

Todas estas vacilaciones, estas incertidumbres (no se olvide que en la portada del libro publicado se indica un título diferente) crean una impresión de puesta en tela de juicio de la verdad establecida en favor de verdades múltiples, de vías y voces diversas, de miradas diferentes. Ello permite que se dé toda su importancia a las intervenciones de los personajes que pueden transformarse en autores, a las de los diversos autores, del traductor y del lector cuya ayuda no deja de solicitarse. Se trata de un texto en constante creación que exige un desciframiento lúdico en conformidad con el lema que figura en el frontispicio de la obra: "Spero lucem post tenebras."

* * *

"Libro de entretenimiento," el *Quijote* de 1605 bien sigue la orientación delineada al principio de este trabajo. De manera festiva, se mezclan en él elementos múltiples que pertenecen tanto a la cultura erudita como a la cultura popular (en particular carnavalesca), pero que remiten también a las formas y a las técnicas narrativas de la literatura de los años anteriores. Gracias a la parodia, deconstruye estos elementos, especialmente los que están vinculados a los "libros de caballerías," y los reconstruye de otra manera, abriendo así nuevos caminos al relato. Valiéndose de un juego continuo, este relato integra tanto la sabrosa conversación (gracias a la cual se elabora el texto) como los cuentos, los casos sucedidos, los donaires, y permite también poner de relieve la novedad, la variedad y el ingenio de una obra que ilustra la capacidad de invención de su creador.

De tal modo, se echan las bases de un sistema en que la escritura, la oralidad, la teatralidad y la representación pictórica se corresponden, en conformidad con la célebre modalidad horaciana: *ut pictura poesis*. Al jugar con la mentira y la verdad, y asimismo con las relaciones entre autor/autores, narrador, traductor y receptor, pero también con las características de la narración (historia/crónica-historia/ficción), el *Quijote* crea un espacio de libertad y de reflexión crítica vinculado tanto al arte de narrar como a los problemas de una España en crisis, la de un héroe problemático que es el protagonista de una nueva poética. "Libro de entretenimiento," sí, pero que conduce a la llamada "novela moderna."

UNIVERSITÉ DE LA SORBONNE NOUVELLE-CRES

Bibliografía

Bataillon, Marcel. *Pícaros y picaresca. "La Pícara Justina."* Madrid: Taurus, 1969.

Bencheneb, S. y Marcilly, Charles. "Qui était Cide Hamete Benengeli?," en *Mélanges à la mémoire de Jean Sarrailh*, 2 vols., Paris: Centre de Recherches de l'Institut d'Études Hispaniques, 1966, I, pp. 97-116.

Cabrera De Córdoba, Luis. *Relaciones de las cosas sucedidas en la Corte de España desde 1599 hasta 1614*, Salamanca: Junta de Castilla y León, 1997.

Cervantes, Miguel de. *Don Quijote de la Mancha*, ed. Diego Clemencín, reproducida en Valencia: Ed. Alfredo Ortells, 1980.

———. *El ingenioso hidalgo don Quijote de la Mancha*, ed. Luis Andrés Murillo, 2 vols., 2ª ed., Madrid: Castalia, 1978.

———. *El ingenioso hidalgo don Quijote de la Mancha*, ed. Francisco Rico del Instituto Cervantes, 1605-2005, 2 vols., Barcelona: Galaxia Gutemberg. Círculo de lectores. — Centro para la edición de los clásicos españoles, 2004.

Chevalier, Maxime. "El cautivo entre cuento y novela," *Nueva Revista de Filología Hispánica*, XXXII, 1983, pp. 403-411.

Correas, Gustavo. *Vocabulario de refranes y frases proverbiales (1627)*, ed. Louis Combet, Bordeaux: Institut d'Études Ibériques et Ibéro-américaines, 1967.

Covarrubias, Sebastián de. *Tesoro de la lengua castellana o española* [1611], ed. Martín de Riquer, Barcelona: Horta, 1943.

Delpech, François. "El hallazgo del escrito oculto en la literatura española del Siglo de Oro: elementos para una mitología del libro," *Revista de Dialectología y Tradiciones Populares*, 53-1, 1998, pp. 5-38.

Domínguez Ortiz, Antonio y Vincent, Bernard. *Historia de los moriscos. Vida y tragedia de una minoría*, Madrid: Biblioteca de la *Revista de Occidente*, 1978.

Flaubert, Gustave. *Correspondance*, ed. Jean Bruneau, t. II, Paris: Gallimard, 1980; Bib. de la Pléiade.

García Gibert, Javier. *Cervantes y la Melancolía. Ensayos sobre el tono y la actitud cervantinos*, Valencia: Edicions Alfons el Magnànim, 1997.

Gil Ayuso, Faustino. *Noticia bibliográfica de textos y disposiciones legales de los reinos de Castilla impresos en los siglos XVI y XVII*, Madrid: Patronato de la Biblioteca Nacional, 1935.

Guillén, Claudio. "Luis Sánchez, Ginés de Pasamonte y los inventores del género picaresco," en *Homenaje a Rodríguez-Moñino*, 2 vols., Madrid: Castalia, 1966, I, pp. 221-231.

Gutiérrez de los Ríos, Gaspar. *Noticia general para la estimación de las artes, y de la manera en que se conocen las liberales de las que son Mecánicas y serviles con una exortación a la honra de la virtud y del trabajo contra los ociosos, y otras particularidades para las personas de todos estados. Por el licenciado Gaspar Gutiérrez de los Ríos, professor de ambos Derechos y Letras humanas, natural de la Ciudad de Salamanca.* Dirigido a don Francisco Gómez de Sandoval y Rojas, Duque de Lerma. Con Privilegio. Madrid: Pedro Madrigal, 1600; BNM: R. 28056.

Horozco, Sebastián de. *El libro de los proverbios glosados,* ed. Jack Weiner, 2 vols., Kassel: Ed. Reichenberger, 1994.

Johnson, Carroll B. "Phantom Pre-texts: *Don Quijote* and the Metafictional Conventions of Chivalric Romance," en *Actas* del Simposio sobre el *Quijote* de la Universidad de Boston, 14-16 de abril de 2005 (en prensa en la revista *Cervantes*).

Klibansky, Raymond, Panofsky, Erwin y Saxl, Fritz. *Saturne et la Mélancolie,* trad. Fabienne Durand-Bogaert y Louis Evrard, Paris: Gallimard, 1989.

López Pinciano, Alonso. *Philosophía antigua poética* [1596], ed. Alfredo Carballo Picazo, 3 vols., Madrid: CSIC, 1953.

Loupias, Bernard. "En marge d'un recensement des morisques de la 'Villa de El Toboso' (1594)," *Bulletin Hispanique,* LXXVIII, 1976, pp. 74-96.

Luque Fajardo, Francisco de. *Fiel desengaño contra la ociosidad y los juegos. Utilíssimo a los confessores y penitentes,* Madrid: Miguel Serrano de Vargas, 1603; BNM: R. 11412.

Márquez Villanueva Francisco. *Personajes y temas del "Quijote,"* Madrid: Taurus, 1975.

Martín Morán, José Manuel. "Don Quijote en la encrucijada oralidad/literatura," *Nueva Revista de Filología Hispánica,* XLV-2, 1997, pp. 337-368.

Moner, Michel. *Cervantès conteur. Écrits et paroles,* Madrid: Casa de Velázquez, 1989.

Oliver Asín, Jaime. "La hija de Agi Morato en la obra de Cervantes," *Boletín de la Real Academia Española,* XXVII, 1947-1948, pp. 245-339.

Ortega Y Gasset, José. *Meditaciones del "Quijote." Ideas sobre la novela,* 3ª ed., Madrid: Revista de Occidente, 1956.

Palau Y Dulcet, Antonio. *Manual del librero hispanoamericano,* t. XI, Barcelona: Librería Palau, 1958.

Percas De Ponseti, Helena. *Cervantes y su concepto del arte,* 2 vols., Madrid: Gredos, 1975.

Pérez de Herrera, Cristóbal. *Amparo de pobres* [1598], introducción y ed. Michel Cavillac, Madrid: Espasa Calpe, 1975, "Clásicos Castellanos," 199.

Pinheiro da Veiga, Tomé. *Fastiginia o fastos geniales,* trad. Narciso Alonso Cortés, Valladolid: Imprenta del Colegio de Santiago, 1916.

Redondo, Augustin. "Acerca de la portada de la primera parte del *Quijote.* Un problema de recepción," en *Silva. Studia philologica in honorem Isaías Lerner,* ed. Isabel Lozano Renieblas y Juan Carlos Mercado, Madrid: Castalia, 2001, pp. 525-534.

———. "El *Persiles,* 'libro de entretetenimiento' peregrino," en *Peregrinamente peregrinos, Actas del V Congreso Internacional de la Asociación de Cervantistas*, ed. Alicia Villar Lecumberri, 2 vols., Barcelona: Asociación de Cervantistas, 2004, I, pp. 67-102.

―――. *Otra manera de leer el "Quijote. Historia, tradiciones culturales y literatura*, 2ª ed., Madrid: Castalia, 1998.

Redondo, Augustin y Rochon, André (eds.). *Visages de la folie (1500-1650)*, Paris: Publications de la Sorbonne, 1981.

Relaciones de pueblos del obispado de Cuenca. ed. Julián Zarco Cuevas; nueva ed. preparada por Dimas Pérez Ramírez, Cuenca: Exc^ma Diputación Provincial de Cuenca, 1983.

Remón, Alonso. *Entretenimientos y juegos honestos y recreaciones christianas*, Madrid: Viuda de Alonso Martín, A costa de Luis Ramírez, 1623; BNM: R. 1028.

Reyre, Dominique. *Dictionnaire des noms des personnages de "Don Quichotte,"* Paris: Editions Hispaniques, 1980.

Riley, Edward Cervantes. *Teoría de la novela en Cervantes* [1962], trad. Carlos Sahagún, Madrid: Taurus, 1966.

Rodríguez de Montalvo, Garci. *Las sergas del muy esforzado caballero Esplandián, hijo del excelente rey Amadís de Gaula* en *Libros de Caballerías*, ed. Pascual de Gayangos, Madrid: Atlas, 1950 [1ª ed.en BAE:1857]; BAE, t. 40, pp. 403-561.

Sito Alba, Manuel. "La *Commedia dell' Arte*, clave esencial de la gestación del *Quijote*," *Arbor*, CXVI, 1983, pp. 7-30

Straparola di Caravaggio, Gian Francesco. *Honesto y agradable entetenimiento de Damas y Galanes. Compuesto por el señor Ioan Francisco Carvacho cavallero Napolitano y traduzido de lengua Toscana en nuestra vulgar, por Francisco Truchado, vezino de Baeça*, Granada: en casa de René Rabut, 1582; BNM: R. 15917.

―――. *Segunda parte del honesto y agradable entretenimiento. Compuesto por el ilustre cavallero Francisco Straparola de Carvacho, Napolitano. Y traduzido de lengua toscana en la nuestra vulgar, por Francisco Truchado, vezino de Baeça*, Baeça: en casa de Iuan Baptista de Montoya, 1581; BNM: R. 15918.

Vila, Juan Diego. "Tráfico de higos, regalados garzones y contracultura: en torno a los silencios y mentiras del capitán cautivo," en *Peregrinamente peregrinos. Actas del V Congreso Internacional de la Asociación de Cervantistas*, ed. Alicia Villar Lecumberri, 2 vols., Barcelona: Asociación de Cervantistas, 2004, II, pp. 1833-1864.

Zúñiga, Francesillo de. *Crónica burlesca del Emperador Carlos V*, ed. Diana Pamp de Avalle-Arce, Barcelona: Crítica, 1981.

Hot in Pursuit: Altisidora and don Quijote in the House of Horrors

ILUMINADA AMAT

> You take the red pill, you stay in wonderland and I show you how far the rabbit hole goes.
> *The Matrix*

FOR WEEKS I'D BEEN in search of the perfect title. Here are three of my favorite runners-up: "The First Time Ever I Saw Your Face," "Full of Sound and Fury Meets the Sound of Silence," and "Still Crazy After All These Years."

Then one day I fell in the rabbit hole and had, what I can only describe as, a hallucinatory reading experience. I sat down to re-read Part II, from the adventure of the enchanted boat to the bitter end. After 13 hours of non-stop reading, two things happened. First, I temporarily lost touch with reality, me sitting on my couch reading a good book. I couldn't get my head out of the textual space; I felt dazed, disoriented. I found myself debating (with myself) who was real, who fictional, who sane, who crazy; my own living room looked odd. Then that night I had a nightmare: I was in a strange place, a guest in a large house; there was a huge room, and I was surrounded by some very "catty" women. After putting up with their innuendos and barbs I exclaimed something to this effect: "Wow, now I know what don Quijote felt like with a bunch of hissing cats loose in the room."

Perhaps I was experiencing some anxiety. I mean what do you say 400 years later? Here are some familiar adjectives used to describe this text and its illustrious protagonist and sidekick: canonical, seminal, foundational, protean, grotesque, unnatural, gluttonous, insatiable, libidinous, ludic, polyphonic, gargantuan. I offer a couple more, products of my own fevered imagination: vortextual, poliphemenal. For me, they describe the text and its significance, its continual hold over the reader, a reader seduced, mesmerized, enchanted, perplexed, annoyed, and most decidedly hooked. I think I've been reading *Don Quijote* too much! And yet, I have always found large portions of the second half of Part II quite absurd, parody notwithstanding: absurd, i.e., I have been incapable of hearing something well, if at all. So, precisely because of my own dissatisfaction and discomfort, I have for the last several months placed myself under obedience to the text: obedience, to listen towards, to lean into it to see what it might yield.

What has been the primary thrust of Cervantine criticism re the ducal palace, Altisidora, and the tales and adventures bracketing don Quijote's two visits? Some studies have brought to our attention the historical context fundamental to an appreciation of these chapters, for example, the importance of the "fiestas palaciegas" and their pageantry (Close), the shadows of the "auto-da-fe" in Chapter 69 (Jehle), the expulsion of the Moors from Spain (Redondo and Márquez Villanueva). Others have focused on questions of intertextuality, sources, genre, the role of the reader (the bibliography for this text is truly staggering). Many of these studies highlight the role of parody, the predominance of the carnivalesque and its "temática del mundo al revés" (Joly *Marginación* 17) as a means of undoing the "noxious influence" of chivalric novels and Cervantes's need to respond to and de-authorize the apocriphal *Don Quijote*. In Márquez Villanueva's words: "...la bufonería sirvió entonces de disfraz para los más arriesgados ejercicios de crítica social, política y religiosa..." (24), i.e., life in the "cortes," Counter-Reformation Spain's obsessions with *limpieza de sangre* and *honra*, its persecution of the Jews, the confrontation between medieval and pre-capitalist economies, among others. For myself, two "critical lenses" have been instrumental in the way I read this text: the insights of psychological and psychoanalytic perspectives with their focus on the erotic and the formation/construction of sexual identity, as evidenced in my own thesis on doubling in *Don Quijote*. The other is the work of those scholars who have produced a significant body of work on the transgressive qualities of the text: its gender-bending, transvestism, homoeroticism and their relationship to alterity/the marginal Other and questions of identity and agency (Louis Combet, Henry Sullivan, Benito Brancaforte, Carroll Johnson, Francisco Márquez Villanueva, Monique Joly, Francisco Ayala, Agustín Redondo, Maurice Molho and George Mariscal, among others).

Within these parameters, I wish to make clear my own positionality: I will not be, for the most part, focusing on what Carroll Johnson has described as "the great questions," "the finer things," or "the higher aspirations of Man" (*Material* 1). In Agustín Redondo's felicitous phrase "los remilgos de la pudibundez" will be given no courtesy here (*Clavijo* 422). I do not read the text like some "con tan religioso fervor que transforman el texto en un verdadero libro sagrado" (Redondo *Clavijo* 421). My fervor is of a different order altogether. Finally, to paraphrase Henry Sullivan, I will try to avoid reifying my own "obsesiones o conclusiones predeterminadas" (*Regalo* 74), although the extent to which any reader can succeed in this enterprise, is highly questionable, in my opinion.

On this 400th birthday celebration, I would like to re-visit don Quijote's psychodelic trip through the ducal badlands to "desenvolver" anew, as it were, our "desenvuelta doncella," a character, as Monique Joly lamented years ago, still "descuidada hoy día por la crítica" (Joly *Etudes* 173), as well as her relationship with don Quijote, in the hopes of finding new surprises, new treasure.

So, friends, colleagues and lovers of Cervantes, I come not to praise Altisidora, but to bury her. There is no need to rehearse here the centrality of the ducal palace to Part II, nor the many parallels with Part I. Nevertheless, the jury is still out where Altisidora is concerned. On the one hand, she is, according to Luis Murillo, a figure both "relentless and frivolous.... calculating and coy.... she is in fact a version of the diabolical female...." (208). For Fred Jehle she is "emparentada" with the Furies Alecto and Tisiphone, "the dreaded goddesses of mythology who punished and pursued evil-doers" (10-11). Márquez Villanueva characterizes her as "uno de los grandes antogonistas..." de don Quijote (300). For Casalduero, on the other hand, she is "esa figura tan frágil y al mismo tiempo tan pulida y dura.... una joven en busca de marido" (321, 324).

What is known of this conflictive figure who appears 14 chapters after don Quijote's arrival in the nobles' "casa de placer" (II: 269)? In the seventeenth century version of a Broadway debut (karaoke night might actually be closer to target) we are given a clear description of, what Michael Casey in another context describes as, "boisterous bodiliness" (21):

> No soy renca, ni soy coja,
> ni tengo nada de manca;
> los cabellos, como lirios,
> que, en pie, por el suelo arrastran.
> Y, aunque es mi boca aguileña

y la nariz algo chata,
ser mis dientes de topacios
mi belleza al cielo ensalza. (which I misread as "suelo")
Mi voz, ya ves, si me escuchas,
que a la que es más dulce iguala,
y soy de disposición
algo menos que mediana.
Estas y otras gracias mías,
son despojos de tu aljaba;
desta casa soy doncella,
y Altisidora me llaman. (II: 374)

A later testimony from dueña Rodríguez: "Porque quiero que sepa vuesa merced, señor mío, que no es todo oro lo que reluce; porque esta Altisidorilla tiene más de presunción que de hermosura, y más de desenvuelta que de recogida, además que no está muy sana: que tiene un cierto aliento cansado, que no hay sufrir el estar junto a ella un momento" (II: 402).

First, her name: For Dominique Reyre she is a gift of the goddess Isis, for Henry Sullivan "regalos o dones del más Alto" (Sullivan 75). As Vila points out, her name is meant to remind us of "el halo precioso del oro y…. los sufijos caballerescos" (Meliador, Beliadoro) perhaps of "Alchisilora, reina del libro de caballerías" el *Caballero de Febo* (469).

Second, her anatomy: Much ink has been spilled on the purported relationship between the size of a man's nose and his "instrumento." Where women are concerned, however, the "nariz chata" has an established pedigree of its own. One *refrán* will here suffice: "Puta y chata, con lo segundo basta" (Francisco Rodríguez Marín qtd. in Redondo *Las dos caras* 158).

Her moral character leaves much to be desired as well. The *Diccionario de Autoridades* defines "desenvoltura" as "desembarazo, despejo, desen-fado…. desvergüenza, deshonestidad, principalmente en las mujeres" (qtd. in Weber 60). She offers, among other things, to rub his feet and scratch away his dandruff. One should recall Ruth's covering of Boaz's feet and, unsavory as it strikes us today, the removal of the beloved's dandruff "funcionaba como una sugestión de máxima sensualidad para la tradición medieval." Márquez Villanueva is here alluding to Grima and her husband in *El caballero Cifar* (317). Today, Altisidora´s physical looks would most likely not land her a centerfold but her implied "pasatiempos" would make her most popular indeed. Oh, and did I forget to mention her breath? Does she live up to her reputation, you ask? I give round one to don Quijote. He roundly rejects Altisidora´s efforts to woe him while, at the same time, praising his ability to attract women: -¡Que tengo de ser tan desdichado andante, que no ha de haber doncella que me mire que de mí no se enamore...! (II: 374). Despite his disclaimer, the next morning, he sallies forth (rosary and all) as if he'd actually added another notch to his belt. For my money there are few passages in all the literary world as perfect and delicious as this:

Dejamos al gran don Quijote envuelto en los pensamientos que le habían causado la música de la enamorada doncella Altisidora. Acostase con ellos y, como si fueran pulgas, no le dejaron dormir ni sosegar un punto....; pero como es ligero el tiempo, y no hay barranco que le detenga, corrió caballero en las horas, y con mucha presteza llegó la de la mañana. Lo cual visto por don Quijote, dejó las blandas plumas, y, no nada perezoso, se vistió su agamuzado vestido y se calzó sus botas de camino, por encubrir la desgracia de sus medias; arrojóse encima su mantón de escarlata y púsose en la cabeza una montera de terciopelo verde, guarnecida de pasamanos de plata; colgó el tahalí de sus hombros con su buena y tajadora espada, asió un gran rosario que consigo contino traía, y con gran prosopopeya y contoneo salió a la antesala, donde el duque y la duquesa estaban ya vestidos y como esperándole. (II: 382-383)

Can you picture Tom Hanks glowing and strutting the morning after "scoring" for the first time? (*Big*)

The very next morning after don Quijote's first rebuff, she pretends to faint, weak with desire:

estaban aposta esperándole Altisidora y la otra doncella su amiga, y, así como Altisidora vio a don Quijote, fingió desmayarse, y su amiga la recogió en sus faldas, y con gran presteza la iba a desabrochar el pecho. Don Quijote, que lo vio, llegándose a ellas, dijo:

—Ya sé yo de qué proceden estos accidentes.

—No sé yo de qué respondió la amiga, porque Altisidora es la doncella más sana de toda esta casa. (II: 383)

It's a close call but I award this round to don Quijote too. He, after all, promises to console her as best he may (II: 383). If she is the most "sana" in the house, heaven help us! The alert reader will not have missed the allusion to the inn in Part I and its most memorable character and her "entretenimientos," Maritornes who "olía a ensalada fiambre y trasnochada..." (I: 203).

Round three: Having failed to elicit an appropriate response, Altisidora is, in turn, subjected to a serenade in which don Quijote suggests she use her hands in traditional women's work (coser y labrar). You know what they say about a woman scorned. Now she literally lets the cats out of the bag and all hell breaks loose: "uno, viéndose tan acosado de las cuchilladas de don Quijote, le saltó al rostro y le asió de las narices con las uñas y los dientes, por cuyo dolor don Quijote comenzó a dar los mayores gritos que pudo" (II: 385). She scores a knock-out punch, and he goes down for the count. Given the connotation of the nose as "common symbol or displacement for the male genitalia," one could say that this cat really has him by the nose! Metaphorical castration indeed! (Sullivan *Grotesque* 148). Couple that with the fact that the female cat "commonly symbolizes the female genitalia" (para. of Greer 1992) and it's a wonder the text is not on the 700 Club's list of prohibited books!

Round four: At the very last moment, as don Quijote and Sancho Panza prepare to make their getaway, she accuses him of stealing several items from among her clothing: "tres tocadores"

> y unas ligas, de unas piernas
> que al mármol puro se igualan
> en lisas, blancas y negras. (II: 468)

From her head to those parts ("blessed be Allah," says our wise Sidi Hamete) which "remain hidden," there is no mistaking her intentions, as Sancho later comments: "Yo de mí sé decir que me rindiera y avasallara la más mínima razón amorosa suya. ¡Hideputa, y qué corazón de mármol, qué entrañas de bronce y qué alma de argamasa!" (II: 475).

How does our hero bear up under this assault? Where is don Quijote, in psychic terms, as he engages in a battle of more than just wits with Altisidora? Many critics have remarked on the profound changes in don Quijote in Part II (in particular his passivity), where adventure after adventure is thrust upon him, to such an extent that he appears to be more and more the victim of "man's inhumanity to man," if you will. Don Quijote traverses "a world increasingly experienced as disoriented" (Brueggemann 51). His sojourn at the palace undoubtedly bears the mark of Dante's sojourn through hell, as Henry Sullivan has so forcefully demonstrated. His time there mirrors the extreme experience of disorientation that Walter Brueggemann charts in the darkest of the Hebrew psalms: "a move first *to the edge* of 'the pit,' then a more intense *entry into the pit* of disorientation, and then finally a *full descent...*" (77). Márquez Villanueva rightly designated the ducal lands as a "región infernal" (32).

It bears remembering don Quijote's words after the disastrous adventure of the enchanted boat: "Dios lo remedie, que todo este mundo es máquinas y trazas, contrarias unas de otras. Yo no puedo más" (II: 267). Shortly thereafter, don Quijote espies a castle and anticipates the rescue of some mistreated princess: "¿Vees? Allí, ¡oh amigo!, se descubre la ciudad, castillo o fortaleza donde debe de estar algún caballero oprimido, o alguna reina, infanta o princesa malparada, para cuyo socorro soy aquí traído" (II: 265). A more salient example of prolepsis would be hard to find, I believe, given that the "caballero oprimido" will in short order be himself. What else do the "máquinas y trazas" anticipate if not the extravagant staging of Altisidora's resurrection, among other productions?

It is, furthermore, no accident that don Quijote first encounters the duchess during a hunt. Recall, the duke's encomium: "La caza es una imagen de la guerra: hay en ella estratagemas, astucias, insidias para vencer a su salvo al enemigo; padécense en ella fríos grandísimos y calores intolerables; menoscábase el ocio y el sueño, corrobóranse las fuerzas, agilítanse los miembros del que la usa, y, en resolución, es ejercicio que se puede hacer sin perjuicio de nadie y con gusto de muchos... (II: 307). Prominent in this quote is the use of war-related terms which, in Redondo's words are reminiscent of "la embestida viril" (*Las dos caras* 153). As we have seen, Altisidora is a relentless hunter.

And yet, I would suggest to you that don Quijote is not simply a victim or the butt of the duchal household's "ocio." On first arriving at the castle, don Quijote soundly refuses to have one of the six serving girls remove his shirt: Pidiéronle que se dejase desnudar para una camisa, pero nunca lo consintió..." (II: 277). Later still, he turns down the four serving girls offered him by the duchess:

En verdad — dijo la duquesa —, señor don Quijote, que no ha de ser así: que le han de servir cuatro doncellas de las mías, hermosas como unas flores.

Para mí — respondió don Quijote — no serán ellas como flores, sino como espinas que me puncen el alma. Así entrarán ellas en mi aposento, ni cosa que lo parezca, como volar…. y no quiero perder esta costumbre (poner una muralla en medio de sus deseos) por la liberalidad que vuestra alteza quiere mostrar conmigo. (II: 369)

When Dueña Rodríguez appears in the dead of night, he exacts a promise of good-behavior on her part before consenting to hear her woes.

Our knight appears to be quite well versed in avoiding temptation. But was he truly able to hear Altisidora's siren call? Consider his dismay upon discovering his torn stocking: Cerró tras sí la puerta, y a la luz de dos velas de cera se desnudó, y al descalzarse — ¡oh desgracia indigna de tal persona! — se le soltaron, no suspiros, ni otra cosa, que desacreditasen la limpieza de su policía, sino hasta dos docenas de puntos de una media, que quedó hecha celosía. Afligióse en estremo el buen señor, y diera él por tener allí un adarme de seda verde una onza de plata; digo seda verde porque las medias eran verdes (II: 370). This discovery takes place immediately before Altisidora decides to play Romeo to his Juliet. As Helena Percas de Ponsetti, Márquez Villanueva, Agustín Redondo and Ruth El Saffar, among others, have remarked, the color green often symbolizes lust and sensuality (*Beyond* 194). One final admission of inedequacy. Perched on Clavileño, he confesses to Sancho: "no sé yo cómo templar esta clavija" (350). Be it the work of repression, impotence or other psychosexual factors (all well-documented elsewhere), my point is that don Quijote is able to hold his own quite well. Despite Henry Sullivan's observation that don Quixote's "celibate resolve is tortured in the flesh and in the spirit by the blandishments of Altisidora..," it is my contention that, despite a skirmish or two, don Quijote bends but does not break (*Grotesque* 56).

What of Altisidora? It is important to recall that despite her strong character (she does manage to "asombrar" the Duchess at one point) she is nevertheless not much more than a glorified servant in the palace. It is imperative that we not overlook questions of social class when reading the text. Sancho's vituperation of all dueñas aside, the economic indigence of those at the mercy of the rich is reflected in dueña Rodríguez´ words: "atenida al miserable salario…. que a tales criadas se suele dar en palacio"

(II: 400). We don't know exactly why Altisidora is there to begin with, perhaps Casalduero's hypothesis (that she is looking for a husband and that she could fall for a *cincuentón*) is not so far-fetched after all. Think of Clint Eastwood and countless others married to much younger women. Life is stranger than fiction, though money doesn´t hurt either. Carroll Johnson has elsewhere noted the strategy of keeping "as many daughters as possible off the marriage market, thus eliminating the need to provide a dowry, which would have to come out of the patrimony" (*Material* 28).

A few final observations. Let me first call your attention to don Quijote's pithy summary of what transpired between them: "Quísome bien, al parecer, Altisidora; ....lloró en mi partida, maldíjome, vituperóme, quejóse, a despecho de la vergüenza, públicamente: señales todas de que me adoraba, que las iras de los amantes suelen parar en maldiciones" (II: 547). On the whole of it, this is not an unreasonable assessment. This time around, I have been struck by two moments in the confrontation between Altisidora and don Quijote that have hitherto gone unnoticed and unremarked, to the best of my knowledge.

First, I refer you to Altisidora's parting words: "Pensáis por ventura, don vencido y don molido a palos, que yo me he muerto por vos? Todo lo que habéis visto esta noche ha sido fingido; que no soy yo mujer que por semejantes camellos había de dejar que me doliese un negro de la uña, cuanto más morirme" (II: 567). Why the vehemence? And what's the camel got to do with anything? Besides the obvious associations with ungainliness and stubborness, Covarrubias' *Tesoro de la lengua castellana* provides a usage for the word "camello" that is suggestive in this context: "Puédese aplicar a los que han tenido abstinencia, y después no se veen hartos ni satisfechos, por ventura de lo que en todo tiempo les es velado" (276-277). Is the abstinence strictly an issue for our knight or could this be an instance of projection as well?

Second, recall Altisidora's comparison of don Quijote and Eneas: "este nuevo Eneas, que ha llegado a mis regiones para dejarme escarnida" (II: 372). I will not linger on Altisidora's "regiones," the text speaks for itself. Altisidora's self-description as "escarnecida" is, of course, parodic. Let me refer you once again to Covarrubias: "Hazer burla del próximo que está en miseria, que puede tenerla sin culpa, y como está en él pudiera estar en mí, que son de su mesma masa y naturaleza, y assí hago burla de mi propia carne." If Márquez Villanueva is correct in calling the ducal court "pervertida" (300), Altisidora also has been degraded and debased , used as bait, cheap entertainment, another commodity in the Baratarias of the world, whose borders are much larger than the ínsula Sancho governed for 10 days. Her devaluation and diminishment is exemplified in the response one of Roque's men makes when Sancho demands the return of Altisidora's "tres tocadores": "yo los tengo, y no valen tres reales" (500). Altisidora's fate in Márquez Villanueva's words is sobering: "…la chispeante Altisidora no es ahora más que una estrella apagada, sin otro destino por delante que interminables días de aguja y 'labor blanca'" (340). "Altisidora me llaman." Perhaps, as María Rosa Lida Malquiel has posited, she is named after a wine "llamado *altissidoriense* o vino de Auxerre, que menciona una obra de Erasmo" (qtd. in Márquez Villanueva 305). Or as Vila has suggested, Altisidora is her *nom de guerre* (306).

Either way, in this tale of misadventure, there are no winners. Don Quijote was right, he can't fly no matter how much he twists at the peg. Altisidore is coy, cunning, fragile, malicious, unpredictable: a fully sketched, breathing, complex human character: as fascinating, "tricksy," and false as each and every one of us. You, me, Altisidora, and don Quijote, ultimately, flesh of the same flesh.

I am caught somewhere in the middle. Like Urbina, Altisidora no longer appears to me to be "un personaje tan bajo y despreciable" (570). Neither do I perceive the "hilaridad sana y democrática" or "la idea de una alegría universal, compartida por los hombres y la naturaleza" which according to Anthony Close is the "tónica esencial" of Part II (476, 483). Carroll Johnson's description of the "maddening ambiguity" inherent in *La gitanilla* (*Material* 104) ultimately captures for me the reason why I/we keep returning to this text.

Hunted, accosted, pummeled, beaten, bruised; more here has been torn than don Quijote's stockings. Despite its ludic and carnivalesque qualities, through don Quijote's sojourn in the Duke's "pleasure dome," the text verbalizes the "resilience of the darkness," a darkness it can neither tame nor eliminate (Brueggemann 53). Ultimately, the text reinforces "how divided and incongruous we all are" (Brueggemann 68). Like don Quijote, we have all experienced moments when Walt Whitman's words would have been balm indeed:

> Oh, to be self-balanced for contingencies,
> To confront night, storms, hunger, ridicule, accidents,
> rebuffs, as the trees and animals do.

("Me imperturbare" *Leaves of Grass*)

Unfortunately, in this house of horrors, this human menagerie, water is scarce. Both the cat and the camel will go thirsty. I had several Simon and Garfunkel songs playing in my head while working on this presentation. I AM A ROCK: the text is the rock against which all interpretations eventually founder, against which all hope of ultimate "MEANING" is Dashed. STILL CRAZY AFTER ALL THESE YEARS: don Quijote, character and text (wild, unwieldy, untamed still), all of us here who love this text passionately and who continue to listen. Right there in the struggle between the twin poles of comedy and tragedy is life, fully lived. Not an insignificant thing to be reminded of 400 years later. Maybe not so crazy after all.[1]

UNIVERSITY OF NORTH CAROLINA
CHAPEL HILL

Works Cited

Ayala, Francisco. "Los dos amigos." *Cervantes y Quevedo*. Barcelona: Seix Barral, 1974. 143-177.

Brancaforte, Benito. "Cervantes' *Tale of Foolish Curiosity* and Hawthorne's *The Birthmark*: the Testing of Women." *Busquemos otros montes y otros ríos: Estudios de la literatura española del Siglo de Oro dedicados a Elias L. Rivers*. Eds. Brian Dutton and Victoriano R. López. Madrid: Editorial Castalia, 1992. 47-57.

———. "El diálogo de Cervantes con la locura." *Homenaje a José Antonio Maravall*. Eds. Carmen Iglesias, Carlos Moya, and Luis Rodríguez Zúñiga. Vol. I. Madrid: Centro de Investigaciones Sociológicas, 1985. 329-42.

Brueggemann, Walter. *The Message of the Psalms: A Theological Commentary*. Minneapolis: Augsburg Press, 1984.

Casalduero, Joaquín. *Sentido y forma del Quijote*. Madrid: Insula, 1949.

Casey, Michael. *Fully Human, Fully Divine: An Interactive Christology*. Liguori, Missouri: Liguouri/Triumph, 2004.

Cervantes, Miguel de. *The History of That Ingenious Gentleman Don Quijote de la Mancha*. Trans. Burton Raffel. New York: W.W. Norton & Company, 1995.

Cervantes, Miguel de. *El ingenioso hidalgo Don Quijote de la Mancha*. Ed. Luis Andrés

---

[1] My most profound thanks to Carroll Johnson for organizing this conference and for his encouragement and support throughout the years.

Murillo. 2 Vols. Madrid: Clásicos Castalia, 1982.

Close, Anthony. "Fiestas palaciegas en la Segunda Parte del *Quijote.*" Actas del Segundo Coloquio Internacional de la Asociación de Cervantistas. Anthropos: Barcelona y Ministerio de Asuntos Exteriores: Madrid, 1989. 475-484.

Combet, Louis. *Cervantès ou les incertitudes du désir.* Lyon: Presses Universitaires de Lyon, 1980.

Covarrubias, Sebastián de. *Tesoro de la Lengua Castellana o Española.* 1611. Rpt. Madrid: Turner, 1984.

Diccionario de autoridades. Real Academia Española. 3 vols. 1726-1739; rpt. Madrid: Gredos, 1979.

El Saffar, Ruth. *Beyond Fiction: the Recovery of the Feminine in the Novels of Cervantes.* Berkeley: U of California P, 1984.

Greer, Margaret Rich. "Phallic Woman in the Novelas of María de Zayas." Unpublished paper read at the Kentucky Foreign Language Conference, Lexington, April 1992.

Jehle, Fred F. "The Resurrection of Altisidora in *Don Quijote.*" *Hispanófila* 75.3 (1982): 9-16.

Johnson, Carroll B. *Cervantes and the Material World.* Urbana and Chicago: U of Illinois P., 2000.

———. *Madness and Lust: A Psychoanalytical Approach to Don Quixote.* Berkeley: U of California P, 1983.

Joly, Monique. *Etudes sur "Don Quichotte."* Paris : Publications de la Sorbonne, 1996.

———. "Erotismo y marginación social en la novela cervantina." *Cervantes* 12.2 (1992): 7-19.

———. "El erotismo en el Quijote: la voz femenina." *Edad de Oro* 9 (1990): 137-148.

Mariscal, George. *Contradictory Subjects: Quevedo, Cervantes, and Seventeenth-Century Spanish Culture.* Ithaca: Cornell UP, 1991.

Márquez Villanueva, Francisco. *Trabajos y días cervantinos.* Alcalá de Henares: Centro de Estudios Cervantinos, 1995.

Molho, Maurice. "Cervantes and the 'Terrible Mothers.'" Eds. El Saffar, Ruth and Diana de Armas Wilson. *Quixotic Desire: Psychoanalytic Perspectives on Cervantes.* Ithaca, NY: Cornell UP, 1993, 239-254.

Murillo, L. A. *A Critical Introduction to Don Quixote.* Paris: Peter Lang, 1988.

Redondo, Augustin. *Otra manera de leer el Quijote : historia, tradiciones culturales y literatura.* Madrid: Editorial Castalia, 1997.

———. Redondo, Agustín. "Las dos caras del erotismo en la primera parte del Quijote." *Edad de Oro* 9 (1990): 251-269.

———. "De las terceras al alcahuete del episodio de los galeotes en el Quijote (I, 22): Algunos rasgos de la parodia cervantina." *Journal of Hispanic Philology* 13.2 (1989): 135-148.

———. "Del personaje de Aldonza Lorenzo al de Dulcinea del Toboso: Algunos aspectos de la invención cervantina." *Anales Cervantinos* 21 (1983): 9-22.

Sullivan, Henry W. *Grotesque Purgatory: A Study of Cervantes's Don Quixote, Part II.*

University Park, Pennsylvania: Pennsylvania State UP, 1996.

————. "Altisidora: ¿Como 'regalo del más alto' acelera la cura de Don Quijote?" *La mujer y su representación en las literaturas hispánicas*. Ed. Juan Villegas. Actas Irvine-92 Asociación Internacional de Hispanistas. Irvine: U of California, 1994, 74-81.

Urbina, Eduardo. "Voluntad, amor y destino: Altisidora, la sin par doncella de don Quijote." Eds. Isaías Lerner, Robert Nival & Alejandro Alonso. *Actas del IV Congreso de la Asociación Internacional de Hispanistas*. Newark, Delaware: Juan de la Cuesta, 2001, 565-571.

Vila, Juan Diego. "Don Quijote y Teseo en el laberinto ducal." *Actas del II Coloquio Internacional de la Asociación de Cervantistas*. Barcelona: Anthropos, 1991, 459-473.

Weber, Alison. "Pentimento: the Parodic Text of *La Gitanilla*." *Hispanic Review* 62 (1994): 59-75.

Cervantine Reflections on *The Matrix*

BRUCE R. BURNINGHAM

THIS ESSAY IS BASED on a chapter of my current book project, *Tinted Mirrors: Baroque Reflections on Contemporary Culture*. Before I launch into my Cervantine analysis of the Wachowski Brothers' landmark *Matrix* trilogy, however, a brief plot summary of a fairly complex narration is in order. The first film in the trilogy tells the story of an alienated office worker named Thomas Anderson (Keanu Reeves) who spends much of his free time surfing cyberspace under the hacker name "Neo," looking for some kind of confirmation that "there is something wrong with the world" (*Matrix* 0:27:16). This confirmation ultimately comes in the form of a demonstration by Morpheus (Laurence Fishburne) that the world as Neo knows it is simply a complex illusion—"the Matrix"—created by a powerful mainframe computer that stimulates Neo's cerebral cortex in order create a virtual reality inside his head. In "real" reality, Neo (along with nearly all the rest of humanity) is actually living in an isolated pod where the heat and electrical impulses produced by his body provide energy for a civilization of machines that have created this elaborate system in order to convert the entire human race into nothing more than an immense collection of imprisoned batteries. (The basic premise here, of course, is Descartes's notion of a malicious demon who deceives us unto perceiving an existence that does not really exist; the original version of what has come to be known in philosophical circles as the "brain in a vat" scenario.) Morpheus—who, along with a small group of others, has managed to "unplug" himself from the Matrix—frees Neo because he believes Neo is the messianic "One" (note the deliberate anagram) who will help liberate all of humanity. Throughout the course of the film, the various "unplugged" characters (having established a vast underground city called Zion) constantly "jack" them-selves back into the Matrix in order to engage in an ongoing battle with the "Agents" whose job it is as programs to police the Matrix and destroy threats to its existence. The climax of the first film occurs when Agent Smith (Hugo Weaving) kills Neo, who according to the logic of the film dies in the "real world" as well. Neo, however, is subsequently "resurrected" thanks to a real-world kiss from his love interest, Trinity (Carrie-Anne Moss), and then goes on to defeat Agent Smith, becoming in the end a kind of Superman who flies around the Matrix world harassing its cybernetic masters.

The second and third films essentially follow the struggle between the machines and the humans, but in doing so, add a couple of significant permutations to the narrative. First, the machines decide that the mere existence of Zion is unacceptable and thus set out to destroy this last human city. Second, Agent Smith somehow disconnects himself from the system — becoming what can only be called a "computer virus" — and spends most of the second and third installments taking over the identity of other individuals within the Matrix, thus effectively replicating himself millions of times over. If Neo is the "One," Smith becomes the "Many." Finally, Neo himself becomes increasingly disconnected from both the real world and the Matrix world as he struggles to discover whether he really is the "One," and if so, just what this means.

A great number of critics have written extensively on the *Matrix* trilogy, focusing particular attention on the Wachowski Brothers' self-conscious engagement with questions of philosophy, religion, Marxism, post-structuralist theory, etc. (The film contains unmistakable elements of Christian allegory, Buddhism, Gnosticism, and even makes explicit reference to the writings of Jean Baudrillard.) For those interested in these topics I recommend a book entitled *The Matrix and Philosophy* (edited by William Irwin). My own interest in these films, however, (as with so many chapters of *Tinted Mirrors*) stems precisely from the *Matrix* trilogy's uncanny re-inscription of Don Quixote's encounter with his own mirror image during his two jousts with Sansón Carrasco first as the Caballero de los Espejos and then as the Caballero de la Blanca Luna. Thus, I would like to focus here on two particular (and doubled) instances of Cervantine reflection involving the ongoing battle between Neo and Agent Smith.

The first of these two doubled encounters takes place on a subway platform at the end of the first film and is clearly meant to function as a homage to the final show down between the good guy and the bad guy of Hollywood Westerns like *High Noon* (a trope which is, itself, taken from the jousting matches of the romances of chivalry). Neo and Smith draw their guns, shooting until each is empty (although neither character inflicts a single wound on the other); after which the battle discourse returns to that of the martial arts, wire-fighting film so prevalent throughout the rest of the trilogy. (The Wachowski Brothers are deeply indebted to such films as *Crouching Tiger, Hidden Dragon*.) At this point, Neo and Smith engage in a highly choreographed fight that ends with Smith holding Neo in a head lock on the subway tracks while the metallic squeal of an oncoming train forebodes what Smith calls the "sound of inevitability," "the sound of [Neo's] death" (*Matrix* 1:57:50-58:01).

Two things tie this scene to Don Quixote's initial battle with Sansón. First, given Smith's overwhelmingly superior strength as an Agent who can literally bend the Matrix code to suit his combat needs, Neo quite unexpectedly defeats Smith by jumping some twenty vertical feet into the ceiling of the subway tunnel in order to free himself from Smith, who then is struck by the train as it speeds by. (As an Agent, of course, this merely kills the vagrant whose identity Smith has opportunistically assumed in order to fight Neo; Smith walks away unscathed from this encounter by transmorphing himself into yet another person). Second, and more importantly, however, what is at stake between Neo and Smith at this point in the film is precisely what is at stake between Don Quixote and Sansón. Early in film one, Agent Smith interrogates Neo and tells him that only one of his two lives (i.e., "Thomas Anderson" as opposed to "Neo") has a future. Thus, when Neo chooses his "hacker" identity over his respectable one, Smith's function throughout the three films becomes that of enforcing this ideological threat: if Neo will not willingly accept his status as Thomas Anderson, Smith will compel him to accept it. Needless to say, readers familiar with *Don Quixote* will recognize the analogy between Smith's relentless pursuit of Neo and Sansón's project throughout the second part of the novel of forcing Cervantes's knight-errant to abandon his self-constructed chivalric self in favor of his original identity as Alonso Quixano. Thus, throughout the course of Neo's subway encounter with Smith, this inquisitorial Agent continues to tauntingly refer to his foe as "Mr. Anderson" precisely because it is this official perspective that the Agent wishes to impose on Neo, regardless of whether or not he has managed to unplug himself from the Matrix. Significantly, then, when Neo makes his Herculean leap upwards in order to loosen himself from Smith's grasp, his biggest gesture of defiance is not so much the leap itself, but the phrase he utters while performing it: "My name is Neo" (*Matrix* 1:58:05-11). For just as Don Quixote insists, "Yo sé quien soy" (106; pt. 1, ch. 5), when confronted by those who challenge his chivalric identity, Neo's defeat of Smith in this scene is more than just physical. It is an ideological victory that resists the hegemony the gatekeepers of the Matrix seek to impose on all those wishing to opt out.

Neo's second face-to-face encounter with Smith in the first film, also mirrors Don Quixote's second encounter with Sansón. Having escaped from Smith's clutches in the subway, Neo races toward a nearby telephone (a device that awkwardly functions within the trilogy as the portal for moving between the real world and the Matrix world), all the while dodging a myriad of Agents who repeatedly assume the identities of various pedestrians. As he opens the door to answer the ringing telephone, Neo unexpectedly finds himself staring down the barrel of Smith's gun. Smith fires a single shot into Neo's heart, which seems to surprise him more than wound him, after which the Agent empties at least ten more rounds into Neo's chest at point blank range. This massive assault, needless to say, instantly kills Neo inside the Matrix, which also means that it kills him in the real world as well. As it would appear to turn out, neither of Neo's two lives have a future. Smith drives home this point by ultimately saying, "Goodbye Mr. Anderson" (*Matrix* 2:03:37-41). And just as "Alonso Quixano the Good" meets his end surrounded by loved ones who beg him not to give up the ghost quite yet, "Neo the Unplugged" dies sitting in a chair onboard a real-world hovercraft surrounded by his comrades-in-arms, none of whom can believe what they have just witnessed, none of whom can believe that Neo is not the "One."

But it is in this that *The Matrix* moves beyond *Don Quixote*. Cervantes himself is very explicit about leaving his protagonist dead and buried at the end of his 1615 second part (due in large measure, of course, to his desire to deter any more unauthorized sequels, like that published by Alonso Fernández de Avellaneda). The Wachowski Brothers, however, not only need the Christ-like Neo to be resurrected in order to become the messianic "One" at the end of the first film, they also need this "One" to move the *Matrix* narrative into the two sequels that will follow. And what ironically provokes Neo's very "un-Cervantine" resurrection is precisely a re-inscription of an uncannily Cervantine mechanism: Dulcinea's function as an ideological inspiration for her knight-errant. Immediately following Neo's two deaths (both of which are confirmed first by an Agent inside the Matrix who checks Neo's pulse and declares him dead and second by a heart monitor in the real world that clearly shows Neo's cardiographic flat line), Trinity whispers in Neo's ear that he simply cannot die because the Oracle has told her that the man with whom she would fall in love would be the "One." And with this, she gives him a kind of inverted "Sleeping Beauty" kiss that revives him not only in the real world, but also within the Matrix world, despite the several gunshot wounds that still ooze blood from his virtual chest. Turning to confront the Agents who have just declared him dead, Neo — like the enlightened prisoners of Plato's metaphoric cave — can suddenly see the Matrix code for what it really is: a trickling stream of binary code that forms the shadowy outlines of the Agents along with the hallway in which they stand. Neo's death and resurrection as the "One" have forever solidified the unorthodox ideological perspective Agent Smith has sought to annihilate. At this point, Neo quite literally jumps into Smith's virtual body, thus causing the Agent to explode into thousands of luminous shards, and he ends the film as a completely untethered force whose ability to fly represents his ultimate defiance of the orthodox laws set down by the Matrix's programmers.

Of course, as Neo himself reminds us in the film's epilogue, this is not the end, it is just the beginning. Thus, in true Cervantine fashion, Neo must face Agent Smith again precisely two more times in the third film of the trilogy. (The two engage in various minor skirmishes over the course of the second film, but none of these rises to the level of Cervantine encounter we find in films one and three, and hence we will pass over them without comment.) As with their two meetings in the first film, the two battles between Neo and Smith in the third film again serve to recapitulate the Don Quixote/Sansón Carrasco encounters. This time, however, Neo's and Smith's function as Cervantine mirror images of each other is made quite explicit. The first of these two meetings actually occurs in the real world itself when Smith manages to take over the body of an unplugged human just as he is coming out of the Matrix world. Very little of this encounter is germane to our immediate analysis, and thus I won't take time to discuss it in detail. I will note in passing, however, that Neo does defeat Smith the first time around, just as Don Quixote initially defeats the Caballero de los Espejos.

Neo's and Smith's second and final encounter occurs inside the Matrix world itself, a Matrix completely dominated by the rogue Agent who by now has turned every virtual man, woman, and child into a carbon copy of himself. Here, Neo finds Smith waiting for him on an urban street lined with thousands upon thousands of identical Smiths who stand as witnesses to their final confrontation. The special effects of this epic confrontation between Neo and Smith are visually impressive (even by the very high standards set by the previous two *Matrix* films), but very little of this thirteen-minute battle is intellectually engaging, and hence again we will simply pass over it. What matters, of course, especially for a culminating film whose tag line is "Everything that has a beginning has an end," is precisely the way this encounter ends. Standing inside an enormous crater in the middle of the street (one created by their very battle), and having beaten Neo nearly to death, Smith demands to know why Neo keeps fighting when his defeat is so clearly inevitable:

> Why, Mr. Anderson, why? Why? Why do you do it? Why? Why get up? Why keep fighting? Do you believe you are fighting for something, for more than your survival? Can you tell me what it is? Do you even know? Is it Freedom? Or Truth? Perhaps, Peace? Could it be Love? Illusions, Mr. Anderson, vagaries of perception. Temporary constructs of a feeble human intellect trying desperately to justify an existence that is without meaning or purpose. And all of them as artificial as the Matrix itself. Although, only a human could invent something as insipid as Love. You must be able to see it, Mr. Anderson. You must know it by now. You can't win. It's pointless to keep fighting. Why, Mr. Anderson? Why? Why do you persist? (*Revolutions* 1:48:44-49:52)

Neo's response to Smith's question — "Because I choose to" (*Revolutions* 1:49:54-56) — is extremely significant. In the first place, it goes to the heart of the entire *Matrix* trilogy's philosophical preoccupation with the issue of free will. Neo has arrived at this point in time (despite his famed predestination as the "One") precisely because he initially chose the blue pill instead of the red pill when Morpheus offered him the choice between finding out "how deep the rabbit hole goes" (an obvious reference to Lewis Carrol's *Alice Through the Looking Glass*), and returning to his quiet life as "Thomas Anderson," virtual software engineer oblivious to the fallen state of humanity. In essence, Neo persists in fighting Smith because that is his purpose *as Neo*, as the "One." Ironically, having chosen to be "Neo" instead of "Mr. Anderson" when he accepted Morpheus's blue pill, Neo can now do nothing else. He might just as well have answered Smith's question in the past tense rather than the present tense: "Because I chose to."

In the second place, Neo's response to Smith (in its present tense form) can be read nearly four hundred years after the fact as a brilliantly succinct summation of Don Quixote's own *raison d'etre*. Smith's indictment of what he calls Neo's "illusions" and "vagaries of perception" perfectly describe Don Quixote's own self-constructed world view. In this regard, Neo is more than just a Christ figure who triumphantly redeems the world after its fall from grace. He is also a quixotic figure who, like his Cervantine predecessor, chooses to battle evil enchanters (in this case, the various Agents) against insurmountable odds, in order to attempt to restore the world to its long-lost Golden Age, one that existed before the machines took control of it. Thus, Smith's inquisitorial skepticism echoes that of the churchman in the palace of the Duke and Duchess in the second part who calls Don Quixote "Don Tonto" and admonishes him to go back home and mind his own business. Of course, as we know, Cervantes's protagonist *does* fight for something more than just his own survival. In fact, if personal "survival" were the central issue, Alonso Quixano would never have left home in the first place. It is precisely because he conceives of a higher purpose that he has ventured out into the world. The question implicit in the churchman's criticism, of course, is exactly that uttered by Smith at the end of his own harangue: Why does Don Quixote persist in fighting for what people like the churchman consider nothing more than illusions? And Don Quixote's response to this churchman's inability to comprehend the values of chivalry amounts to nothing less than Neo's elegant statement of free will directed toward an artificial intelligence who, despite spending much of the *Matrix* trilogy vainly attempting to practice it, proves utterly incapable of understanding the concept: "caballero soy y caballero he de morir" (II: 283; pt. 1, ch. 31).

But this is precisely why Neo's final choice is so important, and why it so perfectly mirrors Don Quixote's own final choice after his defeat at the hands of the Caballero de la Blanca Luna. Readers of *Don Quixote* will remember that the terms of combat Sansón Carrasco imposes on Don Quixote essentially amount to Don Quixote's acceptance of the churchman's previous criticism: "y si tu peleares y yo te venciere, no quiero otra satisfación sino que dejando las armas y absteniéndote de buscar aventuras, te recojas y retires a tu lugar por tiempo de un año, donde has de vivir sin echar mano a la espada" (II: 532-33; pt. 2, ch. 64). Thus, when Sansón finally defeats Don Quixote, the weary knight prefers death to a renunciation of his profession: he *will* die a caballero. And while Sansón ultimately refuses to accommodate this death wish, Don Quixote soon dies nonetheless. In Neo's case, this relationship between death and defeat is inverted. At the end of their long struggle, Neo comes to realize that Smith has been right all along, that his defeat is inevitable. But in this very recognition comes Neo's greatest moment of triumph. He chooses to stop fighting and thus allows Smith to assimilate him (by now, the last non-assimilated individual within the entire Matrix construct). Smith extends his hand into Neo's virtual corporeal space, as we have seen him do so many times before, and with this action Neo becomes a Smith. Shortly thereafter, the Matrix crashes, destroying the entire cadre of renegade Smiths in the process, and then re-boots itself, thus returning the system back to square one for what the film suggests is the seventh time. Where Sansón defeats Don Quixote by becoming a mirror image of the knight-errant, Neo ultimately defeats Smith not just by reflecting his enemy, but by allowing himself to be turned into an exact replica. In this, Neo succeeds against Smith by abandoning all pretense to subjectivity by paradoxically *choosing* to give up his free will in order to accept his fate.

Smith's dialogue leading up to this culminating moment of assimilation is crucial for an understanding of its ultimate Cervantine significance, especially when he says, "everything that has a beginning has an end, Neo" (*Revolutions* 1:51:30-58). This is the only time in the entire *Matrix* trilogy where Smith refers to Neo as "Neo" (rather than calling him "Mr. Anderson," as we have frequently noted), and Smith is completely perplexed by the words he unexpectedly hears coming out of his own mouth. We, of course, have heard these words before. The Oracle uses this nearly exact turn of phrase earlier when she informs Neo that the end is near. Thus, when we hear these words coming out Smith's mouth, we realize—as he ultimately does not—that this particular "Smith" is not the one we have been following throughout the course of the trilogy, not the one who initially defeats Neo in the first film. The Smith who defeats Neo at the very end is precisely the Smith who emerged when the Oracle was, herself, assimilated (a reading confirmed by the fact that, once the system re-boots itself, it is the Oracle whose inert body lies in the mud where this particular Smith had previously lain). And just prior to the Oracle's original assimila-tion, when Neo asks her about the nature of Smith's function within what is clearly a Biblically inspired post-modern morality play, she telling replies: "He is you: your opposite, your negative, the result of the equation trying to balance itself out" (*Revolutions* 0:29:39-47). The Oracle's words, of course, echo those of the Architect, who responds in the second film to Neo's question about his own functionality by saying: "Your life is the sum of a remainder of an unbalanced equation inherent to the programming of the Matrix. You are the eventuality of an anomaly which, despite my sincerest efforts, I have been unable to eliminate from what is otherwise a harmony of mathematical precision" (*Reloaded* 1:50:53-51:11).

But this takes us back to what is essentially *the* central moment of the *Matrix* trilogy, both cinematically and philosophically. In a scene simultaneously evoking Miguel de Unamuno's novel *Niebla* (in which the protagonist, Augusto Pérez, confronts his god-like author in order to engage in a discussion about his free will or lack thereof) and Jorge Luis Borges's stories "El Aleph" and "El jardín de senderos que se bifurcan" (in which Borges explores the notion of self-enclosed and infinitely bifurcating universes, respectively), Neo's interview with the Architect deliberately reduces all of the *Matrix*'s complex themes to a single conversation that takes place in a unique space apart (neither inside the Matrix world nor inside the real world) within which Neo finds himself infinitely surrounded by his own reflection displayed on thousands of television screens that set up a visual mise-en-abîme in which an infinite number of Neos demonstrate an ever-bifurcating series of realities. (In fact, to underscore the infinite multiplicity of this visual mise-en-abîme, the camera seems to pass through various screens — from one parallel reality to another — as this scene progresses.) And the crux of this scene — indeed the crux of the entire *Matrix* trilogy, since everything that happens from this point onward flows from it — comes down to the following piece of dialogue uttered by the Architect as he sends Neo on his final journey:

> Which brings us at last the moment of truth, wherein the fundamental flaw is ultimately expressed and the anomaly revealed as both beginning and end. There are two doors. The door to your right leads to the source and the salvation of Zion. The door to your left leads back to the Matrix, to her [i.e., to Trinity, whose death the Architect insists is inevitable], and the end of your species. As you adequately put: the problem is choice. (*Reloaded* 1:56:20-47)

Needless to say, Neo chooses the door on the left, in part because at this point he still labors under the illusion that he has free will, and in part because a Hollywood blockbuster — however philosophically engaged and postmodern — cannot allow its quixotic hero to abandon his Dulcinea to her untimely demise (a fact which, in an ironically Unamunian way, further calls into question Neo's very subjectivity, since his "choice" is always already over-determined not just by the Wachowski Brothers's screenplay, but by the studio moguls who have financed its production and who call the final shots). Nevertheless, Neo's over-determined choice of doors does result in a double paradox. On the one hand, his choice of the "left" door does *not* result, as the Architect erroneously predicts, in the end of humanity. On the other hand, as we saw with regard to Neo's final confrontation with Smith, his avoidance of the "right" door does not allow him to escape the fate the Architect has in store for him.

But this in and of itself leads us to one final Cervantine reflection. In his highly influential work, *The Order of Things*, Michel Foucault says of Cervantes's gangly protagonist: "He never manages to escape from the familiar plain stretching out on all sides of the Analogue, any more than he does from his own small province. He travels endlessly over that plain, without ever crossing the clearly defined frontiers of difference, or reaching the heart of identity" (46). Substitute the words "Matrix" for "plain" and "Digital" for "Analogue" in the preceding quote, and Foucault's comments emerge as equally apropos of Neo. Try as he might, Neo can never escape his inscription within the Matrix code. (Or, as Jacques Derrida might have said, for Neo "there is nothing outside" the Matrix [158].) Moreover, since Neo is explicitly described in the *Matrix* trilogy as a numerical sign—the remainder of an unbalanced equation—he is not only the anagrammatical, messianic "One," he is also the integer "1," a mathematical sign whose existence, as the Architect so accurately reveals, cannot be separated from the symbolic system within which it is embedded: "The function of the One is now to return to the source, allowing a temporary dissemination of the code you carry, reinserting the prime program" (*Reloaded* 1:54:51-59). Neo's ultimate function is to simply re-boot the system. And in this regard, Neo, the "1," serves as the quintessential postmodern reflection of Don Quixote: "he is himself like a sign, a long thin graphism, [whose] whole being is nothing but language [and who wanders] through the world among the resemblance of things" (Foucault 46). Neo—the remainder, the "unbalan-cer," the 1 among 0s—is the ultimate embodiment of the Cervantine baroque. He is not just a Christ figure; he is quite simply asymmetry incarnate, a postmodern Don Quixote whose function—first and last—is to always upset the ideological equilibrium that exists within the system.

Works Cited

Cervantes Saavedra, Miguel de. *El ingenioso hidalgo Don Quijote de la Mancha*. Ed. Luis Andrés Murillo. 2 vols. Madrid: Castalia, 1978.

Derrida, Jacques. *Of Grammatology*. Trans. Gayatri Chakravorty Spivak. Baltimore: Johns Hopkins University Press, 1976.

Foucault, Michel. *The Order of Things: An Archaeology of the Human Sciences*. New York: Vintage, 1994.

Irwin, William, ed. The Matrix *and Philosophy: Welcome to the Desert of the Real*. Chicago: Open Court, 2002.

The Matrix. Dir. Andy Wachowski and Larry Wachowski. Screenplay by Andy Wachowski and Larry Wachowski. With Keanu Reeves, Laurence Fishburne, Carrie-Ann Moss, Hugo Weaving, and Joe Pantoliano. Warner Brothers, 1999. Color, 136 min.

The Matrix Reloaded. Dir. Andy Wachowski and Larry Wachowski. Screenplay by Andy Wachowski and Larry Wachowski. With Keanu Reeves, Laurence Fishburne, Carrie-Ann Moss, Hugo Weaving, Jada Pinkett Smith, and Gloria Foster. Warner Brothers, 2003. Color, 129 min.

The Matrix Revolutions. Dir. Andy Wachowski and Larry Wachowski. Screenplay by Andy Wachowski and Larry Wachowski. With Keanu Reeves, Laurence Fishburne, Carrie-Ann Moss, Hugo Weaving, and Jada Pinkett Smith. Warner Brothers, 2004. Color, 138 min. Don Quijote, el cuarto centenario y las fuerzas del orden

Que trata de la velocidad de Rocinante y otros asuntos de importancia

DAVID CASTILLO

AL PARECER ALGUIEN DESCUBRIÓ no hace mucho la partida de nacimiento de Alonso Quijano, con lo que cabría suponer que se ha fijado definitivamente la identidad del ingenioso hidalgo manchego a pesar de las dudas del desmemoriado o desganado narrador del capítulo primero del *Quijote*. Nada de Quijada o Quesada, ni siquiera, Quejana, como suponía el narrador "por conjeturas verosímiles." Alonso Quijano y punto. De esta forma, el protagonista dejaría de ser un personaje indocumentado, un sin papeles, para convertirse en ciudadano de pleno derecho. Pero es esta una historia de hace un par de años. Más recientemente un equipo científico internacional ha podido fijar, despues de varios años de trabajo, el lugar silenciado por el narrador, la mítica localidad manchega de cuyo nombre no quiso acordarse.

He aquí en titulares la noticia recogida por numerosos periódicos impresos y electrónicos a finales de diciembre del 2004 y principios de Enero del 2005: "Ubican el lugar de la Mancha de don Quijote," "Profesores de la Complutense sitúan en la localidad de Villanueva de los Infantes la morada de D. Quijote," "Villanueva de los Infantes. Quijote 2005." Y elaboran: "La primera línea de El Ingenioso hidalgo don Quijote de la Mancha, la obra maestra de Miguel de Cervantes, encierra un misterio que ha entretenido por años –400, para ser más precisos– a los estudiosos de la obra: 'En un lugar de La Mancha, de cuyo nombre no quiero acordarme, no ha mucho tiempo que vivía un hidalgo de los de lanza en astillero, adarga antigua, rocín flaco y galgo corredor'. El enigma es ese lugar del que no quiere acordarse el narrador [...] Pero ahora un grupo de investigadores de la universidad complutense de Madrid asegura haber determinado con precision 'ese lugar de la Mancha': la localidad de Villanueva de los Infantes, cerca de Ciudad Real, 220 kilómetros al sureste de Madrid [...] Así, los especialistas han fijado el lugar" (*La Tercera*, Cultura, 14 de diciembre,

61

2004). En otra fuente se lee: "Quixote 2005 [...] Despues de cuatro siglos durante los que ha resultado imposible localizarlo, y aplicando por vez primera una metodología científica y un estudio exhaustivo de las distintas posibilidades, este equipo multidisciplinar ha fijado la mítica localidad manchega en Villanueva de los Infantes [...] Veintisiete pueblos reales que debían encontrarse, como lo exige el texto cervantino, en el Campo de Montiel, fueron estudiados y confrontados a 24 variables, siguiendo hasta once hipótesis de trabajo y valorando cuestiones que llegan hasta la velocidad a la que Don Quijote y Sancho marchaban a lomos de Rocinante y del rucio, que venían a ser, según afirma el estudio, 31 kilómetros en días de verano y 22 en días de invierno" (castillalamancha.es, Villanueva de los Infantes. Quijote 2005).

Ya tenemos entonces convenientemente ubicado, anclado, fijado, al caballero manchego, a pesar de la mala memoria y peor voluntad del narrador. Hay quien dice que el arte de la fijación va unido a otras artes académicas (la limpieza y el dar esplendor) que son propias de las instituciones a las que Julio Baena llama "beneméritas" con un punto de malicia quevedesca que le hace a uno pensar en cuarteles y tricornios. Sea como fuere, cabría hacerse la pregunta ¿y para qué tanto fijar? Quizá las palabras de Mariano Sabina, alcalde de la agraciada localidad de Villanueva de los infantes nos puedan servir de pista, cuando medio en broma pide a la autoridad judicial "que incluya en el código penal como delito no visitar este pueblo manchego en el año cervantino" (castillalamancha.es, Villanueva de los Infantes. Quijote 2005). Digo medio en broma porque lo cierto es que el anuncio de que don Quijote vivió en Villanueva, automáticamente sitúa a esta localidad en el corazón mismo de la Ruta de don Quijote. Se trata de un circuito que parte de Toledo y abarca el Toboso, la citada Villanueva de los Infantes, Almagro, Albacete, los Campos de Montiel, el Campo de Criptana –donde los famosos molinos— y entre otros lugares la casa de Cervantes en Esquivias.

Es ésta una ruta representativa del llamado eco-turismo cultural iluminada por 4,000 señales, unos 200 mapas cartográficos y otras tantas guías interpretativas. Como se dice en *El tiempo* de Bogotá, con lo cual se certifica la internacionalidad de la noticia, la ruta nos lleva "de pueblo en pueblo por los áridos caminos castellanos y manchegos, hasta reencontrar la figura del mítico hidalgo" (2 de febrero, 2005). Desde luego con tanta señal, mapa y guía se podría decir que el camino no tiene pérdida. Es decir que no hay riesgo de perdernos sino que se trata de todo lo contrario de "encontrarnos" siguiendo las huellas de don Quijote. Turismo cultural, una buena razón sin duda para fijar el Quijote, tanto el personaje como el texto. En lo que respecta al texto, una de las manifestaciones más interesantes de esta bendita comunión de eco-turismo y cultura es el *Quijote* de cabecera de los paradores nacionales de turismo, una antología modernizada y condensada que apareció hace poco más de un año con motivo del cuarto centenario. Ernest Hemingway se quejaba en 1921 del tratamiento que recibía entonces el *Quijote* junto con otros clásicos que se veían condensados "para consumición del agotado hombre de negocios" ("Como condensar a los clásicos," recogido en *El Quijote del IV centenario* 33). Las observaciones de Hemingway al respecto del emergente género de las condensaciones pueden considerarse proféticas: "Pero aún hay un modo más rápido de presentar el asunto a quienes han de correr mientras leen: reducir toda la literatura a titulares de prensa, seguidos de una pequeña nota que resuma el argumento. Por ejemplo, El Quijote. Caballero Demente en Una Lucha Espectral. Madrid, España (Agencia de Noticias Clásicas) (Especial). Se atribuye a histerismo de guerra la extraña conducta de don Quijote, un caballero local que ayer por la mañana fue arrestado mientras 'combatía' con un Molino. Quijote no supo dar una explicación de sus actos" (citado en *El Quijote del IV centenario* 33).

La condensación de paradores de turismo, claro está, no llega tan lejos, puesto que se trata de una selección de diez capítulos (4 de la Primera Parte y 6 de la Segunda). De hecho esta antología del centenario está concebida para ocupar el lugar de la Biblia o los evangelios en la mesita de noche de los dormitorios de los paradores. Como escribe el editor, Andrés Amorós en su breve introducción, "sin exagerar mucho podemos decir que nuestra Biblia es el Quijote: un libro con el que se aprendía a leer [...] el mejor resumen de nuestro espíritu y el símbolo de lo español y lo hispánico en el mundo entero" (Introducción 10). Las palabras del editor de la antología vienen precedidas de una presentación institucional firmada por doña Ana Isabel Mariño Ortega, Presidenta Consejera-Delegada de Paradores de Turismo de España. Según la presidenta, la cadena hotelera de paradores nacionales y Cervantes tienen en común "el ser embajadores de la esencia cultural y artística de España y los españoles, espejo que ofrece al mundo lo mejor de nosotros mismos" (9).

Todo esto de los textos solemnes y las esencias de españolidad le recuerdan a uno las enciclopedias de antaño, de los tiempos de Franco (con perdón) cuando se citaban o recitaban las lapidarias palabras de Primo de

Rivera: "Eres español. Por haber nacido en España, eres español, que es una de las pocas cosas serias que se pueden ser en el mundo, como ardorosa y genialmente definió José Antonio. Por ser español perteneces a la nación de más brillante historia del mundo, a la nación que supo escalar las más altas cimas de la voluntad y del pensamiento. Eres hermano de raza de santos como San Vicente Ferrer, el ardiente evangelizador de los judíos valencianos [...] de Santo Domingo de Guzmán, fundador de la Orden de Predicadores para combatir herejías [...] de San Francisco Javier, evangelizador de las Indias Orientales" (Fernández Rodríguez, *Enciclopedia práctica de grado medio*, citada por Luis Otero 123).

En su calidad de caballero escogido para la heróica tarea de resucitar la edad de oro, don Quijote podría ser incluído entre tanto adalid de la salvífica españolidad. Esto es al menos lo que deja entrever el ideólogo fascista Ernesto Giménez Caballero en su *Genio de España: exaltaciones a una resurrección nacional y del mundo* (1932). No deja de ser significativo que en su defensa de la santa españolidad, y en su intento de resucitar nuestra católica e imperial edad de oro, Giménez Caballero se decida por abrazarse a la estatua de don Quijote mientras rechaza el paródico gesto cervantino que resulta más caústico de lo tolerable.

He aquí uno de los pasajes que pudieran haber motivado el adverso juicio de Giménez Caballero en lo que respecta a la ironía cervantina que considera un síntoma de crisis y, al mismo tiempo, un signo inequívoco de bastardía espiritual: " —Dichosa edad y siglos dichosos aquellos a quien los antiguos pusieron nombre de dorados [...] Las doncellas y la honestidad andaban, como tengo dicho, por dondequiera, sola y señora, sin temor a que la ajena desenvoltura y lascivo intento le menoscabasen [...] andando más los tiempos y creciendo más la malicia, se instituyó la orden de los caballeros andantes, para defender las doncellas, amparar las viudas y socorrer a los huérfanos y a los menesterosos. Desta orden soy yo, hermanos cabreros [...] Toda esta larga arenga (que se pudiera muy bien escusar) dijo nuestro caballero, porque las bellotas que le dieron le trujeron a la memoria la edad dorada y antojósele hacer aquel inútil razonamiento a los cabreros, que, sin respondelle palabra, embobados y suspensos, le estuvieron escuchando" (169-171).

Convendría quizá insistir en este juicio del narrador de 1605 que se distancia de la visión de don Quijote y del editor de la antología de paradores para el 2005 quien califica el discurso quijotesco de "hermoso." La actitud socarrona y el tono burlesco con que se contextualiza la utopía regresiva de la edad de oro presenta su versión más radical en el famoso episodio de los batanes. En otro lugar ("Clarividencia tangencial...") establecimos una conexión entre el tipo de inversión paródica que se produce en este capítulo del *Quijote* y la situación paradigmática del grabado anamórfico de motivo bíblico de Edhart Schön *Was siehst du?* (¿Qué ve usted?) (1538), el cual incorpora dos puntos de vista distintos: una escena frontal representando el momento en que Jonás sale de la boca de la ballena, junto a una imagen lateral que resulta indistinguible desde el punto de vista central. Al mirar desde el margen se puede apreciar una escena que poco o nada tiene que ver con la fuente bíblica: se trata del grotesco perfil de un campesino ocupado en satisfacer sus necesidades. El fruto de sus esfuerzos aparece justamente debajo de la figura de Jonás.

En el caso del capítulo XX de la Primera Parte del *Quijote* la incontinencia irreverente de Sancho, que tiene lugar a los pies de su amo, produce una inversión paródica del gesto heróico del caballero de la triste figura y en especial del discurso de la edad de oro que pronunciara al comienzo del episodio cuando se otorga a sí mismo la calidad de encarnación presente de la mítica edad dorada: "—Sancho amigo, has de saber que yo nací, por querer del cielo, en nuestra edad de hierro, para resucitar en ella la de oro, o la dorada, como suele llamarse. Yo soy aquel para quien están guardados los peligros, las grandes hazañas, los valerosos hechos" (246). Quizá no esté de más recordar aquí el momento clave de la recontextualización del discurso quijotesco hacia el final del capítulo:

—Paréceme, Sancho, que tienes mucho miedo.

—Sí tengo –respondió Sancho—; más, ¿en qué lo echa de ver vuestra merced ahora más que nunca?

—En que ahora más que nunca hueles, y no a ámbar –respondió don Quijote.

—Bien podrá ser –dijo Sancho—, mas yo no tengo la culpa, sino vuestra merced, que me trae a deshoras y por estos no acostumbrados pasos.

Flaco favor hacemos a la novela de Cervantes al monumentalizarla, al querer convertirla en embajadora de la esencia mítica de lo español a la manera de la condensación de paradores. Al fin y al cabo el *Quijote* es una obra que nació precisamente en las antípodas de esta noción para burlarse de mitos, utopias regresivas, esencias y reliquias. Como dice Fernando

Vallejo en una conferencia pronunciada en junio en la sede del Instituto Cervantes de Berlín y recientemente impresa en un suplemento de *El País*, "el *Quijote* se burla de todo y cuanto toca lo vuelve motivo de irrisión: las novelas de caballerías y las pastoriles, el lenguaje jurídico y el eclesiástico, la Santa Hermandad y el Santo Oficio, los escritores italianos y grecolatinos, la mitología y la historia, los bachilleres y los médicos, los versos y la prosa..." (*El País*, 10 de septiembre, 2005).

Y si se trata de desenmascarar mitos lo urgente en el año 2005 no es levantar estatuas o crear nuevas reliquias culturales, sino lo contrario, denunciar cruzadas que se hacen en nombre de utopías regresivas, de 'conservadurismos compasivos', ya vengan de nuestro pasado literario o del presente político. ¿Y no es esto lo que ocurre al final del capítulo LVIII de la Segunda parte cuando don Quijote se encuentra con un grupo de estatuas entre las que se incluyen las efigies de San Jorge, San Martín y el santo patrón de España y sus fuerzas armadas, don San Diego Matamoros? "Este sí que es caballero — dice don Quijote — y de las escuadras de Cristo; éste se llama don San Diego Matamoros, uno de los más valientes santos y caballeros que tuvo el mundo y tiene agora el cielo [...] Por buen agüero he tenido, hermanos, haber visto lo que he visto, porque estos santos y caballeros profesaron lo que yo profeso, que es el ejercicio de las armas, sino que la diferencia que hay entre mí y ellos es que ellos fueron santos y pelearon a lo divino, y yo soy pecador y peleo a lo humano" (459). El hecho de que Santiago Matamoros, sea presentado por el propio don Quijote como uno de sus precursores y modelos caballerescos junto al mismo Amadís de Gaula nos debe de hacer repensar el sentido de la utopía quijotesca de la edad de oro.

En este punto nos viene a la memoria el escándalo producido por el gesto desdeñoso de Rodríguez Zapatero durante las ceremonias de celebración de la hispanidad a poco de su investidura como presidente del gobierno español. Al parecer Zapatero se negó a abrazar la efigie del apóstol Santiago, como es uso y costumbre. Que Zapatero, como ciudadano de a pie, se confesase más o menos católico, en el fondo sería lo de menos. El escándalo surge cuando, actuando en calidad de presidente del gobierno español, se niega a abrazar el símbolo patriótico viniendo de esta forma a emborronar los actos de celebración de la fiesta nacional. Como firmaba el columnista Gonzalo de Berceo en *Desde la Fé*: "subió a abrazar la imagen del Apóstol Santiago (que es abrazar la propia tradición, las propias raíces, la propia cultura y los valores mas hondos de la conciencia del pueblo) y no la abrazó." El caso de Cervantes es aún más radical. No es que subiera a abrazar el monumento y no lo abrazara sino que lo tira por los suelos y lo pisotea cuando al final del capítulo, la comitiva caballeril es embestida y pataleada por una manada de vacunos. ¿Será posible que Giménez Caballero no estuviera del todo equivocado cuando afirmaba que el *Quijote* de 1605 es el principio del fin del imperio español, el virus que acabaría por arrasar el orgullo místico y ciego de la España imperial?

Cabría preguntarse en este año de conmemoraciones si es posible celebrar el *Quijote* sin elevarlo al estatus de reliquia cultural o monumento de las fuerzas del orden. Hemingway no era el único que se quejaba de lo que se hacía con el *Quijote* en los albores del siglo XX; tambien se quejaba Miguel de Unamuno. Para él lo urgente era liberar el sepulcro del *Quijote* usurpado por los representates de la razón: "rescatar el sepulcro de Don Quijote del poder de los bachilleres, curas, barberos, duques y canónigos que lo tienen ocupado [...] rescatar el sepulcro del Caballero de la Locura del poder de los hidalgos de la Razón" (*La vida de Don Quijote y Sancho*, citado en *El Quijote del IV Centenario* 29-31). Entre las noticias en torno al *Quijote* y las fuerzas del orden en este año del centenario, destaca un curioso artículo que apareció el 7 de Marzo en *Los Angeles Times*. El periódico nos informaba de que el alcalde de Nezahualcoyotl, circa Mexico City, ha decretado la obligatoriedad de la lectura del *Quijote* entre las fuerzas del orden público. Según la noticia, los oficiales de policía de la ciudad mexicana se ven ahora requeridos a leer la novela cervantina y escribir un reportaje. El artículo viene acompañado de una foto del alcalde, don Luis Sánchez, con el *Quijote* de Porrúa bajo el brazo.

Se puede (se debe) rescatar a *Don Quijote* de entre los brazos de las fuerzas de la razón y el orden como reclamaba Unamuno en 1905, año del tercer centenario? A lo mejor, o a lo peor, le pasa al *Quijote* en los centenarios lo que le pasaba a la pastora Marcela en los rituales funerarios; que tiene su lugar designado en la ceremonia y lo que le compete es dejarse celebrar o vilipendiar en respetuoso silencio, como es uso y costumbre. Por cierto que uno encuentra ciertas similitudes entre el escándalo que produce la réproba pastora Marcela cuando se niega a ocupar el lugar que le corresponde en las solemnidades organizadas por la comitiva pastoril en el capitulo XIV de la Primera Parte y lo que ocurre cuando el rapero Kanye West rehusa ocupar el lugar que le habían designado en la gala de NBC en beneficio de las víctimas de Katrina dejando de lado las palabras prefijadas para expresar otras, las suyas, que naturalmente se salen de contexto. Un corresponsal de

AP Television recoge la noticia: "Kanye West Rips Bush at Hurricane Aid Show. New York -A celebrity telethon for Hurricane Katrina survivors took an unexpected turn when outspoken rapper Kanye West went off script during the live broadcast, declaring America is set up 'to help the poor, the black people, the less well-off as slow as possible' [...]

West began a rant by saying, 'I hate the way they portray us in the media. If you see a black family, it says they're looting. See a white family, it says they're looking for food'. While allowing that 'the Red Cross is doing everything they can' [...] he stated, 'George Bush doesn't care about black people [...] In a statement, NBC said, 'Kanye West departed from the scripted comments that were prepared for him, and his opinions in no way represent the views of the networks' [...] The show, simulcast from New York on NBC, MSNBC, CNBC and Pax, was aired live to the East Coast, enabling the Grammy-winning rapper's outburst to go out uncensored. West's comment about the president was cut from NBC's West Coast airing, which showed three hours later on tape. There was a several-second tape delay, but the person in charge 'was instructed to listen for a curse word, and didn't realize (West) had gone off-script', NBC spokeswoman Rebecca Marks added" (Frazier Moore, AP Television, 3 de septiembre, 2005).

Como se puede ver, el problema aquí es la escasa efectividad de la censura. Seguramente esto no hubiera ocurrido si los encargados de la labor de limpia fueran el cura y el barbero, aquellos beneméritos hidalgos de la razón que con el beneplácito del ama cegaron la puerta de la locura de don Quijote (el aposento de sus libros) en su afán de impedir su segunda salida. Decía Unamuno que los curas, barberos y demás hidalgos de la razón custodian el sepulcro "para que el caballero no resucite" (citado en *El Quijote del IV Centenario* 31).

Hoy en día hay que pensar en el *Quijote* del futuro. Y en esto andan, no ya la cadena de paradores nacionales de turismo, sino empresas españolas de más altas miras. El día 4 de Julio del 2005 *El País* recogía en titulares la siguiente noticia de alcance internacional: "La NASA dispara contra un cometa. La misión Deep Impact estrella hoy un proyectil de 372 kilos contra el Tempel 1." Hacia el fondo de la página, en una sección titulada "Choques naturales y planes para nuevas colisiones" podía leer el desocupado lector lo siguiente: "la Agencia Europea del Espacio (ESA) tiene en estudio una misión [...] elegida entre media docena de propuestas. Se trata de la idea de una empresa española, Deimos, que ha diseñado un proyecto –bautizado Don Quijote– para ir al encuentro de un asteroide y hacer que un módulo choque contra la superficie del mismo, mientras el otro [presumiblemente Sancho Panza] lo estudia en directo a poca distancia." De llevarse a cabo el proyecto no sería de extrañar que el falsario autor arábigo Cide Hamete Benengeli abandonase su retiro para historiar las futuras aventuras del caballero manchego en su póstuma salida espacial.

UNIVERSITY AT BUFFALO, SUNY

Obras citadas:

Baena, Julio. *Discordancias cervantinas*. Newark: Juan de la Cuesta, 2003.

Castillalamancha.es, Villanueva de los Infantes. Quijote 2005.

Castillo, David. "Clarividencia tangencial y excentricidad en El licenciado Vidriera: nueva interpretación de un motivo clásico." *Estas primicias del ingenio. Jóvenes cervantistas en Chicago*. Eds. Francisco Caudet y Kerry Wilks. Castalia, 2003.

Cervantes, Miguel de. *Don Quijote de la Mancha*. 2 Vols. Ed. John Jay Allen. Madrid: Cátedra, 1998.

_____. *Don Quijote de la Mancha. Selección de capítulos y version modernizada*. Ed. Andrés Amorós. Madrid: Paradores de Turismo, 2003.

El Tiempo, 2 de febrero, 2005.

Giménez Caballero, Ernesto. *Genio de España: exaltaciones a una resurrección nacional y del mundo*. Madrid: La Gaceta Literaria, 1932.

La Tercera, 14 de diciembre, 2004.

Moore, Frazier. AP Television, 3 de septiembre, 2005.

Otero, Luis. *En el nombre de Franco, del Hijo y del Espíritu Santo: memoria de un tiempo en que caminábamos por el imperio hacia Dios sabe dónde*. Barcelona: Ediciones B, 2003.

Vallejo, Fernando. Conferencia pronunciada el 7 de junio del 2005 en la sede del Instituto Cervantes de Berlín. Impresa en *El País*, 10 de Septiembre, 2005.

Vizcaíno, Candela, Fernando Tejón y Joan Gonper. *El Quijote del IV Centenario (1605-2005)*. Salamanca: Celya, 2005.

'¡Oh hideputa, bellaco, y cómo es católico!': Sancho, Blasphemy, and the Baroque Public Sphere

WILLIAM CHILDERS

IN BOTH PARTS OF *Don Quixote*, Sancho Panza exemplifies the rural popular classes, which formed a semi-autonomous social world in early modern Europe. Though under siege during the Counter-Reformation, the cultural identity of the Spanish peasantry still retained distinctive beliefs and practices.[1] Sancho's on-going dialogue with Don Quixote and his encounters with a range of people from different walks of life constitute the only sustained image of this crucial social group in the novel. He therefore bears a heavy burden of representation. Cervantes poured a lot of material into this mold, creating a composite of at least three elements. First, Sancho belongs to a conventional literary type, a rural *gracioso*, part wise-cracking clown, part country bumpkin. At the same time, he gives voice to the oral tradition in the proverbs, jokes, and stories he tells. Finally, we should not forget that in Sancho, Cervantes must also have included aspects of peasant life as he observed it. This composite nature of the representation poses a problem for the interpretation of changes in Sancho's behavior. We cannot always decide whether to consider them as an internal development, for example a consequence of his sharing the mad knight's adventures, or as hitherto unexplored aspects of peasant society. Given the transitional historical moment straddled by the first and second parts, we may also consider the possibility that such differences correspond to social changes taking place in early modern Spain.

---

[1] Ginzburg's *The Cheese and the Worms* remains the finest articulation of this dynamic. For Spain, William A. Christian's *Local Religion* and Sara T. Nalle's *God in La Mancha* provide the best accounts along similar lines.

Even within the 1605 *Quixote*, Sancho's speech and behavior vary. His increasingly familiar tone when addressing his master contrasts with his deferential and even embarrassed attitude before the priest or the noble guests at the inn. He makes himself quite at home among the goatherds, helping himself to the wine with an alacrity that demonstrates he is in his element. Yet he appears tongue-tied when he meets up with the priest and barber in Sierra Morena, and speaks in hushed tones to his master concerning his doubts about Dorotea's true identity. Again, when the barber whose harness he stole reappears, he has no trouble asserting his claim to these "spoils." Thus we often see him adjusting his behavior depending on his interlocutors.

The Sancho of Part Two speaks up with greater confidence, even, for example, to the Duchess. As governor of Barataria his ability to express his views openly before large groups of people goes far beyond anything we see in Part One. Variations in his tone and language still persist, however. At times, he is temporarily liberated from the usual constraints of social decorum. In his brief encounters with Tomé Cecial and the Morisco Ricote, he is alone with another member of the peasant class, without Don Quixote or any other social superior present. Each of these scenes contains an irreverent moment, which, without crossing over to the overtly blasphemous, enacts a profanation of sacred categories that still today can produce a shiver of scandalized delight. In the first, he uses the phrase "¡Oh hideputa, bellaco, y cómo es católico!" to praise the wine the Knight of the Woods' squire shares with him. In the second, Sancho enjoys a roadside lunch with a banished Morisco and a group of false pilgrims come from Germany to beg alms for their own enrichment. He joins them in "taking aim at the heavens" with their wineskins, itself a quasi-blasphemous gesture. Then to the affirmation, in *lingua franca*, "Español y tudesqui, tutto uno, bon compaño" which implicitly equates Lutherans and Catholics, Sancho responds with the rather impious ratification: "¡Bon compaño, jura Di!" Though such mild oaths might strike modern readers as harmless, Sancho's irreverence in these scenes certainly contrasts with other moments when he regulates his speech more carefully.

In what follows, I will first discuss the social practice of blasphemy in the context of Counter-Reformation efforts at inculcating a pious attitude among the peasantry, looking at a few specific examples taken from Inquisitorial visits to towns in la Mancha and elsewhere in Spain. I will then return to Sancho's expressions of impiety, to see how this look at the documentary record inflects our reading.

* * *

Impious speech, ranging from casual irreverence to full-blown heresies and explicit insults to God, the Virgin, and the saints, was widespread in Spain long before the Council of Trent called on ordinary Catholics to expose and root out sinful habits in their communities. Even today, many common interjections spoken in anger or in jest amount to profanations of the sacred. Such speech participates in the medieval popular culture Bakhtin termed carnivalesque, a systematic inversion of official Christian doctrine that places the lower organs of the body and their functions above those of the 'spirit' (Bakhtin 303-436). Defiling the holy by means of excrement is typical (Bakhtin 145-76, 223-31). For example, the carnivalesque tone of much Spanish blasphemy appears whenever someone publicly announces the intention to defecate in that most holy of receptacles, the chalice where the priest transforms communion wine into the blood of Christ. I refer, of course, to the popular expression, "¡Me cago en el copón!" Even now, I vividly recall the impression made on me the first time I clearly understood the meaning of these words, spoken, or rather shouted, in a bar in Úbeda. I thought then, and I still think, that it is not sufficient to claim that such language is used merely out of habit, without thinking about what it means. Those who routinely incorporate it into their speech may not be conscious of its literal meaning every time they use it. But irreverence as a cultural practice constitutes a flouting of pious, official doctrine, intended to scandalize. Those excluded from the echelons of power benefit from this practice, a resentful gesture that vicariously defiles the symbols of authority, even as it serves as a sign of horizontal solidarity. By the later Middle Ages, such carnivalesque blasphemy was widespread as a way of marking the separation between the ruling and popular classes, and except for extreme cases, people did not expect to be held to literal meaning of these ejaculations as if they really reflected profoundly held religious views.

Despite its deep roots in Medieval peasant culture, blasphemy underwent a dramatic transformation in sixteenth-century Europe. As Jean Delumeau has shown in his pioneering study *La peur en Occident*, increased attention to the religious life of even the humblest townspeople converged with courtly behavioral norms radiating out from urban centers, to make blasphemy a focal point of emerging social controls. Both ecclesiastical and monarchical authorities became less tolerant of blasphemous speech, erecting a "drastic partition between profane and sacred" (Cabantous 28). Early modern blasphemy thus became, in Olivier Christin's phrase, "a historical construction" (337), resulting from the overlaying of a new set of more restrictive expectations onto a widespread, pre-existing practice. The gradual passage from 'sin' to 'crime' documented by Corinne Leveleux reflects not so much a process of secularization as one of increasing control, with both religious and civil power brought to bear more directly on daily life. The repressive grid through which the behavior of the populace was now scrutinized made blasphemous and irreverent speech appear ubiquitous. Delumeau has gone so far as to refer to this configuration as "a civilization of blasphemy" (525).

Any attempt to reconstruct this process must grapple not only with how official discourses framed blasphemy, but also with the question of how this historical construction related to the actual practice that both pre-dated and outlived it. But this raises the somewhat thorny issue of what blasphemy meant to the blasphemers themselves, as well as to their hearers, their "audience." Was this simply habitual speech, with no real implications for the beliefs of those who used it? Or did it imply, at any level, a rejection of some or all of the teachings of the Church, "superficial Christianity, sympathy for heresy, even secret adhesion to atheism" (Delumeau 522)? One might also acknowledge, with Cabantous, that blasphemy could constitute resistance to new, invasive forms of power: "its use could sometimes translate deep-set anticlerical feeling, particularly after the implementation of certain decisions issued at the Council of Trent" (188). In any case, their sources often limit historians' ability to undertake this reconstruction of the practice of blasphemy, since jurists' sense of decorum generally prevented them from incorporating the actual words spoken or the precise contexts. The records of the Spanish Inquisition provide a uniquely valuable exception, and I will now turn to the comments of a number of scholars who have considered this material, before offering a few examples I myself have gleaned from Inquisitorial archives.

In what remains the most thorough reconstruction of the work of a single tribunal, that of Toledo, Jean-Pierre Dedieu has shown that the serious pursuit of blasphemers began around 1530, as the persecution of Conversos petered out and the immediate Catholic reaction to the Reformation began (Dedieu 246). After about 1560, he perceives a reorientation, in which the focus was less on blasphemers *per se* than on specific heretical statements, euphemistically known as "scandalous words" (349-50). As Dedieu observes, the Inquisition regrouped after the Council of Trent, concentrating its efforts more in the direction of enforcing certain post-Tridentine concerns, such as reining in parishioners' sexual activity, or enhancing the prestige of the clergy. Nonetheless, as the examples I take up later on demonstrate, the punishment of all those who undermined the newly strengthened border between sacred and profane remained a major concern the Inquisition well into the seventeenth century.

In a suggestive article that has stirred up controversy, John Edwards used, not trial records but the collections of testimony gathered by inquisitors on local visits to town in their districts, known as *libros de testificaciones*, to argue that the frequent irreverent speech found in late medieval Soria reflected widespread religious skepticism. At the close of the fifteenth century, on Edward's view, a significant portion of the population used heretical affirmations to mark their distance from orthodox beliefs, such as the virginity of the Mary after giving birth. He generally tends to assume, then, that the heretical views voiced by blasphemers express their deeply held convictions.

Maureen Flynn, working with sixteenth-century examples, arrives at a somewhat different conclusion. She accepts the protestations of many blasphemers that they do not really question the doctrines of the Church, but tries to work out an explanation that goes beyond claiming that they curse God and the saints out of mere habit, with no awareness of what they are saying. Flynn recounts the defense of Juan Gutiérrez, a sacristan accused of blasphemy in the early sixteenth century, who argues that blasphemers make outrageous statements they may not themselves take seriously, in order to scandalize their hearers. She reaches the conclusion that "blasphemers bruised pious sensibilities and travestied conventional images in order to violate the sacred boundaries that otherwise defined their faith" (54). If we recall Cabantous' insistence that strengthening those boundaries was a key facet of the Counter-Reformation project, we may begin to wonder whether blasphemy had become, by the late sixteenth century at least, a form of resistance to the increasing authoritarianism of early modern European societies. But in her pursuit of a psychological model, Flynn stops short of an explanation that would recognize blasphemy as a form of communicative action or social praxis. Her final formulation, though acknowledging that "authoritarian religion" may have fueled them, still considers blasphemous utterances only as "outbursts" that offered merely escapist consolation to the disempowered (55). She does not appear to have seriously considered the possibility that they may have played a significant role in a strategic form of symbolic resistance.

* * *

Building upon the foundation of the work of the French historians cited above, along with Edwards and Flynn, I would like to briefly consider a few examples of blasphemy that I believe suggest both the persistence of medieval skepticism and anticlericalism, *and* their transformation, during the Counter-Reformation, into a coherent practice of resistance to emergent absolutist power structures. While Cabantous speaks, as we have seen, of a "drastic partition" erected "between profane and sacred" (28), actual practice could not be brought into line with this new demand overnight, so a period of transition ensued, during which the Inquisition encouraged neighbors to come forward and describe any verbal offence against God they heard. This resulted in a hypertrophy of the pious attitude, with people denouncing — and confessing — even the most absurdly superficial instances. The following brief enumeration of examples comes mainly from the records of inquisitorial visits to towns of La Mancha. Granted, these denunciations seldom led to trials, but inquisitors kept careful records of all the declarations that were made, no matter how trivial.

The most frequent category are 'reniegos' – *reniego de Dios, reniego de la fe, reniego de la crisma que recibí*. Variations include *descreo en Dios, descreo de la fe de Dios,* and the highly expressive '*soy un puto enemigo de Dios y de sus santos.*' Usually uttered in the heat of anger, these statements could still lead to trouble. In 1565, for example, the Tribunal in Cuenca initiated proceedings against a certain Pedro de Velasco for allegedly crying out 'reniego de Dios' during a street fight. Expressions with 'valga' or 'pese,' are another very common type, such as *valga Dios, valga el Diablo, pese a Cristo, pese al cielo,* etc. These are favorites with gamblers, who often celebrate good luck curse the bad in equally colorful language. One might be inclined to consider them merely empty exclamations, the expression more of the *machismo* of the gaming table than of any attitude toward religious beliefs. However, numerous cases can be found in which the gambler, chided by a more pious onlooker, rather than backing down, openly articulates a heretical rationale. Thus in 1606 Alonso Manuel de Ludeña, an arrogant local *hidalgo* in Quintanar de la Orden, was tried for blasphemy uttered while playing cards.

> Delante de ciertas personas, jugando a los naipes, dijo a los naipes que tenía en la mano, 'Válgate el diablo', y respondiéndole uno de los circunstantes, más vale que le valga Dios, replicó el dicho reo con mucho brio y soberbia, 'No, sino el diablo, que a veces más vale o más puede el diablo que Dios', de lo cual se escandalizaron grandemente los que allí estaban. (Archivo Diocesano de Cuenca [hereafter ADC] Inq. leg. 680, num. 431, fol. 36)

As much as the blasphemy itself, it was his reputation of being "arrojadizo y temerario," combined with his not knowing the articles of the faith, that led to his being fined eight thousand *maravedís*.

Such confrontations between impertinent wit and outraged sensibilities are the stuff blasphemy is made of, in all times and places. But one surprising twist found during the Counter-Reformation is the willingness to switch from implicit camaraderie to accusation. On hearing the *edicto de la fe* read with great pomp at mass, accompanied with threats of punishment in the hereafter for those who do not tell all they know, many may have had a change of heart. Jorge Ramírez came forward in Socuéllamos in 1590 to denounce Luis Martínez for showing disrespect to an image of St. Veronica ten years earlier, when they were classmates at the Jesuit grammar school at Belmonte:

> Un día el susodicho echaba juramentos y decía cosas deshonestas y éste le dijo que no lo hiciese y tuviese respeto a una Verónica qu'estaba en el aposento donde lo susodicho pasaba, y el dicho Luis Martínez volvió la cabeza a la dicha Verónica y dijo, 'Perdóname vuestra merced, señora cara de negro, que no sabía qu'estaba ahí', y este testigo y Francisco de Lara Enriquez, vecino d'esta villa qu'estaba presente le reprehendieron y calló y no pasó otra cosa. (ADC Inq. L-326, fol. 270)

While Ramírez claims he reprimanded his classmate, the irreverent Luis Martínez must have expected them to be only mildly shocked or perhaps impressed by his boldness, and he would have no reason to fear reprisals. In fact, it was only ten years later that Ramírez finally came forward with this accusation.

We may at times surmise an ulterior motive for the decision to denounce. Men on occasion use irreverence in attempts at seduction, perhaps because of its titillating play with the forbidden. If their advances are unwelcome, their violation of religious taboo may be reported. Thus Isabel González, a married woman, came forward during the Inquisitor's 1590 visit to Alcázar de San Juan to declare that one day a year or so before when she was standing in her doorway, Alonso del Campo happened by and among other "palabras de amores" he said to her "En verdad que os vi en misa y que me aficioné grandemente a vos, más que a la madre de Dios porque me pareciste harto más linda y más hermosa que ella" (Archivo Histórico Nacional [hereafter AHN], Inq. leg. 496, exp. 1, fol. 145). Nineteen-year-old Magdalena de Buendía's reversal of attitude appears more treacherous. While flirting with Diego Juárez, she asked him, in jest, whether he believed in God, the Virgin Mary, and the saints, and he said no to everything (ADC, Inq, L-325, fols. 143-144).

These seem to be examples in which the blasphemer rather 'innocently' trusts his interlocutors to take his witticisms in the playful spirit in which he intends them, not as the reflection of his true state of mind. Nonetheless, a certain limit is necessarily crossed, even when one blasphemes in jest. Many, perhaps most, early modern Spaniards would not deny their faith in God, the Virgin, and the saints, jokingly or otherwise. The ever-growing likelihood of being denounced before the Inquisition for speaking this way increasingly marked the behavior of those who did so, producing a dramatic polarization between pious and irreverent attitudes. Under these circumstances, it is interesting to note that a number of individuals openly (one might even say brazenly) denied in public the validity of certain practices and doctrines. These blasphemers apparently sought to wound the self-righteous among their community. The game they played was risky, but the form it takes in different instances is similar enough to warrant considering it a recognizable social role.

The most frequent pattern is that a group of women are discussing some aspect of Christian doctrine, either in church or immediately after attending mass. Usually there was at least one *beata* in the group. The *beatas*, lay women who have taken a vow of chastity and service to God, but live at home, were the self-appointed guardians of religiosity in Castilian towns. The conversation might take as its point of departure a recent event, such as a purported miracle, or they might be commenting on the sermon they had just heard. In any case, at some point the blasphemer breaks in to loudly and forcefully deny the tenet of faith on which the whole discussion is based. For example, in 1590, Catalina Ortiz, of Campo de Criptana, waiting for mass to begin one Sunday during Lent, listened while several local women discussed a miracle in which a woman from their town had her sight restored by an image of St. Christopher in a nearby hermitage. In performing the miracle, the image was reported to sweat. "No puedo creer que un santo de palo puede sudar" (ADC, Inq. L-326, fol. 254v).

During an Inquisition visit to the town of Corral de Almaguer, on May 25, 1585, four local women, one of them a *beata*, declared against someone they knew only as 'la de Francisco Rodríguez.' She had taken the opening of a sepulcher in the church as the occasion to comment, looking at the bones, that she considered the resurrection of the flesh impossible. Evidently she had a reputation in the town. One witness comments, "es tenida comunmente por persona de poco juicio y aun dicen que está loca," while another mentions that she has seen her in church talking to herself and making faces.

In Quintanar, another woman some witnesses consider mad, Mari Díaz, was quoted in one declaration as saying, around 1575, that Hell was only invented to frighten us ("dijo que no había infierno, que por meternos miedo lo decían" ADC Inq. Libro 325, fol 130r). In 1590, she was denounced for denying the virgin birth. After a sermon concerning Joseph's doubts when Mary told him she was pregnant, she asked her friends, "But didn't they sleep together?" ("¿Pues no se acostaban juntos?" ADC Inq. L-326, fol. 169v). On all of these occasions, the inquisitor called in an additional witness to confirm the accusations, but I have found no record of either woman ever having been tried by the Inquisition. In an age of increasing control over religious practice and belief, when their Converso and Morisco neighbors were subject to close scrutiny, they apparently went around for years occasionally making such scandalous statements, presumably as a provocation to sincere believers. Though Old Christians by birth, they carved out a public role for themselves as religious skeptics. And the Inquisition did not judge their performance of that role worthy of a major intervention, though they kept a record of the denunciations against them.

Thus religious identity in early modern Spain partakes of a Baroque performativity. There is a set of obligatory institutionalized behaviors (attending mass, reciting prayers, annual confession) around which are grouped many aspects of social life: genealogy, family tradition, deeply held beliefs about ultimate reality, social status, etc. At the height of the Counter-Reformation, certainly, nothing one does or says in relation to this field will be seen as neutral. But as the above discussion shows, there are subtle ways of communicating alternative positions – and some not so subtle ways. An on-going war of position exists between religious authorities and their official or extra-official 'agents,' on the one hand, and the various groups or individuals who try, in their own small way, to resist the pressure to adhere to an ever-narrower orthodoxy, on the other. More than a single set of beliefs or practices, religion in Counter-Reformation Spain has become a complex field of interacting positions, through which individuals and groups perform identities on which to a large extent their status depends. Under these circumstances, blasphemous and irreverent speech of the type I have been examining became *de facto* a form of public dissent, though without any possibility whatsoever of becoming an active resistance. It was simply limited to an open declaration of inconformity.[2]

Of course, we only have the official records – so for the most part we do not know what people said or how they acted when there were no pious people or *beatas* present. For example, it is interesting to wonder whether the male equivalents to Mari Díaz and Francisco Rodríguez' wife existed, and if they might have remained hidden to us precisely because it was less likely that another man would come forward to denounce them. We do have fictional images of interactions without scrutiny from the other side of the imaginary line separating the pious from the profane. Such images include, for example, Sancho's meetings with Tomé Cecial and Ricote. Yet it must immediately be added that Cervantes creates only the *illusion* of free interaction, for in fact the boundary separating piety and its other still circumscribes the text from outside, in the form of censorship. Despite this invisible constraint, however, these scenes reveal a dimension of social reality not as clearly in evidence in the Inquisition documents.

At the same time, it is worth drawing attention to an example in which the blasphemer himself clearly incorporated into his practice the same reversibility we find in the role of the interlocutor who could pass so easily from accomplice to informer, thus demonstrating the impact on actual practice of the concern to avoid punishment. Cristóbal Hernández, of Huéscar, fifty years old, was accused in 1595 of swearing by the Son of God while playing cards, and of supposedly responding, when scolded for blaspheming, that God had no son, a heretical proposition for which he was

---

[2] For further discussion of the public performance of religious identities, see my forthcoming article "The Baroque Public Sphere."

brought before the Inquisition of Granada. Hernández explained to the Inquisitors that the oath he pronounced – or at least, he later qualified himself, *meant* to pronounce, was, "I swear by the son of the son of God" ("juro al hijo del hijo de dios"). The point being that when they accused him of blasphemy he would answer that God's son had no son ("el hijo de dios no tuvo hijo"), and that he was therefore swearing by something nonexistent. As the case bore out, Hernández had previously been punished by local civil authorities for blaspheming while playing cards. He had said, "reniego de dios y de sus santos," and "los diablos me lleven, que tengo este cuerpo lleno de diablos." Clearly, he had invented his new form of swearing as a way of getting around the prohibition against blasphemy, but this solution turned out to only get him into deeper trouble. In the event, he had to abjure *de levi* and received two hundred lashes and four years banishment, which a member of the Suprema commented in the margin appeared to be "mucho rigor en el sujeto." (AHN Inq leg 1953 num 30, fol 2v) Too clever by half, Hernández was attempting to practice what Bhabha has termed "sly civility," a strategic form of external obedience that masks an underlying rebellious consciousness. Trying simultaneously to blaspheme and to be able to proclaim himself innocent of blasphemy, he invented a Baroque nesting of an oath within an oath that ultimately failed to persuade his hearers. Yet his creative effort reveals better than any example I have yet seen that blasphemy was indeed the site of a culture of resistance to royal and ecclesiastical power. Hernández wants, ultimately to have his cake and eat it too—to achieve the scandalous effect of blasphemy without being susceptible to punishment for it. This is not a spontaneous, unconscious habit of mind, but a calculated strategy for challenging existing structures of power and then pretending not to have done so. Crucial to this strategy is the attempt to invent a form of blasphemy that would be 'reversible': unambiguously irreverent to the ear, but technically defensible in terms of official doctrine. Hernández' simple device of referring to a nonexistent 'son of the son of God' by whom to swear was sophisticated enough to evoke opposite responses in the minds of Inquisitors at different levels in the hierarchy, since the local tribunal sentenced him to two hundred lashes, while the Supreme Council viewed the punishment as a harsh one, considering the individual in question.

* * *

In *Cervantes: raíces folklóricas*, Maurice Molho employed the concept of 'reversibility' to explain the internal dynamic of the popular figure of the *tonto-listo*, the basic model for Sancho Panza. In Molho's conception, such reversibility was a feature of peasant culture for reasons essentially identical to those we saw at work in Cristóbal Hernández' sly blasphemy. Thus, on the one hand, the *tonto* side of the character expressed peasants' passivity in the face of a social hierarchy they could not directly challenge, while the *listo* side stood, at least symbolically, for liberation from this passivity (269-70). Suggestively, Molho ties this tension between obedience and resistance to the question of Sancho's credulity concerning Don Quixote's chivalric fantasies. There is thus in Sancho's relation to his master a give-and-take between belief and doubt (*creer* and *descreer*) that mimics closely the contradictory stances typically held by those accused of blaspheming against the doctrines of the Church (Molho 274). Arguably, then, chivalry serves in this respect as a displaced version of the official Christian belief system, and Sancho's attitudes toward the one could be taken as indicative of the peasantry's attitudes toward the other, as Cervantes chose to represent them. The association in Sancho's behaviour between credulity and passive obedience could then be taken as a hint concerning the ubiquity of religious hypocrisy among the popular classes.

At the beginning of the colloquy between Sancho and Tomé Cecial, Sancho mentions his fifteen-year-old daughter, praising her beauty and virility in terms that inspire an enthusiastic response from the Tomé:

> Partes son esas –respondió el del Bosque – no solo para ser condesa, sino para ser ninfa del verde bosque. ¡Oh hideputa, puta, y que rejo debe de tener la bellaca!
> A lo que respondió Sancho, algo mohino.
> – Ni ella es puta, ni lo fue su madre, ni lo será ninguna de las dos, Dios queriendo, mientras yo viviere. Y háblase más comedidamente, que para haberse criado vuesa merced entre caballeros andantes, que son la mesma cortesía, no me parecen muy concertadas esas palabras. (II.13, 729)

Sancho's initially fails to recognize the other squire's use of insults as compliments, a typically carnivalesque technique termed Billingsgate, which establishes solidarity on the basis of a mutual refusal to take offense at what would normally be considered offensive (Bakhtin 145-95). His own explanation frames this breakdown of class solidarity in terms of the influence of knight errantry on Sancho's expectations concerning social interaction. But there is a little more to it than that. Sancho is on the road in search of adventure, but above all looking to improve his lot in the world and that of his family. As he moves away from his community, he accidentally encounters people he knows on the road and does not recognize them — first Tomé Cecial, then Ricote. True, they are disguised. But in both encounters, as well as having a problem with identifying them physically as his neighbors, Sancho limits his willingness to recognize the social bonds uniting him to them as fellow peasants. In this first scene, Tomé Cecial reminds Sancho of how "achques de alabanzas" work in their linguistic community. Sancho accepts this, and they eventually get to the point where he can burst out with his praise for the wine, "¡Oh hideputa, bellaco, y cómo es católico!" Yet even here Tomé points out to Sancho that he is doing what he had criticized moments earlier: "¿Veis ahí –dijo el del Bosque en oyendo el *hideputa* de Sancho – como habéis alabado este vino llamandole 'hideputa'?" and Sancho answers rather stiffly with an attempt to formulate a rule: "Digo que confieso que conozco que no es deshonra llamar 'hijo de puta' a nadie cuando cae debajo del entendimiento de alabarle" (732). Thus even where two peasants from la Mancha converse in the countryside at night, with no one else to hear them, a newfound sense of suspicion and hesitation have come into play, precisely around those carnivalesque aspects of their speech that border on blasphemy. Sancho initially refuses to take Tomé's inverted praises as their speaker meant them, rather than as what they literally say, and he subsequently insists on defining a rule for interpreting such speech-meaning gaps. This shift in his attitude toward the language games of his social group can be understood, as I have said, in terms of his own desire to ascend in the class hierarchy. However, it can also be read in relation to the changing climate of interaction in early modern Spain. Reversibility of speaker's intention had become a necessary accompaniment to any form of speech having the slightest hint of the illicit. This reading is further supported by the outcome of Sancho's meeting with Ricote, forty chapters later.

Let us recall the improvished luncheon Sancho shares with the band of false pilgrims to which Ricote belongs:

Comenzaron a comer con grandísimo gusto y muy de espacio, saboreándose con cada bocado, que le tomaban con la punta del cuchillo, y muy poquito de cada cosa, y luego, al punto, todos a una, levantaron los brazos y las botas en el aire; puestas las bocas en su boca, clavados los ojos en el cielo, no parecía sino que ponían en él la puntería; y desta manera, meneando las cabezas a un lado y a otro, señales que acreditaban el gusto que recebían, se estuvieron un buen espacio, trasegando en sus estómagos las entrañas de las vasijas.

Todo lo miraba Sancho, y de ninguna cosa se dolía; antes, por cumplir con el refrán, que él muy bien sabía, de "cuando a Roma fueres, haz como vieres," pidió a Ricote la bota, y tomó su puntería como los demás, y no con menos gusto que ellos.

Cuatro veces dieron lugar las botas para ser empinadas; pero la quinta no fue posible, porque ya estaban más enjutas y secas que un esparto, cosa que puso mustia la alegría que hasta allí habían mostrado. De cuando en cuando, juntaba alguno su mano derecha con la de Sancho, y decía:

-Español y tudesqui, tuto uno: bon compaño.

Y Sancho respondía: Bon compaño, jura Di!

Y disparaba con una risa que le duraba un hora, sin acordarse entonces de nada de lo que le había sucedido en su gobierno; porque sobre el rato y tiempo cuando se come y bebe, poca jurisdición suelen tener los cuidados. (II.54, 1070-71)

As I mentioned at the outset, their blasphemous gesture and Sancho's profanation of God's name in order to swear his brotherhood with Protestants (and a half-Muslim) render this scene of communion among these seven men vaguely scandalous for an overly pious sensibility. This is the more true when we recall that these 'pilgrims' are frudalently taking advantage of Spaniards enthusiasm for almsgiving to enrich themselves, and Ricote is an expelled Morisco returning, also, to try to find a treasure he buried before leaving, dig it up, and, presumably, sneak it back out of Spain. Though he swears his companionship with these men, when the one he knows best asks him to do him the favor of returning to their town to help him recover the treasure, offering to split it with him, Sancho invokes the concept of loyal service to the king: "por parecerme haría traición a mi rey en dar favor a sus enemigos, no fuera contigo" (1074). The decision of His Majesty is discussed at some length by the two men, and references to the monarchy appear several times. But nothing in the preceding pages prepares the reader for Sancho's sudden invocation of royal authority as a way of separating himself from Ricote. Sancho identifies unhesitatingly with the king ('mi rey') and thus implicitly accepts that the king's enemies are his own.

There is a brief cosmopolitan space in which Sancho, the Morisco, and the Germans can share food, wine, and a feeling that their mutual recognition transcends the religious differences that separate them. But it is only "sobre el rato y tiempo cuando se come y bebe" that "poca jurisdición suelen tener los cuidados." Afterwards, they return to the characteristically Baroque public sphere, in which caution and prudence have their jurisdiction.

By the end of the novel, Sancho demonstrates a well-developed consciousness of himself as a the king's subject, though he still knows that there are times when he can be irreverent and times when he must not be. His encounters with Tomé Cecial and the Morisco Ricote provide opportunities to hear him speak in confidence. His irreverence in those scenes contrasts with other moments when he regulates his speech more carefully (for example in the presence of the priest). In *Don Quixote*, then, the alternation of carnival license with Lenten asceticism is re-aligned to figuratively represent the calculation one must make when deciding, not at what time of year to behave according to one or another standard, but in what situation, and in whose presence. And this calculation, increasingly, had to be made by ordinary townspeople in order to avoid censure and punishment.

BROOKLYN COLLEGE

Works Cited

Bakhtin, Mikhail. *Rabelais and His Worlds*. Trans. Hélène Iswolsky. Bloomington: Indiana UP, 1984.

Bhabha, Homi K. "Sly Civility." In his *The Location of Culture*. London and New York: Routledge, 1994. 93-101.

Cabantous, Alain. *Blasphemy: Impious Speech in the West from the Seventeenth to the Nineteenth Century*. Trans. Eric Rauth. New York: Columbia UP, 2002.

Cervantes, Miguel de. *Don Quijote de la Mancha*. Dir. Francisco Rico. Barcelona: Crítica, 1998.

Childers, William. "The Baroque Public Sphere." In *Reason and Its Others in Early Modern Spain and Italy*. Ed. David R. Castillo and Massimo Lollini. Nashville, TN: Vanderbilt UP, Forthcoming.

Christian, William A. *Local Religion in Sixteenth-Century Spain*. Princeton, NJ: Princeton UP, 1981.

Olivier Christin, "Le statut ambigu du blasphème au XVIe siècle." *Ethnologie française* 22.3 (1992) 337-343.

Dedieu, Jean-Pierre. *L'Administration de la foi: l'Inquisition de Tolède, XVIe-XVIIIe siècle.* Madrid: Casa de Velázquez, 1989.

Delumeau, Jean. *La peur en Occident (XIVe-XVIIIe siècles). Une cité assiégée.* Paris: Fayard, 1978.

Edwards, John. "Religious Faith and Doubt in Late Medieval Spain: Soria circa 1450-1500." *Past and Present* 120 (1988) 3-25.

Flynn, Maureen. "Blasphemy and the Play of Anger in Sixteenth-Century Spain." *Past and Present* 149 (1995) 29-56.

Ginzburg, Carlo. *The Cheese and the Worms. The Cosmos of a Sixteenth-Century Miller.* Trans. John and Anne Tedeschi. Baltimore: Johns Hopkins UP, 1980.

Leveleux, Corinne. *La parole interdite: le blasphème dans la France médiévale (XIIIe-XVIe siècles): du péché au crime.* Paris: De Boccard, 2001.

Molho, Maurice. *Cervantes: Raíces folklóricas.* Madrid: Gredos, 1976.

Nalle, Sara T. *God in La Mancha. Religious Reform and the People of Cuenca, 1500-1650.* Baltimore: Johns Hopkins UP, 1992.

Palace of the Apes:
The Ducal Chateau and Cervantes's
Repudiation of Satiric Malice
BRYANT CREEL

IN *DQ* 2.30, DON QUIJOTE sees the Duke and Duchess for the first time. They are at a distance, and he sends Sancho to explain who Don Quijote is. When Sancho returns, Don Quijote tries to dismount to go meet the Duke, but Sancho's nervousness and Don Quijote's own ineptness cause them both to fall in a ridiculous way that completely shatters the dignified impression that Don Quijote had hoped to make on these important people. Don Quijote then approaches the Duke and tries to kneel before him, but the Duke stops him and embraces him as an equal. Thus begins the central episode of the second half of the novel, with what on the surface appears to be an attitude of gracious acceptance of Don Quijote and Sancho during their prolonged stay at the ducal chateau. When Don Quijote arrives at the chateau, the hospitality he is shown makes him feel for the first time that he is being treated like famous knights in literature. But the narrator makes it known from the beginning that the Duke and Duchess already know who Don Quijote is and that they plan to lead him on by fueling his delusions. Almost immediately the reader sees the courteous treatment of Don Quijote and Sancho begin to combine with a playful attitude that turns more and more aggressive during the twenty-nine chapters that are devoted to events at the ducal estate.

At first, the ambiguous attitude that the Duke and Duchess have toward Don Quijote seems harmless enough; but as the hoaxes become more bizarre and extravagant, the reader begins to wonder exactly what motivates the Duke and Duchess to go to such lengths.[1] When one considers that Altisido

---

[1] Javier Salazar Rincón sees the Duke and Duchess as making buffoons of Don Quijote and Sancho in order to use them as an antidote against boredom (*El mundo*

ra's cynical and even cruel pranks had to be carried out with the complicity of the Duke and Duchess, the fundamental good will of the ducal pair becomes more and more questionable. By 2.57, when Don Quijote and Sancho leave the ducal chateau, and especially toward the end of the novel,

---

social del Quijote 66). Similarly to Pavel Novitsky, who sees the Duke and Duchess as being motivated by "dull cynicism and decadent cruelty" (*Cervantes and Don Quijote* 15), Luis Murillo regards the Duke's and Duchess's subjection of their guests to subtle, cruel humiliation as being attributable to "a refined perversity," which they conceal with exquisite courtesy (*A Critical Introduction to "Don Quixote"* 178). Ruth El Saffar regards the Duke and Duchess as being motivated by "a disinterested desire to be entertained" (*Distance and Control* 97). Anthony Close views the Duke and Duchess as cultivating the art of the *burla* as a sort of masque and as doing so with the innocent intention of paying homage to *Don Quijote* and participating communally in the comic merriment afforded by the novel ("Seemly Pranks" 71-73, 87). Close argues that any malicious mischief that characterizes the pranks organized by the Duke and Duchess is inherent in the spirit of the devilry that is a conventional element of the *burla* and the civilized good fun that it provides (70, 72). Part of the basis of his argument is his claim that Cervantes saw the *burlas* at the ducal estate in a positive light (70). However, he arrives at that view by incurring the fallacy of identifying Cide Hamete Benengeli with Cervantes (70) and overlooking the fact that the fictional Arab historiographer can be perceived as being motivated by an intention to ironically ridicule an "exemplary" Christian hero. It is interesting that Azorín expresses impatience toward the circumstance that, in spite of the fact that since the end of the eighteenth century the "stupid cruelty" of the Duke and Duchess had been recognized by critics (he cites the example of Vicente de los Ríos's *Análisis del Quijote*), "hoy existen todavía comentadores que encarecen la afabalidad y generosidad y cortesía de los duques" (*Obras completas* 2: 944). Those words were originally published in 1914. The fact that almost one hundred years later critics still admire the Duke and Duchess can be seen as a tribute to Cervantes's subtlety. To continue reviewing critical opinion as to the motives of the Duke and Duchess, Stanislav Zimic takes the same view of those motives as Salazar Rincón and, in addition, sees their obsessive need for jokes and laughter as a symptom of the lack of worthy pursuits in their lives (*Los cuentos y las novelas del "Quijote"* 277). Henry Sullivan refers to the "jocose cruelty" to which Don Quijote is subjected at the ducal estate as a "theater of sadism" (*Grotesque Purgatory* xi, 57, 147). Francisco Márquez Villanueva regards the Duke and Duchess as seeking the pleasure of humiliating Don Quijote and of enlisting Altisidora's assistance for that purpose. Above all, he notes, they want to prove that love would be defeated by sensuality. Márquez Villanueva's perspective is similar to the view I will present here, that the Duke and Duchess want to mock higher values that they themselves do not cultivate.

when in 2.69-70 the Duke and Duchess briefly intercept Don Quijote and Sancho with elaborate and mysterious histrionics as they return to their village, what initially began as Don Quijote's treatment as an honored guest has degenerated into crass insults and scapegoating. The ducal country house reveals itself to be the home of malicious ridicule, base frivolity, and aggressive ill-will. As such, it can be regarded as a metaphor for the domain of malicious satire. That type of satire and the spirit that underlies it stand in conspicuous contrast to both the childlike goodness of Don Quijote and the delicately reproving attitude with which Cervantes himself subtly and implicitly places the Duke and Duchess in an unfavorable light. My main purpose in the present comments is to explore further some of the broader implications of the pranks organized by the Duke and Duchess at Don Quijote's expense and the relation of those events to Cervantes's aesthetic ideas. I wish also to address some metaphorical dimensions of certain paradoxical motifs in the second part of the novel, such as Dulcinea's "enchantment" and Sancho's role in her "disenchantment."

In portraying the ducal household, Cervantes seems to have represented a typical phenomenon of the period. Werner Sombart, in *Luxury and Capitalism*, discusses the Spanish-Dutch era of the seventeenth century as a stage in the development of modern luxury (82). He notes that an important factor contributing to the impoverishment of the nobility in that period was that, as plebeian elements in the society became enriched, the old families tried to equal the parvenus in ostentatious display (82-83). We know that the Duke in *Don Quijote* had incurred debt because he borrowed money from the wealthy land owner whose son seduced Doña Rodríguez's daughter before escaping to Flanders, a betrayal that the Duke abetted out of self-interest. According to Sombart, the forms of domestic luxury that typically caused the nobility of the period to experience economic decline were spectacular events such as tournaments, pageants, processions, and public banquets (95). During Don Quijote's visit with the Duke and Duchess, there is a tournament (in which Tosilos is supposed to combat Don Quijote); but in depicting the spectacles organized at the ducal estate, Cervantes seems to have intended above all to draw attention to their insolent frivolity. They include—in addition to the tournament already mentioned—the occasion of the lavish announcement of the formula for disenchanting Dulcinea, that of the extravagant presentation of the story of the *dueña* Dolorida (or Countess Trifaldi), the Clavileño episode, the elaborate reception of Sancho at Barataria, and Altisidora's mock funeral and revival in 2.69. From the point of view of the Duke and Duchess, the sole purpose of these events is to provide entertainment by inciting Don Quijote's fantasies and taking advantage of Sancho's simplicity while the two are guests at their estate. The novel presents specific instances of crass insensitivity to values on the part of the Duke, such as his high-handed treatment of Doña Rodríguez and her daughter and his accusing Don Quijote of stealing from the maidservant Altisidora while Don Quijote was a guest in his house (2.57); but the most damning symptom of his degeneracy is his attitude of false sincerity towards the people to whom he extends his hospitality, Don Quijote and Sancho. Certainly the expected norm of behavior in an aristocratic country retreat (a "casa de placer" or "casa de recreo") would be one of high courtesy and affable socializing. Georg Simmel, in his analysis of the valuable sociological art form known as "sociability" (*The Sociology of Georg Simmel* 40-57), explains that its first condition is "tact" based on a superficial avoidance of attentions to reality and on an avoidance of ego-stresses and personal and even individual attitudes in deference to a collective, common consciousness. Simmel holds that the symbolic ritual of sociability is ultimately grounded in a tacit recognition of social realities such as the interdependence of the individual and the collectivity. I would suggest as well that "sociability" reinforces certain types of moral aware-ness, such as the principle of universal human solidarity.[2] In any case, Simmel also notes that sociability is of a democratic nature and thus requires that one treat others not only as equals but as being more valuable or even superior. The *eclesiástico* (chaplain) at the home of the Duke and Duchess is the first to violate the requirements of tact when he inveighs against Alonso Quijano on a personal level (he does not acknowledge the persona Don Quijote); but the Duke and Duchess follow suit in their general behavior toward Don Quijote, both by being insincerely courteous toward him and by amusing themselves at Don Quijote's expense. They transgress the democratic spirit of sociability by treating Don Quijote as an inferior, with the result that, in Simmel's words, the sociological art form of sociability is made to "degenerate into a sociological naturalism" (Simmel 47) in which the naive formalism of an elevating histrionics is displaced by crude factuality (lavish enactments of a farcical theatricality — the hoaxes — notwith stand ing).

---

[2] For Scheler's views on what he terms "the principle of universal human moral solidarity," see his *Formalism in Ethics* 279, 368, 496, 527-38.

My emphasis on the issue of propriety may seem to trivialize the broader ethical implications of the subject under discussion. However, as Nicolai Hartmann points out in his observations on the values of social intercourse, the existing forms of social intercourse are profoundly necessary to life; and all human relationships, even those that are external and seemingly unimportant, are based on trust and the power of good faith. Hence, "all propriety in social encounter with others calls for a like propriety in them," and one who violates the forms of social intercourse "refuses to others what he claims from them for himself" (*Ethics*, 2: 304-305). Such a transgressor in little things, by offending against social forms, offends against the inner ethos, which reappears in those forms in a way that is diminished but unmistakable. So it is that—to cite examples that could be applied to the Duke—an inconsiderate man shows himself to be immodest: like a real criminal, such person is rightly "subject to condemnation and punishment, to boycott and ostracism" (Hartmann, 2: 304-305). In an observation that is reminiscent of Simmel's mention of "degeneration into a sociological naturalism," Hartmann notes that "without established social custom mankind sinks into formlessness and savagery" (2: 302).

Specifically relevant to the Duke's and Duchess's behavior toward Don Quijote and to possible sources drawn on by Cervantes for the ethical perspective presented in the episode with the Duke and Duchess is a passage in Aristotle's *Nicomachean Ethics* mentioned by Hartmann as concerning the virtue of social deportment that consists in "the rightly balanced, tactful relation to jesting, which is dignified and yet is appreciative of humor" (Hartmann, *Ethics*, 2: 308). One of the two deficient extremes of that attitude fits the Duke. In Aristotle's words, "Those who go to excess in raising laughs seem to be vulgar buffoons. They stop at nothing to raise a laugh, and care more about that than about saying what is seemly and avoiding pain to the victims of the joke" (*Nicomachean Ethics*, 1128a 5-8) (trans. Irwin, 112). Such a tactless intrusion of personal motives contrasts with the genial tact implied both in Alonso Quijano's masking (as in a costume party) of his own real personality with the identity of Don Quijote and with the respectful hospitality that Don Quijote had been shown shortly before by Diego de Miranda. Stanislav Zimic has observed that for perceptive readers the impression of insensitivity on the part of the Duke and Duchess is heightened by what seems to be a subtly implied attitude of indulgence on the part of Don Quijote, and he notes that several critics have pointed out that at the home of the Duke and Duchess Don Quijote sometimes seems to be conscious of the attempts to deceive him.[3]

---

[3] *Los cuentos y las novelas del "Quijote"* 272. See also 270 and 270 n.3 for Zimic's own emphasis on the ambiguity with which the degree of Don Quijote's awareness is presented and for references to overstatements as to evidence of Don Quijote's lucidity at the ducal estate on the part of G. Torrente Ballester and M. Van Doren. I would suggest that Torrente Ballester and Van Doren might have been influenced by Miguel de Unamuno's view (presented in his "Vida de Don Quijote y Sancho," 84) that Don Quijote's "madness" is of the imagination but not of the understanding, or by Francisco Maldonado de Guevara's "Del *Ingenium* de Cervantes al de Gracián," in which it is asserted that Don Quijote consciously and creatively imitates his own madness. In general, Cervantes makes the issue of Don Quijote's awareness of the malice of the Duke and Duchess ambiguous. A good example of that ambiguity is Don Quijote's response to Altisidora's tirade. Don Quijote tells the Duchess,

> ...todo el mal desta doncella nace de ociosidad, cuyo remedio es la ocupación honesta y continua. Ella me ha dicho aquí que se usan randas en el infierno; y pues ella las debe de saber hacer, no las deje de la mano; que ocupada en menear los palillos, no se menearán en su imaginación la imagen o imágenes de lo que bien quiere, y ésta es la verdad, éste mi parecer y éste es mi consejo.. (2.70: 1045. See note 6 below)

These words would fit a situation in which Don Quijote believed that Altisidora did mean her insults (because she was just pretending to love him) as much as one in which he believed she did not mean them (because she was embarrassed by his not having reciprocated her advance). Incidentally, the mention of "el infierno" in Don Quijote's words cited above can be interpreted as an oblique reference to the ducal estate, in spite of the fact that on the surface it refers to elements of Altisidora's description of a scene in hell in which a dozen devils were playfully kicking Avellaneda's second part of Don Quijote as though it were a ball because it was so bad (2.70: 1043). In any case, it would seem that ultimately Cervantes wants the reader to see Don Quijote's belief that he has been well treated by the Duke and Duchess partly as being a result of his capitulating to his own megalomania, and not merely to hold him up as a model of good will and of presenting oneself as appreciative toward one's host as a matter of principle. When Don Quijote and Sancho, on their way back to their village, experience anxiety as they are escorted to the ducal chateau under duress, Don Quijote recognizes the place and says with surprise, "sí en esta casa todo es cortesía y buen comedimiento; pero para los vencidos el bien se vuelve en mal y el mal en peor" (2.69: 1034). His memory of his previous stay with the Duke and Duchess is thus represented as being positive.

More important for the present comments, however, is — I repeat — the fact that the malicious spirit in which the Duke and Duchess satirize Don Quijote is conspicuously opposed to the spirit and attitude with which Cervantes satirizes the Duke and Duchess. In fact, Cervantes even manages to endow the Duke and Duchess with certain exemplary qualities: for example, in 2.57, before Don Quijote and Sancho go to Barcelona, the Duke gives Sancho two hundred gold *escudos*. If one surveys passages in *Don Quijote* that can be interpreted as subtle clues to Cervantes' aesthetic ideas, one repeatedly encounters references that take implicit exception to such attributes of malicious satire as crude naturalism and a disposition of vengeful ill will. I will limit myself to a few representative examples. When Don Quijote discusses the greatness of Homer's and Virgil's portraits of Ulysses and Aeneas, he says that those poets painted their heroes "no como ellos fueron, sino como habían de ser, para quedar ejemplo a los venideros hombres de sus virtudes" (1.25: 237)[4]. In Don Quijote's advice to Sancho before Sancho's governorship, he tells him, "Cuando te sucediere juzgar algún pleito de algún tu enemigo, aparta las mientes de tu injuria y ponlas en la verdad del caso .... Al culpado ..., muéstratele piadoso y clemente; porque aunque los atributos de Dios son todos iguales, más resplandece y campea a nuestro ver el de la misericordia que el de la justicia" (2.43: 842). In a conversation with Don Diego de Miranda, Don Quijote takes issue with satiric malice partly because of its tendency to be personal:

> Riña vuesa merced a su hijo si hiciere sátiras que perjudiquen las honras ajenas, y castíguele y rómpaselas ...; porque lícito es al poeta escribir contra la invidia y decir mal de los invidiosos ...con que no señale persona alguna; pero hay poetas que a trueco de decir una malicia se pondrán a peligro que los destierren a las islas del Ponto." (2.26: 650-51)[5]

(We have already noted that an analogous assertion of personal attitudes has been seen as being incompatible with sociability). The

---

[4] Passages quoted from *Don Quijote* are from the 1969 edition by Martín de Riquer; any translations are mine.

[5] The specific reference is to Ovid's exile to the coasts of the Black Sea, but the general sense could also be a reference to Lope de Vega, who in 1588 was exiled from Madrid and the Kingdom of Castile for writing libelous verses against Elena Osorio.

narrator refers to the lion that Don Quijote challenges as "más comedido que arrogante" (2.17: 657). The following observation, which the narrator applies to the *eclesiástico* at the home of the Duke and Duchess could also be applied — partly because of the ambiguous meaning of the word "sus" — as an apt description of the Duke and Duchess, and their disparagement of Don Quijote: "destos que quieren que la grandeza de los grandes se mida con la estrecheza de sus ánimos" (2.31: 765). The foregoing passages, in addition to having specific relevance to the contexts in which they appear, create a critical perspective for viewing the behavior of the Duke and Duchess, as well as generally what Cervantes terms "maliciosa sátira": both that of such minor poets as Vicente Espinel[6] and of great mockers and iconoclasts of heroism like Góngora and Quevedo. Ramón Menéndez Pidal has observed of such mocking of the heroic that, unlike Góngora and Quevedo, "Cervantes nunca hizo esto" ("Cervantes y el ideal caballeresco" 226).

The malicious ridicule of Don Quijote extends to Sancho as well, such as that which occurs in relation to the bizarre events surrounding the "disenchantment of Dulcinea." When that motif is interpreted metaphorically, it becomes less enigmatic. Dulcinea represents the suprasensible ideal. In ugly peasant form,[7] she is "enchanted" in the sense that her "true" (in the sense of "ideal") form is distorted by empirical accident -- specifically, I would propose, by the degrading effects of poverty. One argument in support of this interpretation is that it finds its logical basis in the circumstance that peasants are usually of low social status and hence poor. Yet this reading of the enchantment motif is also supported by clues in the text. When Don Quijote speaks to the young peasant woman who Sancho says is Dulcinea appearing to Don Quijote in enchanted form, Don Quijote says to her, "…el maligno encantador …ha puesto nubes y cataratas en mis ojos …y ha transformado tu sin igual hermosura y rostro en el de una labradora pobre…" (2.10: 607). Also, in the Cave of Montesinos the "enchanted"

---

[6] See 2.8: 592 and 592 n.9.

[7] At the home of the Duke and Duchess, Don Quijote describes the enchanted Dulcinea as follows: "…halléla encantada y convertida de princesa en labradora, de hermosa en fea, de ángel en diablo, de olorosa en pestífera, de bien hablada en rústica, de reposada en brincadora, de luz en tinieblas, y finalmente, de Dulcinea del Toboso en una villana de Sayago" (2.32: 776).

Dulcinea has a companion borrow money from Don Quijote on her behalf. It is interesting also that when Don Quijote gives her his last four *reales* (Dulcinea had asked for six), he tells her, "Decid ...a vuestra señora que ...me pesa en el alma de sus trabajos, y que quisiera ser un Fúcar para remediarlos..." (2.23: 711). The reference, of course, is to the Fuggers, the great German banking family that was the chief supporter of Charles V. In his *Outline of History*, H. G. Wells writes, "Charles V was not so much a Habsburg emperor as a Fugger emperor" and that Charles's election was secured by a vast amount of bribery (737). It is understandable that these references would be made in this novel in the context of attention to the issue of poverty among the common people. J. H. Elliott (*Imperial Spain* 199-200) explains that Charles V's dangerous credit transactions had incalculably disastrous consequences for sixteenth- and seventeenth-century Spain. Those actions led to the mortgaging of Spain's resources and establishing the domination of foreign bankers over the nation's sources of wealth. The *servicios* that the Crown compelled the *Cortes* to impose to pay for those loans ultimately had to be paid by the common people, who, as a consequence, were unable to pay their rents and were reduced to utter misery, many wandering naked or filling the prisons. In any case, Dulcinea's "enchantment" is the displacement of her ideal essence, including its physical manifestations, by non-essential qualities that arose from the accidental, extrinsic causes of social circumstances. From this point of view, the "enchantment of Dulcinea" motif has the broader metaphorical implication that just as wealth has the power to turn an ordinary reality into an ideal image, poverty can turn an ideal image into an ordinary reality.[8]

Metaphorical interpretation also helps to clarify Sancho's role in the "disenchantment of Dulcinea." In general, insofar as Sancho corresponds to an aspect of the character Don Quijote (his attachment to practical reality),

---

[8] As Karl Marx observed in relation to the power of money, "*money* transforms the *real essential powers of man and nature* into what are merely abstract conceits and therefore *imperfections*—into tormenting chimeras—just as it transforms *real imperfections and chimeras* ...into *real powers* and *faculties*" (*Economic and Philosophic Manuscripts* 168-69; emphasis in original). In the former case, one thinks of the transformation of Aldonza Lorenzo into a princess, an event that makes an actual relationship with her as unrealizable for Don Quijote as if she were an ugly and ordinary rustic. In the latter case, one thinks of how the ordinary behavior of the Duke and Duchess is disguised in a veneer of prosperity and elegance.

his privation while in Don Quijote's service represents Don Quijote's own repudiation of the practical demands of everyday life that nevertheless accompany him wherever he goes. The afflictions that Sancho experiences while he is governor dramatize the idea that people in government posts must conform to the whims of the powerful. Since Sancho represents, among other things, the principle of surrender to the material, natural order, his being whipped or whipping himself can be seen to be logical as a way to disenchant Dulcinea when it is interpreted as a repudiation of subjection to natural necessity, such as that which entraps the "enchanted Dulcinea." Because the Duke and Duchess seek to amuse themselves by aggravating Don Quijote's madness, it is also logical that they would impose a solution to Dulcinea's enchantment that would not be practicable because of the strain it places on relations between Don Quijote and Sancho.[9] Don Quijote is determined axiologically, and so he defines Dulcinea in ideal terms. She thus becomes a projection of Don Quijote's freedom of will. One could argue that the efforts of the Duke and Duchess to make Don Quijote a puppet in charades that entail the "enchanted Dulcinea" (in a manner reminiscent of the way Ginés de Pasamonte exploits the naiveté of others and manipulates them by aping their fantasies) is motivated not just by a malicious desire to compromise the source of Don Quijote's freedom of will but also by an aggressive wish to discredit his idealism by mocking and debunking the values that inspire it.[10] One has to be careful not to infer too much about the Duke and Duchess on the basis of what we know from seeing them at their country estate, but it seems accurate to assert that they have little serious regard for the kind of idealism that drives Don Quijote, given both their willingness to make sport of it and their own neglect of it. Their interest in idealism seems to be limited to a desire to disparage it for the sake of entertainment. The Duke and Duchess seem to want to make Don Quijote look ridiculous because they want to justify their repudiation of the old, high conception of noblesse. While it would be incorrect to refer to "quixotic" tendencies on the part of the Duke and Duchess that are similar

---

[9] For a discussion of the antagonism between Don Quijote and Sancho that develops in relation to the disenchantment of Dulcinea, see Carroll Johnson, *Cervantes and the Material World* 32-36.

[10] Joaquín Casalduero comes close to this view with his observation that in Part II of *Don Quijote*, "toda confirmación del espíritu [del hombre de acción] es siempre paródica" (*Sentido y forma del "Quijote"* 294).

to those of Don Quijote, in this confrontation between two instances of megalomania it would be hard to determine which is the more pathological. Perhaps one could say that the monomania of Don Quijote is more psychopathic, while the smug irreverence of the Duke and Duchess is more sociopathic, especially by the standards of high courtesy.

The lack of a genuine idealism on the part of the Duke and Duchess is, then, the key to understanding the thematic import of their game of obstructing the "disenchantment of Dulcinea," of preventing Don Quijote from restoring Dulcinea to mythopoeic form so that he can resume his former relationship with her. With that obstruction the Duke and Duchess increase Don Quijote's feelings of impotence and drive a wedge between him and Sancho, whom Don Quijote depends upon to maintain his practical links to the real world. Since the "enchanted" Dulcinea is trapped in the empirical order and Don Quijote is unable to renounce his devotion to her, the actions of the Duke and Duchess have the effect of confining Don Quijote's emotional center in the empirical order as well, a situation that ultimately leads to his demise.

In general, Don Quijote's preoccupations remain impervious to the trivializing finiteness of everyday reality, yet he maintains a deep and loyal relation to that reality. In contrast, the Duke and Duchess, with their wealth and their cajoling elitism, hover "above" the real world; but they are "imprisoned" by that world in the same way that the master can be said to be enslaved by the bondman. By shedding their idealism, they have become reduced to the same paltriness that they seek to rise above. Alonso Quijano's physical death prevents Don Quijote from succumbing spiritually, and he remains "in a higher place"; yet the Duke and Duchess remain confined in a lower one, in the sphere of "ambición soberbia" (2.32: 770, referred to in similar terms by Sancho in 2.53: 926 and by Don Quijote in 2.42: 840 as a "golfo profundo de confusiones") that was repudiated by Sancho when he left his governorship.[11] The narrow-mindedness of the Duke and Duchess

---

[11] It is in this sense only that Ruth El Saffar's view that the Duke and Duchess "often find themselves trapped in their own illusions" (*Beyond Fiction* 120) would seem to me to be accurate. In the book in which that observation appears, El Saffar does not explain her meaning; but in *Distance and Control* she observes that the Duke and Duchess are trapped in the sense that they "are controlled to some extent from within their play by the very characters whom they intend to manipulate" (93). Such developments (described by El Saffar on 93-98) occur to such a small extent that to

explains their puerility and their efforts to compensate for their own pettiness by mocking a social inferior who in the arena of subjective culture is actually their superior (as Don Quijote observes, "la sangre se hereda y la virtud se aquista, y la virtud vale por sí sola lo que la sangre no vale": 2.42: 841). The Duke's and Duchess's malicious urge to debunk the naive high-mindedness or innocence of social "outsiders" culminates in the final episode involving Altisidora, where she pretends to have died of unrequited passion for Don Quijote and appears lying on a bier at her own mock funeral. When the prank is over, she tells Don Quijote (I will translate her words, since the translations I have seen by Putnam, Cohen, and Rutherford seem to me to be inadequate),

> Good God alive, Don Codfish, mind of mortar, like a date stone, more stubborn and hard than a peasant with a one-track mind when he's got his sights set on something — if I come at you I'll scratch your eyes out. Do you in any way think, Don Vanquished and Don Beat-to-a-Pulp, that I died because of you? Everything you've seen tonight has been staged — I'm not a woman who for a hunched-over old camel like you would let myself feel pain in the dirt under one of my fingernails, let alone die for you. (2.70: 1044)[12]

One could suspect that what Altisidora says is true, that since Don Quijote is old, gaunt, and poor he is not desirable to women, which is why his mistress has to be a fantasy. Is Altisidora completely blind to Don Quijote's extraordinary spiritual stature? Perhaps she is not.[13] She may recognize that

---

say that the Duke and Duchess are "trapped" by them seems to me to be an exaggeration. Trapped they are, but in a different way — in an ethical bind. The main value of El Saffar's observations is that they record the fact that the Duke and Duchess are susceptible to their own insecurities at betraying the social norms by which they are supposed to live.

[12] "Vive el Señor, don bacallao, alma de almirez, cuesco de dátil, más terco y duro que villano rogado cuando tiene la suya sobre el hito, que si arremeto a vos, que os tengo de sacar los ojos! ¿Pensáis, por ventura, don vencido y don molido a palos, que yo me he muerto por vos? Todo lo que habéis visto esta noche ha sido fingido; que no soy yo mujer que por semejantes camellos había de dejar que me doliese un negro de la uña, cuanto más morirme." (2.70: 1044)

[13] Carroll Johnson observes that Altisidora "appears actually to fall in love with ...[Don Quijote]. At the very least, she is truly offended and hurt when he announces

quality enough to find Don Quijote even less desirable, and her tirade may have the subtly ironic implication that, unlike in literature, in the world of reality ethical idealists are not prized as mates because their reluctance to rely on cunning to advance themselves in life makes them less reliable as providers. As Don Quijote himself observes, "el mundo [es] enemigo siempre de premiar los floridos ingenios ni los loables trabajos" (2.62: 998).

The novel *Don Quijote* as a whole can be seen as an elaborate tribute to the feeling of ethical idealism, as a value of the self that is opposed to values of means. For Don Quijote, knight errantry is spirituality. However, ethical idealism is also profoundly practical. It addresses the crucial human concerns of what is valuable in life and what can be done to attain it.[14] The negative opposite of Don Quijote's orientation is represented in the ethical inertia of the Duke and Duchess, their stagnation in a luxurious world of sensuous pleasure, histrionics, and indifference to values and ends. These are characteristics that the Duke and Duchess share with Don Diego de Miranda, whose preening manner of dress compares to that of the Duchess and contrasts so comically with Don Quijote's greasy leather jerkin and student's shirt that are described when he disrobes at Don Diego's house (in 2.18).[15] Whereas Don Quijote represents an ideal of self-abnegation and self-transcendence, Don Diego and especially the Duke and Duchess represent the urge to exalt themselves by what Thorstein Veblen refers to as a display of invidious pecuniary emulation. In this way they represent, respectively, earlier and later stages in the rise and decline of aristocratic culture. As Sombart notes,

...old aristocratic principles [of probity, candor, and disinterestedness] declined rapidly in all countries during the seventeenth and eighteenth

---

he would rather be true to Dulcinea than to have a fling with her" (*Don Quixote: The Quest for Modern Fiction* 66). F. Márquez Villanueva would seem to agree with Johnson's observation concerning Atisidora's injured vanity, but not with the view that Altisidora might have fallen in love with Don Quijote: "Claro que ni ella ni nadie iba a morirse por amores de Don Quijote, pero sí que su perversa comedia descarrila irremisiblemente ante la entereza sin mella ni doblez del caballero." (*Trabajos y días* 331)

[14] See Nicolai Hartmann 1: 1-46 on the practical character of philosophical ethics.

[15] See my *Don Quijote, Symbol of a Culture in Crisis* 53-62 for a discussion of Diego de Miranda and a survey of how criticism has interpreted him.

centuries…. [T]he changed outlook of the nobility was bound to swell the great stream of luxury …. (*Luxury and Capitalism* 85)

It is not the case, however, that—for all his nobility of soul and his attainments in the sphere of subjective culture—Don Quijote represents the good and the Duke and Duchess the bad in black and white terms. Just as the Duke and Duchess know how to act like genteel hosts if they choose to do so, Don Quijote knows how to act violent and barbaric. Apart from the many instances of his gratuitous attacks on unsuspecting travelers, he joins the Duke in the predatory ritual of killing a wild boar; and, like the Duke, he turns a deaf ear to Sancho's objections. Also, Don Quijote is not without his elitist tendencies, even if they are limited to occasional comically defensive reflexes in relation to such matters as Sancho's loquacity or engaging plebeians in combat. In their way, the Duke and Duchess are direct descendants of Don Quijote's culturally atavistic tendencies. As Veblen notes, "In the later barbarian culture society attained settled methods of acquisition and possession under the quasi-peaceable régime of status. Simple aggression and unrestrained violence in great measure gave place to shrewd practice and chicanery …." (*The Theory of the Leisure Class* 236). In the new order, good-nature, equity, and indiscriminate sympathy become hindrances to self-advancement, success now being the reward for a freedom from scruple, sympathy, honesty, and regard for life (Veblen 223). "Strategy or cunning is an element invariably present in games, as also in warlike pursuits and in the chase" (Veblen 273). It is no accident that one finds in the context of the stay at the ducal chateau, when Sancho makes the rounds of his "ínsula" in 2.49, that gambling and the deceit that accompanies it are met with earnest, civic-minded disapproval and penalized accordingly.

In the eyes of the Duke and Duchess, Don Quijote's arrival at their chateau is an opportunity for them to exercise their cunning in a series of farces in which Don Quijote is the leading dupe. In his essence, Don Quijote represents the Renaissance affirmation of an inspired civic and religious morality based on a striving for the realization of higher values. Yet in spite of his amazing erudition and high character, he is impulsive and emotionally determined. This characteristic makes him easy for the Duke and Duchess to manipulate and exploit for the purposes of their entertainment. Even when he is about to depart from their country house in 2.57, Don Quijote seems to remain oblivious to having been made the butt of irony. In answer to the Duke's accusation that he stole three nightcaps and two garters from Altisidora, his first words are, "No quiera Dios ...que yo desenvaine mi espada contra vuestra ilustrísima persona, de quien tantas mercedes he recibido..." (2.70: 951). Don Quijote seems, again, restrained by a scruple of manners of which the decadent Duke is incapable. Is a broader implication of Don Quijote's discourse on the difference between an offense and an affront (in 2.32, after his rebuttal to the *eclesiástico*) that the ridicule he and Sancho are subjected to at the ducal chateau actually constitutes an affront? He says that unlike when one is merely offended, a man is affronted when the person who injured him "sustentó lo que había hecho, sin volver las espaldas y a pie quedo" (2.32, 772). Perhaps one can see in such contrasting characteristics a series of stages and variants in the pattern of the aristocracy's cultural evolution, and perhaps these stages are represented in a series of characters in this novel. There would seem to be a movement from Don Quijote (the pristine, tonic, old heroic stage, revived in the high morality of the great figures of the Renaissance); to Diego de Miranda (noble turned prosperous private citizen given to self-centered and trivial Epicurean pursuits[16]); to Ricote (a merchant representing the economic force of wealth, the basis of a new aristocracy and a condition for the erosion of old aristocratic ideals: Sancho encounters Ricote while he and Don Quijote are still guests at the home of the Duke and Duchess); to the Duke and Duchess (the stage of lavish waste, self-trivialization, and hollow elitism, which the image of Don Quijote occasionally parodies and makes appear ridiculous).

Yet in order to avoid stereotyping the high nobility, Cervantes has Don Quijote and Sancho, soon after they leave the ducal estate, encounter in 2.58 a group of young nobles engaged in the culturally healthy activity of dressing as shepherds and reciting the eclogues of Garcilaso and Camões. The incompatibility of this situation with the decadence at the ducal chateau is suggested chapters later, when Don Quijote refers to verses of Garcilaso that were being sung when he and Sancho arrived at Altisidora's mock funeral in 2.69. He says, "¿qué tienen que ver las estancias de Garcilaso con la muerte desta señora?" (2.70: 1045). Also, the motifs in 2.58 of becoming

---

[16] For a discussion of the critical tradition of interpreting Diego de Miranda as a Christian Epicurean (in the works of authors such as Vicente Llorens, Marcel Bataillon, and Francisco Márquez Villanueva), see my *Don Quijote, Symbol of a Culture in Crisis* 56-57.

entangled in invisible nets (deceit) in a "feigned Arcadia" (false paradise) and trampled by bulls (subjected to vile abuse) hearken back metaphorically to the recent visit with the Duke and Duchess. In the *societas leonina* (or "sociation with a lion") of the relationship between the Duke and Duchess on the one hand and Don Quijote and Sancho on the other, the Duke and Duchess assume that all the advantage is on their side. In contrast, in the earlier "Adventure of the Lions," the lion that was confronted by Don Quijote acted like a gracious host and displayed his superiority precisely by deferring to his unexpected visitor. In contrast, the inferiority of the Duke and Duchess makes itself evident precisely in the disadvantage at which they place their unsuspecting guests. A broad and quite bitter, though subtle, satirical implication of the entire episode involving the ducal chateau is that the only way frivolous people like the Duke and Duchess could have respect for heroic idealism is as a practical joke; and the only way a heroic figure like Don Quijote could be highly regarded in the real world of cunning manipulation is, also, as a practical joke. Can the lack of virility of character at the Duke's estate be seen to be figuratively suggested in the baroquely flamboyant effeminacy of the bearded *dueñas*? Perhaps the Clavileño episode was intended to imply the degree to which the malicious pranks of the Duke and Duchess are earthbound and unconvincing, except for simpletons like Sancho, who believe that it is in their interest to pretend to be convinced when they see themselves being manipulated.

In sum, the general purpose of the episode involving the stay of Don Quijote and Sancho at the ducal chateau is to contrast two opposed attitudes: Don Quijote's scrupulously ceremonious high-mindedness and self-effacement are contrasted with a world in which the standard is smug contempt and idle malice—a world where naively sincere good faith is countered by mocking duplicity, where kind earnestness is met by ridicule and smugness, and a noble indifference to worldly possessions is contrasted to frivolous luxury and waste. On another level, the contrast is between differing degrees of sensitivity to the ethical implications of form, insofar as form is determined by spiritual essence. A low degree of such sensitivity is represented by the Duke and Duchess, and a high degree is represented by Don Quijote. Northrop Frye notes that satire is both an attitude and a form (*Anatomy of Criticism* 310). The degeneration of comic gaiety is represented by the *eclesiástico*'s personal attack against Don Quijote that clashes with a festive occasion, but especially by the grotesque and malicious farces enacted by Altisidora. Frye, again, defines decorum in literature as "the suiting of style to …a subject." It is "the poet's *ethical* voice, the modification of his own voice …to the vocal tone demanded by a subject or mood" (*Anatomy* 269). The requirements of tone can be determined by the genre of a work, and comedy requires a prevailing comic mood (*Anatomy* 171-72, 269). *Don Quijote* is a comic epic, and Cervantes observes the requirements of comic tone and avoids pathos by never evoking either the laughter that Don Quijote's gullibility provokes or any pain that Don Quijote might be experiencing. The principles of sociability can be seen as being similar to comic decorum in literature. Both sociability and comedy are aesthetic forms of play in which the serious problems of social interaction in the real world are on the surface largely subordinated to conventional form-laws in order to achieve an equilibrium between the purposes of the individual and those of the collectivity (Simmel, *Sociology* 53-56). Pathos is incompatible with the decorum of comedy, just as it is incompatible with the decorum of sociability. Far from confronting the Duke and Duchess because of their neglect, Don Quijote never indulges the poignancy of his personal feelings when he finds himself being maliciously ridiculed. So successfully does he resist doing so that the reader must wonder if he ever even experiences such pain. An analogous phenomenon is the difficulty in this novel of identifying the author's attitude toward the events portrayed. Simmel regards the character of an author's or narrator's personality in literature as being comparable to the way the giver or host of a party becomes completely absorbed in a group in order to defer to the cultivation of pure sociable form (Simmel, *Sociology* 53). With his dignified and healthy restraint during the hoaxes organized by the Duke and Duchess, Don Quijote actually sets a tone of congenial sociability even after the Duke and Duchess have abused and compromised that tone. So it is that Don Quijote, as a guest at the ducal chateau, can be seen as the image of Cervantes the author discreetly observing the requirements of comic decorum as he elaborates a subtle discourse of satiric irony. Like Don Quijote, Cervantes—the consummate ironist—almost never asserts his personal attitudes toward his characters, even when he is describing characters who inappropriately insist on asserting such personal attitudes themselves.

THE UNIVERSITY OF TENNESSEE,
KNOXVILLE

Works Cited

Aristotle. *Nicomachean Ethics*. Trans. Terence Irwin. Indianapolis: Hackett, 1985.

Azorín (Martínez Ruiz, José). "Sobre el *Quijote*." In *Obras completas*, II. Madrid: Aguilar, 1959, 941-46.

Casalduero, Joaquín. *Sentido y forma del "Quijote."* Madrid: Ínsula, 1949.

Cervantes de Saavedra, Miguel. *El ingenioso hidalgo don Quijote de la Mancha*. 1605, 1615. Ed. Martín de Riquer. Barcelona: Editorial Juventud, 1968.

Creel, Bryant L. *Don Quijote, Symbol of a Culture in Crisis*. Valencia: Albatros Hispanófila, 1988.

Close, Anthony. "Seemly Pranks: The Palace Episodes in *Don Quixote* Part II. In *Art and Literature in Spain, 1600-1800: Studies in Honor of Nigel Glendenning*. London: Tamesis, 1993.

Elliott, J. H. *Imperial Spain, 1469-1716*. New York: St. Martin's Press, 1964.

El Saffar, Ruth. *Beyond Fiction: The Recovery of the Feminine in the Novels of Cervantes*. Berkeley: U of California P, 1984.

———. *Distance and Control in "Don Quijote": A Study in Narrative Technique*. Studies in the Romance Languages and Literatures 147. Chapel Hill, NC: U of North Carolina Department of Romance Languages, 1975.

Frye, Northrop. *Anatomy of Criticism: Four Essays*. Princeton: Princeton UP, 1957.

Hartmann, Nicolai. *Ethics*. 1926. Trans. Stanton Coit. 3 vols. London: Unwin, 1932.

Johnson, Carroll. *Don Quixote: The Quest for Modern Fiction*. Boston: Twayne, 1990.

———. *Cervantes and the Material World*. Urbana, IL: U of Illinois P, 2000.

Maldonado de Guevara, Francisco. "Del *Ingenium* de Cervantes al de Gracián." *Anales Cervantinos* 6 (1957): 97-111.

Márquez Villanueva, Francisco. *Trabajos y días cervantinos*. Alcalá de Henares: Centro de Estudios Hispánicos, 1995.

Marx, Karl. *The Economic and Philosophic Manuscripts of 1844*. Trans. Martin Milligan. New York: International Publishers, 1964.

Menéndez Pidal, Ramón. 1948. "Cervantes y el ideal caballeresco." In *España y su Historia*. 2 vols. Madrid: Ediciones Montauro, 1957. 2: 213-34.

Murillo, Luis. *A Critical Introduction to "Don Quijote."* New York: Peter Lang, 1990.

Novitsky, Pavel I. *Cervantes and Don Quixote: A Socio-historical Interpretation*. Trans. Sonia Volochova. New York: The Critics' Group, 1936.

Salazar Rincón, Javier. *El mundo social del Quijote*. Madrid: Gredos, 1986.

Scheler, Max. *Formalism in Ethics and Non-Formal Ethics of Values*, (1913-1916). Trans. Manfred S. Frings and Roger L. Funk. Evanston, IL: Northwestern UP, 1973.

Simmel, Georg. *The Sociology of Georg Simmel*. Trans. and ed. Kurt H. Wolff. Glencoe, IL: The Free Press, 1950.

Sombart, Werner. *Luxury and Capitalism*. 1913. Trans. W. R. Dittmar. Ann Arbor: The U of Michigan P, 1967.

Sullivan, Henry W. *Grotesque Purgatory: A Study of Cervantes' "Don Quijote," Part II*. University Park, PA: Penn State UP, 1996.

Unamuno, Miguel de. "Vida de Don Quijote y Sancho, según Miguel de Cervantes Saavedra explicada y comentada." 1905. In idem, *Ensayos*, ed. Bernardo G. de Candamo. 2: 66-361. Madrid: Espasa-Calpe, 1958.

Veblen, Thorstein. *The Theory of the Leisure Class: An Economic Study of Institutions.* New York: The Modern Library, 1934.

Wells, H. G. *The Outline of History, Being a Plain History of Life and Mankind.* New York, Macmillan, 1921.

Zimic, Stanislav. *Los cuentos y las novelas del "Quijote."* Madrid: Iberoamericana, 1998.

Mangled in La Mancha: *Don Quijote* Meets the Spanglish of Ilán Stavans

JAMES IFFLAND

"IN UN PLACETE DE La Mancha of which nombre no quiero remembrearme, vivía, not so long ago, uno de esos gentlemen who always tienen una lanza in the rack, una buckler antigua, a skinny caballo y un greyhound para el chase." Thus begins the "translation" into "Spanglish" of the first chapter of the *Quijote* carried out by Professor Ilán Stavans of Amherst College. As the reader probably knows already, Stavans's text provoked a true *cause célèbre* with its first appearance in the newspaper *La Vanguardia* of Barcelona on July 3, 2002.[1]

The notion of analyzing this incident precisely when we're trying to honor the quadricentennial of the publication of Cervantes's masterpiece might seem somewhat out of place. Nevertheless, I believe that it's worthwhile on such a transcendent occasion to take a serious look at what I've referred to elsewhere as the "social destiny" of the *Quijote*.[2] By this I mean the very many ways in which the work has been appropriated and mobilized within the sociopolitical and cultural dynamics not only of the Spanish-speaking world, but the world at large.

In the precise case that concerns us, the question of the social destiny of the *Quijote* branches out in several directions. First, the episode forces us to reflect on that peculiar status of the *Quijote* as a cornerstone of Hispanic culture—a kind of "Bible," as it were. As a consequence of that enormous

---

[1] A casual web search will give the reader an idea of the proportions of what Stavans himself calls an "international controversy" (*Spanglish* 252).

[2] See "On the Social Destiny of *Don Quijote*: Literature and Ideological Interpellation" (also available in Spanish as "Sobre el destino social de *Don Quijote*: literatura e interpelación ideológica").

cultural status, the Spanish language itself is frequently referred to as the "language of Cervantes" (just as English is dubbed the "language of Shakespeare").

Second, it reveals a great deal about the peculiar dynamics of academia in the United States. The act of translating the *Quijote* into so-called Spanglish must be seen as forming part of the problematique of how to get ahead in this country's academic world, that is, by astutely linking one's scholarly activity with certain core themes that are currently in fashion (in this instance, those of identity, ethnicity, hybrid subjects, the bicultural, etc.).

Quite clearly, introducing the study of "Spanglish" into the institutional circuitry of the U.S. academy confers on it an air of legitimacy that it would not otherwise enjoy. And here we pass from the inoffensive little world of the ivory tower (at least according to some) to the world of politics in the strictest sense.

The translation that provoked so much controversy is now found in a new book by Stavans entitled *Spanglish: The Making of a New American Language*. The greater part of the book is comprised of a lexicon of some 3,500 words supposedly belonging to Spanglish.[3] It's preceded by a "theoretical" essay ("*La jerga loca*" 1-54) in which Stavans explores the phenomenon of Spanglish not only within the U.S., but in the Spanish-speaking world at large. Although Stavans asserts that his interest is primarily "scientific" in nature, the reader doesn't take long to realize that the book is actually an ideological *celebration* of Spanglish.

And it's here where we run into the significance of the growing Spanish-speaking population of the United States for the country's society in general. More precisely, I'm referring to the "problem" caused by the supposed lack of assimilation on the part of the new Hispanic immigration, especially the Mexican, with its excessive adherence to its native language, Spanish. Hence their role as the "bad guys" in the insidious recent book by Professor Samuel

---

[3] I say "supposedly" because even a quick survey of the lexicon produces many surprises. For example, classified as Spanglish in just the "A" section are words like "acequia," "adobe," "aficionado," "agente," and "aguardiente." A full analysis of the lexicon—a task that falls outside the focus of this essay—would reveal a host of theoretical and methodological shortcomings in Stavans's whole approach to his subject.

Huntington of the Kennedy School of Government at Harvard University, entitled *Who Are We? The Challenges to America's National Identity.*[4]

---

[4] Let's remember that Huntington enjoys great prestige within the ideological apparatuses in Washington for having "forecasted" in his famous previous book, *The Clash of Civilizations*, that, after the fall of the Soviet Union, the next great challenge for American democracy was going to be the Islamic world. Six or seven years after the publication of this work, we find the U.S. occupying two Muslim countries… Huntington's views on Hispanics are complemented by a wide range of discursive practices typical of the U.S. media, as studied very well in Otto Santa Ana's *Brown Tide Rising: Metaphors of Latinos in Contemporary American Public Discourse.* See particularly Chapter VII, "Disease or Intruder: Metaphors Constructing the Place of Latinos in the United States" (253-94). The "brown tide" alluded to in the title of the book is an example of the many aquatic metaphors found in public discourse referring to Hispanic immigrants. See also Wayne Cornelius's perceptive essay entitled "Ambivalent Reception: Mass Public Responses to the 'New' Latino Immigration to the United States" where the author points out that "there is an 'ethno-cultural' objection to the most recent wave of Latin immigration that underlies persistent U.S. public concern about immigration levels, regardless of the state of the macroeconomy. Native-born residents of states and local communities affected by heavy immigration are increasingly concerned about the potential of immigrants from Latin America and the Caribbean to shift the ethnic, cultural, and linguistic balance within their communities" (165-66). As Ana Celia Zentella points out in "Latin@ Languages and Identities," the "threat" of Spanish has been exaggerated: "Contrary to the inflammatory charges made be proponents of 'English-only' laws, who claim that Latinas do not know English and do not want to learn it, the English language is in no danger of being supplanted by Spanish or any other language. Instead, Spanish is being lost" (332). Here the author bases herself on the many studies that confirm the loss of Spanish among Hispanic youth. As Barbara Zurer Pearson affirms in "Bilingual Infants: Mapping the Research Agenda:" "It is an amazing fact that in the U.S., bilingual ability is rarely seen as an asset but more often as a handicapping condition. Mainstream schools spend millions of dollars and thousands of hours of nearly fruitless effort unsuccessfully teaching a second language to high schoolers; the same school systems suppress second-language abilities in preschool and elementary school children in the name of hastening their acquisition of English" (309). As Otto Santa Ana affirms: "It may be in the public school contexts that the social costs are dearest. The bilingual Latino child is not viewed simply as an American child, or an American child with an advantage of two languages and cultures. Rather, such a child is considered a linguistically impaired student at best—at worst, a racialized foreigner" (290).

Now, some readers might be thinking that I'm lending way too much importance to Stavans and his book by having brought up the thorny issues just cited. To assuage doubts in that regard, I'll sketch a quick profile of this fellow member of the profession. Having studied at the Universidad Autónoma Metropolitana, Xochimilco, Stavans emigrates to New York from Mexico City at the age of twenty five in the mid-eighties. He receives his doctorate from Columbia University and in very little time ends up occupying the prestigious Lewis-Sebring Chair at Amherst College, the elite private college located in picturesque central Massachusetts. But he racks up even more points for having managed to establish himself, before reaching the age of forty, as the "czar of Latino culture" in the U.S., in the frequently cited words of the *New York Times*.[5] Stavans's presence in the American media is very widespread — a true "public intellectual" who functions as a mouthpiece of the Latino community in this country. As many readers know, he has his own cultural program on PBS television — "La Plaza: Conversations with Ilán Stavans." The compliments he has received from well-known members of the American intelligentsia — "Skip" Gates, Richard Rodríguez — have bestowed on him a particularly compelling halo.[6]

Stavans also has his many critics, of course, especially among Latino intellectuals that have more direct experience with the marginalized "barrios" of large U.S. cities and the country's neglected rural areas.[7] After

---

[5] The *New York Times* article by Lynn Richardson, entitled "How to Be Both an Outsider and an Insider: 'The Czar of Latino Literature and Culture' Find Himself Under Attack," appeared on November 13, 1999. As it turns out, the "czar" moniker actually appears in a negative comment by Professor Juan Flores of Hunter College (see below). This doesn't prevent it from being cited over and over again in a positive sense, including within advertisements for Stavans's books. "The New York Times described Ilan Stavans as 'the czar of Latino literature in the United States'" runs the web blurb for *Ilan Stavans: Eight Conversations*, published by the University of Wisconsin Press (2004).

[6] See the comments that appear strategically placed on the dustcover of *Spanglish*: "Cantankerous and clever, sprightly and serious, Stavans is a voracious thinker ... unafraid to court controversy, unsettle opinions, make enemies.... He is an old-fashioned intellectual, a brilliant interpreter of his triple heritage — Jewish, Hispanic, and American" (Gates); "Ilan Stavans is the rarest of North American writers — he sees the Americas whole. Not since Octavio Paz has Mexico given us an intellectual so able to violate borders, with learning and grace" (Rodríguez).

[7] Several examples are found in the aforementioned *New York Times* article:

all, Stavans himself confesses in his much-commented earlier book, *The Hispanic Condition: The Power of a People* that he lived with his back turned toward Mexican society during the twenty five years he spent there, in large part because he belonged to a Jewish community characterized, according to Stavans, by deep, self-imposed isolation.[8] Although our author responds to his critics by asserting that his social class, his white skin and blond hair, and his Jewish origin should not disqualify him as a potential Latino spokesman, it's not too difficult to understand the bitter reaction he has provoked among Latino intellectuals who have suffered directly from U.S. racism.[9]

"'He's becoming the czar of Latino literature and culture,' said Juan Flores, a professor of black and Puerto Rican studies at Hunter College. 'This guy comes in, and he's the one who is the spokesman, the canon-former who is making the ultimate decisions about what is worthy of readership on the part of the American audience. It's astounding the quick move to that kind of prominence'" (Richardson A 17). Tey Diana Rebolledo of the University of New Mexico comments: "'He's not Chicano. He's a Mexican. He hasn't been in the movement since it started, so he's a little bit of an outsider'" (Richardson A 17). Francisco Lomeli of the University of California, Santa Barbara summarizes the reaction in question as follows: "'People have worked so hard against the grain, and to have somebody come in almost like a character out of theater, deus ex machina, there's a little bit of resentment'" (Richardson A 17).

   [8] Stavans describes the Jewish community in Mexico City as "a secure, self-imposed Jewish ghetto, an autistic island where Gentiles hardly existed and Hebraic symbols prevailed. [...] What made me Mexican? It's hard to know: language and the air I breathed, perhaps. Early on I was sent to Yiddish day school, the Colegio Israelita de México [...] where the heroes were Shalom Aleichem and Theodor Herzl; people like Lázaro Cárdenas and Alfonso Reyes were our neighbors' models, not ours. Together with my family and friends, I inhabited a self-sufficient island, with imaginary borders built in agreement between us and the outside world, an oasis, completely uninvolved with things Mexican" (*Hispanic* 238- 39).
   [9] "'Some people attack me because I wasn't born in the barrio [...]. I've been attacked for not being dark skinned and for being young. If you paid attention to all this, you would be naked, walking in the street, without a name and a telephone number'" (Richardson A 17). Stavans points out that his status as a "Latino" was essentially thrust upon after arriving in the U.S.: "Suddenly, I ceased to be Mexican and became, much to my surprise, a Latino—and what's worse, a white Latino, something most people have difficulty understanding [...]" (*Hispanic* 240). Nevertheless, it should be noted that Stavans doesn't shy away from situating

Now, we must take into account the fact that in his campaign in favor of Spanglish, Stavans positions himself precisely as a "defender of the people."[10] While he admits that Hispanics must learn English to improve their life in the U.S., and that it would, in fact, be preferable that they maintained their Spanish more or less intact, he ends up asserting that we mustn't look down on this "new American language" that is emerging and that even functions as a proud identifying mark among young Hispanics from *all* social classes.[11]

Stavans constantly praises the verbal creativity displayed by the speakers of Spanglish, even comparing it with Afro-American jazz.[12] He goes on to link its "hipness" with other aspects of Latino culture that are

---

himself as a spokesman of mestizo Latinos: "As native Americans, we were in these areas before the Pilgrims of the *Mayflower* and understandably keep a telluric attachment to the land" (*Hispanic* 5).

[10] "I realize, obviously, that for many impoverished Latinos the possibility of speaking el inglés, el español and Spanglish isn't really an option. But should that curtail our constructive analysis? And for how long will the so-called educated insist that los pobres don't speak a tongue, they simply destroy it? Class is an integral component of our way of life. When it isn't Spanglish we're complaining about as we address those that we portray as less worthy than us, it is something else [...]" (*Spanglish* 50-51)

[11] "It was thanks to them [Stavans's Latino students at Amherst] that I understood that Spanglish cuts across economic terrain. It isn't spoken only por los pobres, the disposed [sic]. The middle class has embraced it as a chic form of speech, una manera moderna y diverstida de hablar. This is in sharp contrast with other slang more often than not defined by turf: the language of drugs, for instance. Spanglish, instead, is democratic: de todos y para todos" (*Spanglish* 20). Spanglish is "not defined by class, as people in all social strata, from migrant workers to upper-class statements [sic] like congressmen, TV anchors, comedians, use it regularly. South of the Rio Grande, Spanglish also knows no boundaries at it permeates all levels of the economic ladder" (*Spanglish* 43).

[12] "Yes, it's a hodgepodge... But its creativity astonished me. In many ways, I see in it the beauties and achievements of jazz, a musical style that sprung up among African-Americans as a result of improvisation and lack of education. Eventually, though, it became a major force in America, a state of mind breaching out of the ghetto into the middle class and beyond. Will Spanglish follow a similar route?" (*Spanglish* 3). Later on, in the same vein, Stavans states that "Latinos in los Unaited Esteits are the ones in the linguistic avant-garde. They are in charge of revolutionizing language through sheer improvisation" (*Spanglish* 58-59).

currently in fashion in the U.S. — salsa music, well-known actors, actresses, and singers like Ricky Martin and Jennifer López, Mexican food, and even the Spanish-language soaps.[13] The growing and increasingly influential Spanish-language mass media outlets appear as heroes within Stavans's argument, in part because of their role in disseminating Spanglish.[14] That prestige enjoyed by certain elements of Hispanic culture will help to pave the way for the future society Stavans refers to as "Caliban's Utopia" in *The Hispanic Condition.* There he narrates a "dream" (see xiv-xv) he had which propels us to the year 2061, a moment by which a more or less peaceful version of the world depicted in *Blade Runner* (his comparison--xvii) has come about, one in which the border between the U.S. and Mexico has disappeared and in which the lingua franca is now Spanglish). In "Caliban's Utopia," the children of Aztlán have established their definitive hegemony over the marginalized Anglo population. There is no doubt that the "dream" is presented with humorous overtones, but it also clearly evokes an emancipatory political project.[15]

---

[13] In *The Hispanic Condition* Stavans describes the increasing popularity of things Latino in the following terms: "And what is more exciting is that the Anglos are beginning to look like us — enamored as they are of our bright colors and tropical rhythms, our self-immolating Frida Kahlo, our mythological 'Che' Guevara. [...] No more reticence, no more isolation: Spanish accents, our peculiar *manera peculiar de ser,* have emerged as exotic, fashionable, and even enviable and influential in mainstream American culture" (4).

[14] "It is in the media [...] where Spanglish travels faster and the creation of a 'common ground' becomes tangible. Univisión and Telemundo are the fastest-growing television networks in the United States. *El Show de Cristina, Sábado Gigante,* and *Noticiero Univisión,* to name only three of the most popular programs — and to obviate [sic] the ubiquitous soap operas to be found on prime time every weekday — are watched by millions. [...] Add to this the impact of radio. It is well-known fact that there are more Spanish-language radio stations in the state of California alone than in all of Central America together. El impacto, pues, es asombroso [...] The lingo de la calle y la montaña, then, penetrates people's minds, and their vocabulary, at an astonishing speed. La revolución lingüística es imparable — the verbal transformation is unstoppable" (*Spanglish* 14-15)

[15] The more directly political implications of Caliban's Utopia, including the reference to Aztlán, are more fully highlighted in the letter to Stavans's son, which serves as an afterword to *The Hispanic Condition* ("Letter to My Child"): "When you become an adult, Latinos will have ceased to be marginal. Instead, we'll have become protagonists. The Rio Grande will not divide: Latin and North America will

Now, let me declare at this point that I'm incensed by all the anti-immigrant and anti-Hispanic measures that have materialized in the "English only" referenda or in the successful campaigns of the millionaire Ron Unz to eradicate bilingual education (yes, even in Massachusetts, my progressive home state...). And to tell the truth, I would love it if Hispanics were able to establish real social and political hegemony in this country, preventing it from going to hell in a hand-basket as it seems to be currently headed. But, quite frankly, I doubt that the route sketched by Stavans would be smoothed out by the flourishing of Spanglish. Rather, I would suggest that the complete opposite is true.

Faced by a truly worrisome sociopolitical situation, the Hispanic population in the U.S. desperately needs a strong cultural backbone, and much of the "calcium" needed to strengthen it will come from pride in its culture and the language that has been its vehicle for centuries.

To make this argument may seem a paradoxical gesture for many readers. Everyone who resides here in the U.S. is more than familiar with the relative lack of prestige of Spanish within the hierarchy of foreign languages. In a curious way, at the same time that Spanish enjoys enormous popularity in high school and college classrooms, it continues in its role as a kind of "ugly duckling" in the collective American imaginary.[16]

---

become a single unity." (244). "It is Moctezuma's revenge: they shall infiltrate the enemy, we shall populate its urban center, marry its daughters, and reestablish the kingdom of Aztlán. They are here to reclaim what we were deprived of, to take revenge. This isn't a political battle, a combat often stimulating to the liberal imagination, but a cosmic battle to set things right" (246). Needless to say, what Stavans describes *is*, indeed, a political battle, despite whatever cosmic dimension he wishes to project upon it.

[16] A good synthesis of the phenomenon in question is found in Liesl Schillinger's article for the *Washington Monthly* entitled "Spanish Disquisition": "I often have encountered other linguists, non-linguists, professors, and people in other professions who confess that they [...] dislike the sound of Spanish. 'It's ugly,' a typical Spanish-averse friend—an elegant woman with an advanced degree and knowledge of two other foreign languages—once declared to me without embarrassment. She passed on a bit of gossip she had heard and found amusing. Apparently, Ivana Trump's son, Donald Jr., once told his mother he wanted to learn Spanish. 'Why?' she had retorted. 'So you can speak with the servants?' [...] The Spanish language suffers from an unaddressed image problem in this country, connected to Southwestern and urban impressions of Hispanicity that sink the language and

Even if we look toward the European cultural context, we find Spaniards still subject to their centuries-old linguistic inferiority complex vis à vis English, French and German, a complex reinforced even further by their literature's precarious position within the universal canon.

And here, of course, we return to the *Quijote*... As we all know, it is the only Spanish work that has entered without problems in that aforementioned canon. In a certain sense, the *entire* great edifice of literature written in Spanish, whether on the Iberian Peninsula or in the Americas, rests on the poor backs of Don Quijote and Sancho.[17] And if as a Cervantes scholar I feel proud in my role as exegete of the Hispanic "Bible." at times I feel that virtually the entire Spanish cultural Establishment has committed an enormous error by having invested virtually all of its cultural capital in this single work.

It's not a question of downplaying the importance of the *Quijote* in the world literary pantheon, but rather of working harder to publicize the other wonders of Spanish and Latin American literature. In other words, *after* this quadricentennial celebration is over we should all roll up our sleeves and begin to spread the news about the *Libro de Buen Amor*, the *Celestina*, *Fortunata y Jacinta* and *La Regenta*, on the one hand, and on the other, about Sor Juana Inés de la Cruz, Rulfo, Lezama Lima, and Vallejo.

Moreover, by insisting so much on the *Quijote*'s status as a "monument," we can't help but invite the intervention of graffiti artists. Turning our eyes now to Ilán Stavans's translation, let's remember the circumstances in which it came about.

---

culture in the grim border zones of Texas and California and in the ghettoes and elevators of metropolises."

[17] The notion that Spanish literature "only" has the *Quijote* is widespread. A succinctly put but very representative example appears in the aforementioned article by Liesl Schillinger: "Indeed, historically, Americans and Europeans alike have often skipped Spain when they considered countries responsible for the creation of Western culture. A casual scan of high culture tells the story [...]. Great literature? With the single exception (and what an exception!) of Cervantes, the canon does not speak Spanish; Stendhal, Balzac, Goethe, Mann, Tolstoy, Dante, Dickens, Chaucer, and others drown it out" ("Spanish Disquisition"). Stavans himself, it should be noted, adds fuel to the fire with comments of his own: "Spaniards are known to be obsessed with language, but, after *Don Quixote*, they have not been particularly talented in producing a first-rate literature" (*Spanglish* 20).

Stavans is touring in Spain, obviously enjoying the notoriety caused by the news that he's giving a college course on Spanglish. During his stay in Barcelona, he participates in a radio broadcasted debate in which a member of the Real Academia Española de la Lengua also takes part, adopting a very dismissive attitude toward Spanglish. At a given moment this member of the Royal Academy (whom Stavans never identifies) states that Spanglish will never be considered a legitimate language until it is capable of producing a work of the stature of the *Quijote*. Not to be out-maneuvered, Stavans quickly shoots back –Who knows? Maybe at some point in the future a masterpiece like the *Quijote* might well appear. Immediately thereafter, the interviewer asks Stavans how the *Quijote* itself would sound in Spanglish, and our author responds with an improvised version of the first few lines. Subsequently, an editor of the cultural section of *La Vanguardia* of Barcelona requests a translation of the whole first chapter – a request that Stavans honors. Its subsequent dissemination in newspapers around the Spanish-speaking world and on the web sparks the scandal that is the object of these reflections.[18]

It's true, in fact, that the translation of a culture's central texts has always been surrounded by tension, and even by certain very real dangers, as is seen clearly in the paradigmatic case of this phenomenon – the translation of the Bible into the vernacular languages.[19] Translating the *Quijote* is fraught with similar perils, and even more so in the case of a "translation" into a controversial derivative of its original language.

---

[18] The basic details related here appear on 251-52 of *Spanglish*.

[19] "Translation has to do with authority and legitimacy and ultimately, with power, which is precisely why it has been and continues to be the subject of so many acrimonious debates. [...] No wonder nations have always felt they needed some person or persons they could trust enough to entrust him or her with the task of translating: the Horatian 'fidus interpres' or 'trustworthy interpreter.' [...] Obviously, trust is more important when the most central text of a culture is concerned, a text invoked to legitimize the power of those who wield it in that culture. It may just be possible that the West has paid so much attention to translation because its central text, the Bible, was written in a language it could not readily understand, so that it was forced to rely on translators to legitimize power" (Lefevere 2-3). "If a text is considered to embody the core values of a culture, if it functions as that culture's central text, translations of it will be scrutinized with the greatest care, since 'unacceptable' translation may well be seen to subvert the very basis of the culture itself" (Lefevere 70).

The numerous attacks aimed at this translation have allowed Stavans to present himself as a victim of the habitual intolerance of the Spaniards. The Real Academia Española ends up being the "bad guy" — that galvanizing champion of all the "purists" of the language of the "Madre Patria." Stavans, on the other hand, appears first in the role of the defender of the Spanish of the Americas, and then, of all the underprivileged groups among which Spanglish acquired its initial impetus.[20]

Now, many could indeed argue that there is nothing wrong in trying to bring Cervantes's masterpiece closer to Hispanic adolescents stuck in the ghettos of the U.S., "speaking to them in their own language" and thereby sparking in them an interest in classic works of Spanish literature which in turn would result in an increase of their battered self-esteem. The question that arises immediately is whether the translation Stavans offers us has, in fact, fulfilled the objectives just mentioned. I believe that the answer must be a resounding "no."

To begin with, we must ask ourselves whether the term "translation" is really applicable to Stavans's final product. In principle, we should be dealing with an "interlinguistic" translation, according to the tripartite classification of Roman Jakobson, that is, from one established language into another.[21] Here we're confronted by the whole problem of whether

---

[20] "How many Chicanos in the San Fernando Valley know of the mere existence of the Real Academia Española de la Lengua, an institution created in the 18th century to legislate—some would say promote—the well-being of the Spanish language? A miniscule number, no doubt. And how many Nuyoricans see their linguistic roots in Castile? An even smaller amount..." (*Spanglish* 20). For an example of his "populist" stance, see footnote 10 above. It's worth noting, in passing, that Stavans asserts that Latin Americans are much less concerned about the issue of linguistic purity because of their past experience with colonization: "In the Americas, Spanish is [still] somewhat foreign, a sign of the imperial expansion of the Catholic Kingdom of monarchs Isabella and Ferdinand. El español como lengua extranjera. To show that this is the case, it is enough to look at the reaction to Spanglish on the two sides of the ocean: whereas Spaniards are often puritanical about their tongue, los americanos are altogether less hysterical about the issue as a whole. This, in my view, is because the population in Latin America is well acclimated to the act—y el arte—of colonization. They know by experience what it means to be subjugated by an alien tongue" (*Spanglish* 26).

[21] For Jakobson's distinction between "intralingual," "interlingual," and "inter-semiotic" translation, see 145.

Spanglish is a language or not. On this point Stavans engages in the widest possible gamut of ambiguities, although he generally tends to affirm that it's a dialect on the road to becoming established as a language. (His most constant paradigm is Yiddish, which Stavans spoke as a child).[22]

Even if we accept the notion that his translation occurs between a language and a species of dialect, we still have the fact that Spanglish has many variants. Stavans has no problem in recognizing the existence of Cubonics (spoken by the Cubans in Miami), Dominicanish (spoken by the Dominicans of New York), etc.[23] But he also insists that a process of standardization is under way (*Spanglish* 13-15), in large part due to the Spanglish-language mass media, whose anchormen, D-J's, etc. are stabilizing linguistic usage at the national level ("rufo" instead of "techo," for example). But to the degree that Stavans has to recognize that the Spanglish-speaking community is by no means a unified phenomenon, we have to ask ourselves the question: Who, exactly, is the reader to whom this translation is addressed?

---

[22]In an interview published in *El País* Stavans states "No, el spanglish no es todavía un idioma. Está en proceso de convertirse en dialecto. Es una jerga que noce del choque o del encuentro entre el español y el inglés, y que no se restringe al territorio geográfico de EE UU" (Carbajo 34). At one point in *Spanglish*, Stavans offers this formulation of the term: "**Spanglish, n.** The verbal encounter between Anglo and Hispano civilizations" (5). When he chooses to become somewhat more specific, he says the following: "Yes, Spanglish shows the characteristics of an internal tongue, at least in the United States: it is often used by Latinos to define their own turf. But it has many other uses too: it is a transitional stage of communication in the process of English-language acquisition, it is a fashion, too. But in Latin American and the Caribbean the category of lengua intra-étnica, internal tongue, falls apart altogether, and another set of categories is brought to the fore: margin vs. center, imperial culture vs. colonies" (*Spanglish* 45). For the Yiddish comparison, see *Spanglish* 44-47, for example: "Upon my arrival in New York City in the mid eighties, I sensed that strange affinity between Spanglish and Yiddish. The explanation might have to do with my upbringing: Yiddish, another mishmash of languages, was part of my early education in the small Jewish enclave in Mexico in which I came of age. [...] Is Spanglish the Yiddish of today? Un poco sí, un poco no... At first sight, the equation appears ridiculous. But is it?" (44) "[...] Spanglish, to be fully understood, ought to be compared to Ebonics and Yiddish. Not that they are the same, but they have elements in common" (47). See also Stavans's comments in *Hispanic* 162.

[23] See *Spanglish* 12-13, where he says, among other things, that "there is really not one Spanglish, but many" (13).

It goes almost without saying that a translation is normally produced for a community of readers that isn't fluent in, or knowledgeable about, the original language.[24] Can we say that the Hispanic population of the U.S., even its second- or third-generation members, is not capable of deciphering the Spanish of Cervantes, especially in an annotated edition? Moreover, the premise that the translator should be a native speaker — or at least a true master — of the language into which he/she translates is very widely accepted.[25] Can it be said that Stavans, even after his four energizing years in New York City, is a "native speaker" — or "master" — of Spanglish?

Stavans admits that he has had to improvise a great deal in his role as translator, coining new terms — "neologisms," one might say — in Spanglish. For him, it's simply a healthy extension of that "jazzy" creativity characteristic of Spanglish.

I suppose that more than one reader might end up thinking that Iffland has lost his famous sense of humor and that he has obviously not detected that Stavans has carried out, in fact, an ingenious spoof, making fun of the retrograde old fogies of the Real Academia Española (gachupines todos ellos…). I fully recognize that a translation into Spanglish of the first chapter of the *Quijote* carried out, say, by the recently deceased Guillermo Cabrera Infante could be a ludic masterpiece of the first magnitude.[26] But given the

---

[24] "If a translation is, indeed, a text that represents another, the translation will to all intents and purposes function as that text in the receptor culture, certainly for those members of that culture who do not know the language in which the text was originally written. […] Let us not forget that translations are made by people who do not need them for people who cannot read the originals" (Lefevere 1).

[25] Dryden's formulation runs as follows in his classic essay on translation: "No man is capable of translating poetry [in the wide sense], who, besides a genius to that art, is not a master both of his author's language, and of his own […]" (Schulte and Biguenet 20). "The qualification of a translator worth reading must be a mastery of the language he translates out of and that he translates into […]" (Schulte and Biguenet 30).

[26] In that vein we might even want to look at the recent translation into police code carried out by officers in the hard-scrabble streets of Nezahualcóyotl, just outside Mexico City, as part of their elaborate celebration of the quadricentennial: "Los policias Emilio Hernández Castro y Gerardo García Márquez haciendo uso de […] claves — utilizadas para evitar que civiles que interceptan las señales de intercomunicación sepan qué asunto se transmite y para agilizar la misma comunicación con el puesto de mando — buscaron hacer más entendible al Quijote

theoretical piece that accompanies the translation, along with all the essays, interviews, etc. that Stavans has carried out in his promotion of Spanglish, the only conclusion one can reach is that, yes, indeed, this whole thing is meant to be taken seriously.[27]

The moment has arrived to take a look at our text.[28] The reader will note, for starters, the enormous presence of conventional English throughout the text. Let's return to just the famous first sentence: "*In* un placete de La Mancha *of which* nombre no quiero remembrearme, vivía, *not so long ago*, uno de esos *gentlemen who always* tienen una lanza *in the rack*, una *buckler* antigua, a *skinny* caballo, y un *greyhound* para el *chase*" (*Spanglish* 253). What we find here is plain and simple "code-switching" of the type that is, in fact, typical of bilingual Hispanics living in the U.S. But even if we are willing to accept this as part of the "new language" in question, we would have to ask ourselves whether it would manifest itself in this precise manner among "native speakers." The many sociolinguistic studies on the phenomenon of code-switching show that people don't normally change several times within the same sentence as is seen here.[29]

But even if we accept the notion that people can go along peppering their Spanish with many isolated words in English, we can ask ourselves

---

para aquellos policías que no que no les interesaba el mundo de la lectura. 'En el 22 de la Mancha de cuyo 62 no quiero acordarme, no hace muchos micros vivía un hidalgo de los de lanzas en astilleros, un armero para guardar 81s" (Ramón 4a). There's obviously more than a little playfulness being displayed here by our police translators.

[27]For examples of the vigorous campaign Stavans has carried in the dissemination of his position on Spanglish, see his essays "The *Gravitas* of Spanglish" and "Latin Lingo." For examples of his interviews, see "The Meaning of Spanglish" (with Silvana Paternostro in *Newsweek*) and "Spanglish" (with Ray Suárez on PBS's "New Hour"), as well as the previously cited interview with Juan A. Carbajo in *El País*,

[28]Page numbers cited correspond to the original and to this essay's appendix, respectively. Tom Lathrop and I would like to thank Professor Stavans for granting permission to reproduce his translation as it appears in its totality in *Spanglish*. The reader may also find it online at *Cuadernos Cervantes de la Lengua Espanola: La Revista del Español en el Mundo*.

[29] See, for example, Carol Myers-Scotton, Pieter Muysen, and Lesley Milroy/Pieter Muysken (eds.). (I would like to thank Carol Neidle, good friend and colleague, for directing my attention to these works.)

whether they would be such everyday words as "always" (seen in the sentence cited above), "with," "new," "thanks," "good," "happy," etc. [30]

Now, if we look for "authentic" Spanglish terms — those that in principle should appear in Stavans's lexicon — we find hardly any at all. We do have "felo" ("fellow"), "bró" ("friend"), "sondáu" and "sonóp" ("sundown" and "sunup"), but not much more. [31] What do appear abundantly, on the other hand, are what I've called Spanglish "neologisms" — that is, words that Stavans coins as he goes along. Among them we encounter "huntear," "saddlear," "pleasura," "sallyinguear," "desappointeado," "readear" and many, many more. [32]

This modality of Spanglish will, indeed, sound familiar to many colleagues who have had to teach Spanish language classes here in the United States. This tendency to make up new words based on English is something we have to confront every single day we teach. On not being able to remember a word in Spanish, the lazy student usually lets fly, with malicious playfulness, his new espanglishado term, provoking the complicit laughter of many of his classmates. Frequently we're dealing with the student who really doesn't want to take *any* foreign language. And given

---

[30] " "A cazuela *with* más beef than mutón" (253); "al nuevo orden de cosas y a la *new* profesión that was to follow" (257) [notice the use of the Spanish "nuevo" in the same phrase]; "Pero daba *thanks* al autor por concluir el libro" (254); "El remarcaba que el Cid Ruy Díaz era un caballero very *good*" (255); "Pero remembreando que el valiant Amadís no era *happy* que lo llamaran así" (257).

[31] "El *felo* habló d'esto muchas veces with el cura" (254); "it had to be Don Galaor, *bró* de Amadís of Gaul" (254) [note that Don Galaor was a biological brother of Amadís, not just a friend or buddy]; "En short, nuestro gentleman quedó tan inmerso en su readin that él pasó largas noches — del *sondáu y sonóp*" (255).

[32] "La gente sabía that él era un early riser y que gustaba mucho *huntear*" (253); "Un ladino del field y la marketa que le *saddleaba* el caballo" (253) ["ladino" is apparently Stavans's rendition of the English "lad," which appears in whatever unacknowledged English translation he's using as his base]; "tenía el hábito de leer libros de chivaldría with tanta *pleasura*" (253); "especialmente when él saw him *sallyingueando* hacia fuera of su castillo" (255); "quedó desappointeado" (256); "especialmente cuando *readeaba* esos cuentos de amor" (254) [note that Stavans also uses "readiar" — "había readiado" (255)]. Others include "employar" (253); "wieldear" (253); "foregetear" (253); "awakear" (254); "understandear" (254)); "refrainear" (256).

that he wants to fulfill the language requirement in the easiest way possible, he chooses an "easy" foreign language—*par excellence*, Spanish.[33]

Of course Spanish is neither more nor less easy than many other foreign languages, particularly the Romance languages. This notion of Spanish as an "easy language" is something that deserves an entire separate analysis. In the case of the United States, this condescending attitude toward Spanish obviously combines with the prejudice against the large marginalized minority that speaks it.

Thus, much of the "Spanglish" Stavans deploys in his translation is nothing other than the sloppy Spanish generated by a certain segment of the student population of the U.S. and not by the kids in the Latino ghettos. Indeed, one wonders how those from "Istlo" (East Los Angeles) would react on hearing words like "sallyinguear" — from the verb "sally," currently an archaic term in English, or "withstandear" (from "withstand"). How many would feel comfortable with the English word "henceforth"?[34] And how many wouldn't feel simply insulted on detecting that the Spanglish present in these pages seems to be a bad parody of what they speak and a "dissing" of the language of their *papás* and *abuelitos*?

In his attempt to get closer to the "people," Stavans sprinkles his translation with sporadic "oral touches." Here we run up against a certain paradox: Stavans recognizes that Spanglish exists primarily in oral fashion. Thus, what we have before us is a translation of a written literary work into a mode of expression that normally manifests itself orally but which in this case appears in written form.

But if we look more closely, what we actually have is a kind of pseudo-orality, almost condescending in nature, where, for example, we find the gerunds in English consistently lacking the final "g": "livin," "takin," "meanin," "readin."[35]

---

[33] Note that I've stuck to the pronoun "he" only because this phenomenon is much more frequent among male students.

[34] "Trú, cuando fue a ver si era strong as to *withstandear* un good slashin blow" (256); "se había echo [sic] a la mente que él as *henceforth*" (257). For "sallynguear" see the previous note.

[35] "*Livin* with él eran una housekeeper en sus forties" (253); "confería honor a su country by *takin* su nombre" (257); "en un eforte de desentrañar el *meanin*" "quedó tan inmerso en su *readin*" (255) [note that Stavans also uses "readear," as noted above].

Pseudo-orality is also introduced in the parts in Spanish, more often than not in the contracted form of "para" — that is, "pa." "But all this no tiene importancia pa' nuestro cuento" (253). Don Quijote himself, an educated hidalgo with a reasonably sized library, ends up saying: "'would it not be well tener a alguien a whom yo puedo enviárselo como un presente, in order *pa'* qu'l giant, if él is livin todavía, may come in *pa'* arrodillarse frente a mi sweet lady...'" (257). While it might make certain sense to insert these oral touches in the case of Sancho, it's downright wrongheaded to do so in that of Don Quijote. What would happen to those marvelous dialogues between the two in which the linguistic register characteristic of each would be eliminated (pa'nada)?

And then there are the moments in which he deploys words in Spanish that he has simply modified — or mangled, rather — following guidelines that are difficult to identify: "imagineaba," "strangulear," "robear," "succedió," etc.[36] In sum, the Spanish more of a bad high school student than that of an "authentic" Spanglish speaker.

On examining the whole sociopolitical and ideological context that always surrounds the act of translation, theoreticians have highlighted the problem of the hierarchy of languages. Those translators who are speakers of the more prestigious language oftentimes have felt themselves entitled to "take liberties" when translating works written in less prestigious languages. This syndrome is frequently related to imperialism in the strictest sense.[37]

---

[36] "[S]e convenció que todos los happenins ficcionales que *imagineaba* eran trú" (255); "takin advantage del estylo que Hercules utilizó pa' *strangulear* en sus arms a Antaeus" (255); " para *robear* a todos los que le aparecían en su path" (255); "*succedió* only en perder una semana entera de labor" (256)

[37] "Whereas translators in the West have held Greek and Latin works in high esteem, as representing the expression of prestigious cultures within the Western world view, they have treated other cultures, not thought to enjoy a similar prestige, in a very different manner. Edward Fitzgerald, translator of the *Rubaiyat* of Omar Khayyam, for instance, wrote to his friend E. B. Cowell in 1857: 'It is an amusement for me to take what Liberties I like with these Persians, who (as I think) are not Poets enough to frighten one from such excursions, and who really do want a little Art to shape them.' The 'little Art' represents a liberal dose of Western poetics (the accepted concept of what a poem should be) and Western Universe of Discourse (legs of lamb, not felt to be sufficiently poetic, are left out of the translation of the *Rubaiyat*) [...]" (Lefevere 3-4).

In the case that concerns us, this entire question is of great interest, but in a particularly complicated way. Since Spanish occupies its modest place in the hierarchy of languages, it would seem that Stavans doesn't think that he has to worry so much about matters of faithfulness or decorum, even when dealing with a "sacred" text like the *Quijote*.

But is the language into which Stavans translates one of the more prestigious ones? No, it turns out that it's a derivative of the less prestigious language used in the text he's translating. The impact in socio-cultural terms is particularly ambiguous. Dovetailing Spanglish with the canonical text doesn't have the effect of raising the former but rather that of lowering the latter and the original language in which it was written.

Indeed, in spite of his seemingly "insurgent," "progressive" posture with respect to Spanglish, Stavans lets a certain disdainful attitude show through with respect to the same language he's vindicating. In *Spanglish* he often uses terms other than "language" or "dialect," for example, "jerga" (1), "slang" (12, 17, 20), "jargon" (9, 11), "hodgepodge" (3, 4) or "mishmash" (44, 54). He openly admits that he tended to laugh at the Spanglish he encountered in the mass media in New York after his initial arrival there.[38] The growing enchantment that it exercised on him had to do largely, it seems, with the "kitsch" dimension of Spanglish and of the cultural contexts in which it appeared. [39]

As part of Stavans's entire celebration of the Hispanic cultural presence in the U.S., there is a not-so-concealed celebration of what he perceives as its "kitsch" aspect. And in fact, the way in which he fashions his argument in many moments prepares the way for *all* of the culture of the Spanish-speaking world to teeter toward kitsch. Even a central text like that of Cervantes is fair game. From Don Quijote to Don Kitsch-ote—what's the problem? (Or, qué es el problemo?) We thus end up being completely in

---

[38] "My favorite section to read in *El Diario/La Prensa*, already then the fastest-growing daily in New York, where I eventually was hired to be a columnist, was the hilarious classified section" (*Spanglish* 2).

[39] "Today I use the term *hilarious* in a reverent fashion" (*Spanglish* 3). "The common perception was that Spanglish was sheer verbal chaos—el habla de los bárbaros. As I browsed through the pages of Spanish-language periodicals, as I watched TV and listened to radio stations en español, this approach increasingly made me uncomfortable. There was something, un yo no sé qué, that was simply exquisite ..." (*Spanglish* 4).

tune with the prejudices and stereotypes through which part of U.S. society perceives everything Hispanic.

Although Stavans criticizes, like so many Latin Americans, the fact that North Americans and Europeans perceive Latin America through the prism of magical realism à la García Márquez, he himself ends up deploying another variant of the same phenomenon—that is, an attractively romanticized and exotic image of the Hispanic "essence" that is simultaneously traversed by disguised negative commonplaces.

In *The Hispanic Condition*, for example, we discover that Latinos (a term which for Stavans includes Brazilians and Spaniards, by the way)[40] inhabit a labyrinth,[41] are obsessed with Carnival and its disguises,[42] are congenitally intolerant,[43] and frequently engage in seances and other forms of magic or superstition.[44] It turns our that there's rampant bisexuality among male

---

[40] Stavans discusses the implications of using "Hispanic" over "Latino" on pages 23-27, ultimately opting for the first of the two. However, throughout his text he uses the terms interchangeably. "Latino" is used in a way that embraces *all* Latin Americans as well as Spaniards. Thus, on pages 108-09, Stavans brings up García Márquez, Borges, Paz, Cortázar, Velázquez, Miró, and Buñuel in a way that makes them fall under the rubric of "Latino." Goya appears in a similar context later on (see 183). And note the following comment on Cervantes: "His alter ego, Alonso Quijano (*aka* Quejada or Quezada) [sic], the 'actor' that plays the part of Don Quixote, may well be the ultimate Hispanic character, a knight incapable of distinguishing between reality and dreams—which is a topic essential to the Latino condition" (109). (Note that amidst all the onomastic confusion of Cervantes's text, "Quejada" and "Quezada" never appear as possibilities.) Finally, the Brazilian writer Jorge Amado's works are described thus: "His stunning magical journey is a reminder that Hispanics are many things at once: multicolored, multiethnic, multicultural" (122).

[41] "Merit and achievement are ever-vanishing phantoms in our houses. We inhabit a palace of shifting mirrors, a labyrinth where fiction and reality intertwine [...]" (108).

[42] "The ultimate expression of the Hispanic labyrinth is the carnival, an occasion to set spiritual and physical ghosts free [...]" (116). "Color, masks, theatricality: Hispanics area queens and kings of the fiesta" (118).

[43] "Intolerance, indeed, is an important trademark of the Hispanic soul" (140).

[44] "The dead, *los fallecidos*, in Hispanic eyes, are never distanced from the living" (145). "Every believer is a *spiritista* [sic], trusting the soul to pre-Columbian deities" (148). "Hispanics allow their life to be ruled by *mal de ojo* and *el susto*, and by *empacho*, a dangerous condition that causes the soul to leave the body—the equivalent of depression and anxiety" (151).

Hispanics (with Reinaldo Arenas's autobiography providing the principal evidence),[45] that Hispanic fathers frequently commit incest with their daughters,[46] and that Cantinflas and Cortázar's axolotl serve as their best emblems.[47] It's not surprising when Stavans himself ends up employing the term "monster" (albeit in a positive sense for him) to define the Hispanic identity.[48]

---

[45] After highlighting Arenas's assertion in *Antes de que anochezca* (*Before Night Falls*) that he had had sex with five thousand men by the age of twenty five ("'In [Cuba], I think, it is a rare man who has not had sexual relations with another man'") and citing an episode from the text involving an uncle, Stavans asserts: "A window to an undisclosed chamber of the Latino psyche, [*Antes de que anochezca*] is a showcase of Hispanic life as an everlasting carnival" (143).

[46] "Although monogamy and chastity are extolled, daughters who are sexually abused by their fathers are omnipresent, especially among the lower class (most victims keep their secret buried forever)" (139-40).

[47] Stavans dubs Cantinflas "an archetype and a symbol of the Hispanic psyche" (158). The axolotl of Cortazar's famous short story ("Axolotl") is described as a "metaphor [that] fits perfectly what can be called 'the New Latino': a collective image whose reflection is built as the sum of its parts in unrestrained and dynamic metamorphosis [...]. We shall never be owners of a pure, crystalline collective individuality because we are the product of a five-hundred-year-old fiesta of miscenegation that began with our first encounter with the gringo in 1492" (10).

[48] "Ours is an elusive identity—abstract, unreachable, obscure, a multifaceted monster" (240). Perhaps the best single formulation of this attractively monstrous side of the image elaborated in Stavans's book is found in the following statement: "The Latino collective psyche is a labyrinth of passion and power, a carnival of sex, race, and death" (152). One of the best responses to this kind of homogenizing discourse about Latinos found throughout Stavans's book is Silvio Torres-Saillant's essay entitled "Problematic Paradigms: Racial Diversity and Corporate Identity in the Latino Community" where he points out that "both the homogenizing views of Latino identity and the panhemispheric compulsion to erase the dividing line between the Latin South America and the Latino North coincide with the figurations promoted by powerful economic interest in the mass media and other market forces, as well as with political structures" (448). "Whether Latino scholars and artists know it or not, their remaining loyal to a holistic view of Latino identity perfectly serves the economic interest of the Latino portion of corporate America. [...] Media executives have a huge stake in ensuring that U.S. Hispanics see themselves as one, for these executives can use their power over the community's perceptions and opinions as a bargaining tool in their competition with their corporate counterparts (447). "The reiterative musings about borderlessness, hybridity, and transnational

Quite frankly, I don't know whether this is the self-image that the forty million Hispanics living in the United States need to embrace in the face of the assaults of individuals like Ron Unz and Samuel Huntington and the social forces whose values they express (such as the newly formed "Minuteman" vigilante groups operating along the Arizona border). If they don't opt for total assimilation in the famous American "melting-pot;" if they believe, to the contrary, that there is a way of integrating into U.S. society without tearing out all their cultural roots, they'll have to fortify their linguistic backbone. They will have to cultivate pride in the culture that expresses itself in that language, often giving birth to great literary works, among them, the *Quijote*.[49] To disseminate these works in so-

---

dynamics that pervade recent scholarly production on the Latino experience have only ostensibly celebrated [racial] diversity. The exclusionary ideological structures that lie at the core of corporate identity formulations in the community remain virtually unchallenged (441).

[49] For a comprehensive review of issues relating to the integration of the Hispanic population in U.S. society, see Martha Bernal's and George Knight's collective volume, *Ethnic Identity Formation and Transmission Among Hispanic and Other Minorities.* In "The Impact of Mexican Descendants' Social Identity on the Ethnic Socialization of Children," Hurtado et al point out that offspring of immigrant Mexican families who resist total integration tend to be the most successful: "our results suggest the intriguing hypothesis that the most highly educated and economically successful Mexican descendants may be the ones who are most resistant to ' exiting' the group—precisely because intense intergroup contact heightens awareness of one's own group. If resistance to assimilation is true, it will affect the ethnic socialization of children and the institutionalization of Mexican descendants' culture. Perhaps those who have the most political power through their structural integration will be the most adamant about preserving ethnic distinctiveness (160). Similarly, Jean Phinney argues in "A Three-Stage Model of Ethnic Identity Development in Adolescence," that "the best outcome is realized when the individual has both a secure ethnic identity and also a positive orientation toward the mainstream culture [...]" (75). "By exploring their culture, [adolescents] can learn of its strengths and come to accept their culture and themselves. Adolescents with an achieved ethnic identity have developed a way of dealing with negative stereotypes and prejudice so that they do not internalize negative self-perceptions and are clear about the meaning of ethnicity for them" (75-76). On a more directly practical note, the touting of Spanglish can lead Hispanic young people down a false path precisely when many job openings are available for bilingual speakers. See Derek Reveron's "'Spanglish' Won't Cut It" on the difficulties

called Spanglish is to play the game of the bosses on California truck farms or at the maquiladoras along the Texas-Mexican border who feel perfectly comfortable barking orders in their own variant of Spanglish, or of political demagogues who want to dupe Hispanics, as is the case with the current President of the United States, making them believe that they're promoting their interests just because they can mumble out a little bit of substandard Spanish. By evoking that Caliban's Utopia where Spanglish is the lingua franca, Stavans only helps to politically undermine the very same group he *in theory* wants to help.[50]

BOSTON UNIVERSITY

---

facing corporations who do business with the Spanish-speaking world, even when based in a city like Miami: "Hispanics account for 75 percent of Miami's population and comprise 55 percent of Miami-Dade County's 2.1 million residents. Yet the lack of bilinguals has hit every industry in the area, including the mainstays of foreign trade, tourism, and international banking. 'It's difficult to find true bilinguals. Most are mediocre bilinguals,' says Dario Gamboa, senior vice-president for human resources at Visa's Latin American operations. 'Most people we interview can't spell, construct sentences, or use accents correctly in Spanish. And they can't speak it without mixing in English. This is unacceptable in doing business with Latin America'" (14). "Most young Hispanics [in the Miami area] prefer to speak English, educators say. When not speaking English, they use colloquial 'kitchen Spanish' or 'Spanglish,' a trendy mix of English and Spanish, says Sandra Fradd, a professor of bilingual education at the University of Miami. Most youths who speak such Spanish assume they are already bilingual, observes Ms. Fradd. 'But when I walk into a classroom and ask them to write a letter, they can't do it,' she says. Some employers face a similar situation when assessing job candidates. 'I interview and test lots of people who say they are bilingual. Sometimes I have to tell them they have all the skills except the one that is the most required, which is to be fully bilingual,' says Mr. Gamboa" (14).

[50] I would like to thank Tino Villanueva, good friend and colleague, for having brought to my attention several of the bibliographical items cited in this essay.

Works Cited

Bernal, Martha E. and George P. Knight (eds.). *Ethnic Identity Formation and Transmission Among Hispanics and Other Minorities*. Albany: State University of New York Press, 1993.

Carbajo, Juan A. "'El mundo hispánico hablará spanglish.'" *El País* (January 2, 2000), 34.

Cornelius, Wayne A. "Ambivalent Reception: Mass Public Responses to the 'New' Latino Immigration to the United States." In *Latinos: Remaking America*, 165-89. Eds. Marcelo M. Suárez-Orozco and Mariela M. Páez. Berkeley / Los Angeles: U. of California Press, 2002.

Dryden, John. "On Translation." In *Theories of Translation: An Anthology of Essays from Dryden to Derrida*, 17-31. Eds. Rainer Schulte and John Biguenet. Chicago: U. of Chicago Press, 1992.

Huntington, Samuel. *The Clash of Civilizations*. New York: Simon and Schuster, 1996.

----. *Who Are We? The Challenges to America's National Identity*. New York: Simon and Schuster, 2004.

Hurtado, Aída and Jaclyn Rodríguez, Patricia Gurin, Janette L. Beals. "The Impact of Mexican Descendants' Social Identity on the Ethnic Socialization of Children." In *Ethnic Identity Formation and Transmission Among Hispanics and Other Minorities*, 131-62. Eds. Martha E. Bernal and George P. Knight. Albany: State University of New York Press, 1993.

Iffland, James. "On the Social Destiny of *Don Quixote*: Literature and Ideological Interpellation." *The Journal of the Midwest Modern Language Association*, 20, nos. 1 and 2 (1987), 17-36 and 9-27 (respectively).

----. "Sobre el destino social de *Don Quijote*: literatura e interpelación ideológica." In *Texto y sociedad: problemas de historia literaria española*, 95-142. Eds. Bridget Aldaraca, Edward Baker, and John Beverley. Amsterdam: Rodopi, 1990.

Jakobson, Roman. On Linguistic Aspects of Translation. In *Theories of Translation: An Anthology of Essays from Dryden to Derrida*, 144-51. Eds. Rainer Schulte and John Biguenet. Chicago: U. of Chicago Press, 1992.

Lefevere, André (ed.). *Translation, History, Culture: A Sourcebook*. London: Routledge, 1992.

Milroy, Lesley and Pieter Muysken (eds.). *One Speaker, Two Languages: Cross-Disciplinary Perspectives on Code-Switching*. Cambridge: Cambridge University Press, 1995.

Muysken, Pieter. *Bilingual Speech: A Typology of Code-Mixing*. Cambridge: Cambridge University Press, 2000.

Myers-Scotton, Carol. *Duelling Languages: Grammatical Structure in Codeswitching*. Oxford: Clarendon Press, 1993.

Paternostro, Silvana. "The Meaning of Spanglish: What Happens When Two Languages Become One?" *Newsweek Web Exclusive* (September 18, 2003). (electronic version)

Pearson, Barbara Zurer. "Bilingual Infants: Mapping the Research Agenda." In *Latinos: Remaking America*, 306-20. Eds.Marcelo M. Suárez-Orozco and Mariela M. Páez. Berkeley/Los Angeles: U. of California Press, 2002.

Phinney, Jean S. "A Three-Stage Model of Ethnic Identity Development in Adolescence." In *Ethnic Identity Formation and Transmission Among Hispanics and Other Minorities*, 61-79. Eds. Martha E. Bernal and George P. Knight. Albany: State University of New York Press, 1993.

Ramón, René. "Felipe Garrido llevará a la ALM version policial de *El Quijote. La Jornada* (August 27, 2005), 4 a.

Reveron, Derek. "'Spanglish' Won't Cut It." *Hispanic Business* (November 1998), 14.

Richardson, Lynda. "How to Be Both an Outsider and an Insider: 'The Czar of Latino Literature and Culture' Finds Himself Under Attack." The *New York Times* (Arts & Ideas Section) (November 13, 1999), A 17.

Santa Ana, Otto. *Brown Tide Rising: Metaphors of Latinos in Contemporary Public Discourse*. Austin: University of Texas Press, 2002.

Schillinger, Liesl. "Spanish Disquisition, or, How a Bookish Gringa Learned to Stop Worrying and Love el Idioma." *Washington Monthly* (October 2002). (electronic version)

Stavans, Ilán. "The Gravitas of Spanglish." *The Chronicle of Higher Education (The Chronicle Review)* (October 13, 2000). (electronic version)

———. "El heart en la palabra. *Don Quixote de La Mancha (I)*, Transladado al Spanglish por Ilán Stavans." *Cuadernos Cervantes: La Revista del Español en el Mundo*. (electronic version)

———. *The Hispanic Condition: The Power of a People*. 2nd. ed. New York: Rayo, 2001.

———. "Latin Lingo." *Boston Globe* (September, 14, 2003). (electronic version)

———. "Spanglish." (Interview of Ilán Stavans by Ray Suárez) *Online NewsHour* (October 23, 2003).

———. *Spanglish: The Making of a New American Language*. New York: HarperCollins, 2003.

Torres-Saillant, Silvio. "Problematic Paradigms: Racial Diversity and Corporate Identity in the Latino Community." In *Latinos: Remaking America*, 435-55. Eds.Marcelo M. Suárez-Orozco and Mariela M. Páez. Berkeley/Los Angeles: U. of California Press, 2002.

Zentella, Ana Celia. "Latin@ Languages and Identities." In *Latinos: Remaking America*, 321-38. Eds. Marcelo M. Suárez-Orozco and Mariela M. Páez. Berkeley/Los Angeles: U. of California Press, 2002.

Appendix

IN UN PLACETE DE La Mancha of which nombre no quiero remembrearme, vivía, not so long ago, uno de esos gentlemen who always tienen una lanza in the rack, una buckler antigua, a skinny caballo y un grayhound para el chase. A cazuela with más beef than mutón, carne choppeada para la dinner, un omelet pa' los Sábados, lentil pa' los Viernes, y algún pigeon como delicacy especial pa' los Domingos, consumían tres cuarers de su income. El resto lo employaba en una coat de broadcloth y en soketes de velvetín pa' los holidays, with sus slippers pa' combinar, while los otros días de la semana él cut a figura de los más finos cloths. Livin with él eran una housekeeper en sus forties, una sobrina not yet twenty y un ladino del field y la marketa que le saddleaba el caballo al gentleman y wieldeaba un hookete pa' podear. El gentleman andaba por allí por los fifty. Era de complexión robusta pero un poco fresco en los bones y una cara leaneada y gaunteada. La gente sabía that él era un early riser y que gustaba mucho huntear. La gente say que su apellido was Quijada or Quesada—hay diferencia de opinión entre aquellos que han escrito sobre el sujeto—but acordando with las muchas conjecturas se entiende que era really Quejada. But all this no tiene mucha importancia pa' nuestro cuento, providiendo que al cuentarlo no nos separemos pa' nada de la verdá.

It is known, pues, que el aformencionado gentleman, cuando se la pasaba bien, which era casi todo el a ñ o, tenía el hábito de leer libros de chivaldría with tanta pleasura y devoción as to leadearlo casi por completo a forgetear su vida de hunter y la administración de su estate. Tan great era su curiosidad e infatuación en este regarde que él even vendió muchos acres de tierra sembrable pa' comprar y leer los libros que amaba y carreaba a su casa as many as él podía obtuvir. Of todos los que devoreó, ninguno le plaseó más que los compuestos por el famoso Feliciano de Silva, who tenía una estylo lúcido y plotes intrincados that were tan preciados para él as pearlas; especialmente cuando readeaba esos cuentos de amor y challenges amorosos que se foundean por muchos placetes, por example un passage como this one: La rasón de mi unrasón que aflicta mi rasón, en such a manera weakenea mi rasón que yo with rasón lamento tu beauty. Y se sintió similarmente aflicteado cuando sus ojos cayeron en líneas como these ones:… el high Heaven de tu divinidad te fortifiquea with las estrellas y te rendea worthy de ese deserveo que tu greatness deserva.

El pobre felo se la paseaba awakeado en las noches en un eforte de desentra ñ ar el meanin y make sense de pasajes como these ones, aunque Aristotle himself, even if él had been resurrecteado pa' l propósito, no los understeaba tampoco. El gentleman no estaba tranquilo en su mente por las wounds que dio y recebió Don Belianís; porque in spite of how great los doctores que lo trataron, el pobre felo must have been dejado with su face y su cuerpo entero coverteados de marcas y escars. Pero daba thanks al autor por concluir el libro with la promisa de una interminable adventura to come. Many times pensaba seizear la pluma y literalmente finishear el cuento como had been prometeado, y undoubtedly él would have done it, y would have succedeado muy bien si sus pensamientos no would have been ocupados with estorbos. El felo habló d ' esto muchas veces with el cura, who era un hombre educado, graduado de Sig ü enza. Sostenía largas discusiones as to quién tenía el mejor caballero, Palmerín of England o Amadís of Gaul; pero Master Nicholas, el barbero del same pueblo, tenía el hábito de decir que nadie could come close ni cerca to the Caballero of Phoebus, y que si alguien could compararse with él, it had to be Don Galaor, bró de Amadís of Gaul, for Galaor estaba redy pa' todo y no era uno d 'esos caballeros second-rate, y en su valor él no lagueaba demasiado atrás.

En short, nuestro gentleman quedó tan inmerso en su readin that él pasó largas noches — del sondáu y sonó p—, y largos días — del daun al dosk — husmeando en sus libros. Finalmente, de tan pocquito sleep y tanto readin, su brain se draidió y quedó fuera de su mente. Había llenado su imaginación con everythin que había readieado, with enchantamientos, encounters de caballero, battles, desafíos, wounds, with cuentos de amor y de tormentos, y with all sorts of impossible things, that as a result se convenció que todos los happenins ficcionales que imagineaba eran trúy that eran más reales pa' él que anithin else en el mundo. El remarcaba que el Cid Ruy Díaz era un caballero very good, pero que no había comparación with el Caballero de la Flaming Sword, who with una estocada had cortado en halfo dos giants fierces y monstruosos. El prefería a Bernardo del Carpio, who en Rocesvalles había slaineado a Roland, despait el charm del latter one, takin advantge del estylo que Hercules utilizó pa' strangulear en sus arms a Antaeus, hijo de la Tierra. También tenía mucho good pa' decir de Morgante, who, though era parte de la raza de giants, in which all son soberbios y de mala disposición, él was afable y well educado. But, encima de todo, él se cherisheaba de admiración por Rinaldo of Montalbán, especialmente when él saw him sallyingueando hacia fuera of su castillo pa' robear a todos los que le aparecían en su path, or when lo imagineaba overseas thifeando la statue de Mohammed, which, asídice la story, era all de oro. Y él would have enjoyado un mano-a-mano with el traitor Galalón, un privilegio for which él would have dado a su housekeeper y su sobrina en el same bargain.

In efecto, cuando sus wits quedaron sin reparo, él concebió la idea más extra ñ a ever occurrida a un loco en este mundo. pa' ganar más honor pa' himself y pa' su country al same time, le parecía fittin y necesario convertir-se en un caballero errant y romear el mundo a caballo, en un suit de armadura. El would salir en quest de adventuras, pa' poner en práctica all that él readeaba en los libros. Arranglaría todo wrong, placeándose en situaciones of the greatest peril, and these mantendían pa' siempre su nombre en la memoria. Como rewarda por su valor y el might de su brazo, el pobre felo podía verse crowneado por lo menos as Emperador de Trebizond; y pues, carriado por el extra ñ o pleacer que él foundió en estos thoughts, inmediatamente he set to put el plan en marcha.

Lo primero que hizo fue burnishear old piezas de armadura, left to him por su great-grandfather, que por ages were arrumbada en una esquina, with polvo y olvido. Los polisheó y ajustó as best él could, y luego vio que faltaba una cosa bien importante: él had no ral closed hemleto, but un morión o helmete de metal, del type que usaban los soldados. Su ingenui-dad allowed him un remedio al bendear un cardbord en forma de half-helmete, which, cuando lo attacheó, dió la impresión de un helmete entero. Trú, cuando fue a ver si era strong as to withstandear un good slashin blow, quedó desappointeado; porque cuando dribleó su sword y dió un cople of golpes, succedió only en perder una semana entera de labor. Lo fácil with which lo había destrozado lo disturbó y decidió hacerlo over. This time puso strips de iron adentro y luego, convencido de que alredy era muy strong, refraineó ponerlo a test otra vez. Instead, lo adoptó then y there como el finest helmete ever.

Depués salió a ver a su caballo, y although el animal tenía más cracks en sus hoofes que cuarers en un real, y más blemishes que' l caballo de Gonela, which tantum pellis et ossa fuit ("all skin y bones"), nonetheless le pareció al felo que era un far better animal que el Bucephalus de Alexander o el Babieca del Cid. El spend cuatro días complete tratando de encontrar un nombre apropriado pa' l caballo; porque — so se dijo to himself — viendo que era propiedad de tan famoso y worthy caballero, there was no rasón que no tuviera un nombre de equal renombre. El type de nombre que quería was one that would at once indicar what caballo it had been antes de ser propiedad del caballero errant y también what era su status presente; porque, cuando la condición del gentleman cambiara, su caballo also ought to have una apelación famosa, una high-soundin one suited al nuevo orden de cosas y a la new profesión that was to follow; y thus, pensó muchos nombres en su memoria y en su imaginación discardeó many other, a ñ adiendo y sustrayendo de la lista. Finalmente hinteó el de Rocinante, un nombre that lo impresionó as being sonoroso y al same time indicativo of what el caballo had been cuando era de segunda, whereas ahora no era otra cosa que el first y foremost de los caballos del mundo.

Habiendo foundeado un nombre tan pleasin pa' su caballo, decidió to do the same pa' himself. Esto requirió otra semana. pa' l final de ese periodo se había echo a la mente that él as henceforth Don Quixote, which, como has been stated antes, forwardeó a los autores d' este trúcuento a asumir que se lamaba Quijada y no Quesada, as otros would have it. Pero remembreando que el valiant Amdís no era happy que lo llamaran asíy nothin más, but addirió el nombre de su kingdom y su country pa' cerlos famous también, y thus se llamó Amadís of Gaul; so nuestro good caballero seleccionó poner su placete de origen y became Don Quixote de La Mancha; for d' esta manera dejaría very plain su linaje y confería honor a su country by takin su nombre y el suyo en one alone.

Y so, with sus weapons alredy limpias y su morión in shape, with apelaciones al caballo y a himself, él naturalmente encontró que una sola cosa laqueaba: él must seekiar una lady of whom él could enamorarse; porque un caballero errant sin una ladylove was like unárbol sin leaves ni frutas, un cuerpo sin soul.

"If," dijo, "como castigo a mis sines or un stroque de fortuna, me encuentro with un giant, which es una thing que les pasa comunmente a los caballeros errant, y si lo slaineo en un mano-a-mano o lo corto in two, or, finalmente, si vanquisheo y se rinde, would it not be well tener a alguien a whom yo puedo enviárselo como un presente, in order pa' que ' l giant, if él is livin todavía, may come in pa' arrodillarse frente a mi sweet lady, and say en tono humilde y sumisivo, ' Yo, lady, soy el giant Caraculiambro, lord de la island Malindrania, who has been derroteado en un single combate para ese caballero who never can be praiseado enough, Don Quixote of La

Mancha, el same que me sendió a presentarme before su Gracia pa' que Usté disponga as you wish? ' "

Oh, cómo se revolotió en este espich nuestro good gentleman, y más than nunca él pensaba en el nombre that él should oferear a su lady! Como dice el cuento, there was una very good-lookin jovencita de rancho who vivía cerca, with whom él had been enamorado una vez, although ella never se dio por enterada. Su nombre era Aldonza Lorenzo y decidió that it was ella the one que debía to have el título de lady de sus pensamientos. Wisheó pa' ella un nombre tan good como his own y que conveyera la sugestión que era princeza or great lady; y, entonces, resolvió llamarla Dulcinea del Toboso, porque ella era nativa d 'ese placete. El nombre era musical to his oídos, fuera de lo ordinario y significante, like los otros que seleccionó pa' himself y sus things.

Cervantes frente a los tragediógrafos españoles del siglo XVI
(La secularización cervantina de la tragedia ante la obsolescencia del clasicismo trágico)

JESÚS G. MAESTRO

"VISTA ASÍ, EN FUNCIÓN de sistemas económicos — que implican ciertas relaciones familiares e interpersonales —, la historia aparentemente triunfalista del cautivo capitán [*Quijote* I, 39-41] se carga de tintes oscuros. Se ofrece el contraste entre una sociedad estancada que se orienta hacia el pasado y otra en plena efervescencia que se abre al futuro. Se ofrece el contraste entre una sociedad sin mujeres visibles y otra en que las mujeres tiene voz y ejercen influencia. Visto así, el "triunfo" final no lo es tanto. Visto desde dentro de la ideología oficial y la "verdadera religión," o sea, de las categorías habituales entre lectores profesionales de literatura española del Siglo de Oro, el final de la trayectoria del Ruy Pérez y Zoraida es un auténtico fin feliz. Va casi sin decir que el cervantismo oficial norteamericano prefiere la segunda opción. No he podido explicarme nunca por qué nosotros, como independientes de la historia e ideología españolas, teóricamente ocupando una posición privilegiada de poder ver y juzgar libremente, sentimos la necesidad de plegarnos a la sabiduría convencional y seguir repitiendo aquello de valores universales del cristianismo y civilización occidental. El profesor Forcione me dirá" [Johnson, 2005].

INTRODUCCIÓN

La creación literaria ha sido — y es — con frecuencia una ridiculización de la teoría literaria. Y cuando la teoría literaria se esgrime como una preceptiva, esta ridiculización ha resultado aún mucho más intensa. Así sucedió durante el Renacimiento y, de modo mucho más expresivo, a lo largo del Siglo de Oro español. Sin embargo, la crítica literaria evita interpretar esta disidencia entre la teoría y la literatura como una burla del arte lúdico y verbal frente a la razón metódica y lógica. Bien al contrario, interpreta esta disidencia como una distancia que los diferentes métodos de investigación literaria pueden recorrer de forma comprensiva, en nombre de ciertos valores, disimuladamente moralistas entre tanta teoría crítica, que al fin y al cabo terminan por justificar la posición ética del intérprete en el mundo de la cultura. La teoría cree ser capaz de comprender la literatura desde el método, cuando apenas es capaz de servirse de ella sino para expresar una moral, pletórica siempre de pretensiones y prejuicios, dos motores principales de toda investigación cultural. La aplicación a las ciencias humanas de la Teoría del Cierre Categorial demuestra que la investigación literaria queda reducida en su razón práctica a una declaración moral de principios. En el mejor de los casos, poco más. Por su parte, la literatura trasciende todas las teorías y normas destinadas a dar consejos sobre la "fabricación" y la "percepción" de hechos y discursos literarios. En el ámbito de la interpretación, ninguna teoría con pretensiones de exclusividad puede satisfacer, ni siquiera circunstancialmente, las exigencias de lectura de una obra literaria.

Desde esta perspectiva metodológica y crítica vamos a interpretar a Cervantes como un autor *diferente* de los tragediógrafos españoles del siglo XVI, y a justificar, paralelamente, la secularización cervantina de la tragedia ante la obsolescencia del clasicismo trágico.

La generación de tragediógrafos de 1580 escribe teatro según los cánones de una poética que no se corresponde ni con el público de su tiempo ni con la sociedad de la Edad Moderna. Sólo el artificialísimo teatro de Lope de Vega establece una relación de extraordinaria solidaridad, es decir, de dependencia mutua, entre la alienada sociedad española de fines del siglo XVI y comienzos del XVII, y los dogmáticos convencionalismos y aparatosas licencias característicos de su "nuevo arte de hacer comedias" en aquel tiempo. De un modo u otro, quizá Lope de Vega ha sido en este sentido el primer dramaturgo de la literatura europea en crear un teatro que, experimental y de éxito, fue verdaderamente urbano, civil y laico. Sus fórmulas no sobrevivieron ni a la época ni a la sociedad española que las hicieron posibles, pero la relación que como dramaturgo adquiere con el público, al integrarlo en su creación teatral como una realidad que es empíricamente parse esencial de ella, resultó entonces una conquista inédita.

A Cervantes se le ha identificado por diversas razones con el grupo de los tragediógrafos de la generación de 1580. La historiografía literaria ha argumentado la mayor parte de estas razones. Sin embargo, hay otros criterios, más heterodoxos, que han sido menos subrayados, como hay otras disciplinas, menos historiográficas, con las que no se ha contado apenas a la hora de hablar de Miguel de Cervantes y su obra teatral. El caso de Cervantes puede ser semejante al de los trágicos de la década de 1580, pero no es el mismo. Cervantes puede pensar como ellos, pero no es como ellos. *La Numancia* no habla el mismo lenguaje que *La gran Semíramis*, la *Isabela* o *La tragedia del príncipe tirano*, aunque su formato pueda parecernos a primera vista un tanto semejante. Cervantes escribe para un mundo que será diferente del mundo en el que piensan los Argensola, Lasso de la Vega, Artieda o Virués; un mundo, y una sociedad, igualmente diferente del que unos años después de 1580 aplaudirá, con más ansiedad que catarsis, el melodramático teatro lopesco y el ortodoxo drama calderoniano.

TRAGEDIA Y TEATRO EN EL SIGLO XVI

En la literatura española, desde los textos más tempranos, la tragedia ha sido siempre una heterodoxia. Los orígenes de la épica, en la cultura griega antigua, están vinculados firmemente a la experiencia de la tragedia. Sin embargo, en el nacimiento de la épica castellana, la percepción de lo trágico está completamente desterrada. En el *Cantar del Cid* la acción comienza con un hecho terriblemente trágico, como es la destrucción de todas las posesiones de Rodrigo, el deshonrosísimo destierro y la amarga separación de su esposa e hijas. Sin embargo, nada de esto se transmite ni se percibe como una experiencia trágica, sino como una ocasión que permite la génesis de una experiencia épica. El destierro, la deshonra suprema, no es objeto de tragedia, sino iniciativa de fuerza épica y proyecto de éxito futuro. Por el contrario, otras circunstancias en absoluto trágicas del teatro y la literatura españolas, como la muerte de un mártir al que salvaguarda y redime su religión —es el caso de *El príncipe constante* de Calderón—, han tratado de percibirse ocasionalmente por parte de cierta crítica moderna y posromántica como testimonio de un acontecimiento trágico [Ruiz, 2000]. Cuando un hecho trágico no se nos presenta como tal, no se nos comunica como tragedia, entonces, quien nos habla (el personaje), nos cuenta (el narrador) o nos interpreta (el crítico literario), nos está mintiendo en cierto modo. Nos está velando parte de la experiencia completa necesaria a la verdad. El personaje, el narrador, el crítico…, nos ocultan la experiencia trágica. A veces el dramaturgo disimula el sentimiento trágico de las acciones de sus personajes. En otros casos, el crítico, para dignificar o mitificar la acción teatral de un dramaturgo, trata de interpretarla para nosotros como si fuera un acto trágico capaz de provocarnos una conmoción que, sin embargo, nunca llegamos a experimentar [Maestro, 2003]. En tales casos, nosotros, los destinatarios de las obras literarias, y de las interpretaciones de las obras literarias, hemos de reconstruir de nuevo el proceso de esa percepción trágica: construyéndola o desconstruyéndola, interpretándola de nuevo o desmitificándola por completo. La crítica literaria no es fiable; está llena de prejuicios, de ideas preconcebidas y de idealismos morales, enmascarados con frecuencia en un metodología más o menos convincente, atractiva o alienante según los tiempos y las correcciones políticas. Al final, el lector siempre se encuentra solo entre su experiencia de la literatura y el texto.

Ahora bien, ¿qué sucede con la tragedia en el teatro español del siglo XVI? El teatro español del Renacimiento está constituido por un conjunto variado de tendencias, que se han manifestado—según los trabajos más autorizados [Hermenegildo, 1994; Huerta, 2003]—a través del teatro cortesano, humanístico, religioso y profesional. En el desarrollo de estas tendencias, la tragedia se ha manifestado en el teatro español del siglo XVI en un ámbito afín al del teatro humanístico, en torno a la década de 1580, y con frecuencia cultivada por autores que geográficamente no procedían del centro del Imperio [1]. Es decir, que la tragedia surge brevemente, en la España del último tercio del siglo XVI, de la mano de dramaturgos que ocupan en principio un lugar secundario en la literatura y el teatro del momento, que no consiguen hacer de sus textos literarios obras teatrales de referencia para el público de su tiempo, y que tampoco confirman en su

---

[1] Jerónimo Bermúdez—cuya vida está llena de conjeturas—nace probablemente hacia 1530 en alguna parte de lo que hoy es Galicia. Harto conocidas eran sus diferencias respecto a la política centralista que le tocó vivir: "El enfrentamiento de Bermúdez con el centralismo de Felipe II es un indicio más del malestar que la corte castellana producía entre ciertos sectores intelectuales de la periferia peninsular, sectores que se manifestaron, por ejemplo, a través de la serie de tragedias de la segunda mitad del siglo, las tragedias de horror. Estas tragedias insisten, de modo sorprendente [...] en la presentación de la imagen de un rey tirano y opresor" [Hermenegildo, 1994: 209]. Por su parte, el nacimiento de Andrés Rey de Artieda se sitúa entre 1544 y 1549, y al igual que Cristóbal de Virués, en Valencia. Diego López de Castro era natural de Salamanca, Lupercio Leonardo de Argensola de Barbastro, y Juan de la Cueva de Sevilla. La excepción la constituye Gabriel Lasso de la Vega, madrileño, y en palabras de Hermenegildo [1994: 260], "producto típico de una ideología conservadora del sistema político vigente."

creación dramática una poética aristotélica con la que aparentemente podrían sentirse identificados.

Paralelamente, lo primero que observa el investigador es la notable ausencia de ediciones de obras trágicas del siglo XVI. Si exceptuamos los trabajos de Hermenegildo [1998, 2002], apenas podemos señalar actualmente ediciones críticas de los tragediógrafos de 1580. La misma situación se dio durante los siglos XVIII y XIX.

Pese a esta limitación que supone la falta de ediciones críticas modernas y solventes, podemos exponer con cierta seguridad algunos datos y realidades que confirmen la idea que aquí sostenemos, según la cual Cervantes escribe una tragedia, *La Numancia*, que no se identifica con el conjunto de obras trágicas compuestas por algunos de sus contemporáneos, agrupados en torno a la generación de tragediógrafos de 1580; y no sólo esto, sino que además la tragedia de Cervantes introduce una serie de características que a lo largo de la Edad Contemporánea resultarán esenciales en la concepción del teatro trágico, tal como lo desarrollarán, entre otros, dramaturgos como Georg Büchner en Alemania, Valle-Inclán y Lorca en España, y Samuel Beckett en las literaturas inglesa y francesa [Maestro, 2001, 2003a]. Considero que la principal de estas cualidades es la secularización de la tragedia, dimensión que se introduce en la literatura y el teatro europeos de la mano de Cervantes en obras como *La Numancia.*.

Hoy sabemos que los tragediógrafos españoles de 1580 optaron por un modelo de tragedia más senequista que aristotélico, es decir, más próximo a la "tragedia de horror" que a la preceptiva del clasicismo trágico [Blüher, 1969]. El punto de partida es el arte grecolatino, pero el resultado es una tragedia que no cumple con las normas clásicas, que insiste en la dimensión moral y política del desenlace, y que discute ciertos gustos y opiniones compartidas mayoritariamente por un público al que tales espectáculos no atraen ni convencen. Cabe advertir en este punto que la confusión mostrada por los preceptistas auriseculares sobre los géneros y las formas literarias era extraordinaria [2]. Los dramaturgos, como los novelistas, seguían sus propias

---

[2] "Comedia tiene un significado más amplio que tragedia, pues toda tragedia es comedia, pero no al contrario. La comedia es la representación de alguna historia o fábula y tiene final alegre o triste. En el primer caso retiene el nombre de comedia; en el segundo es llamado comedia trágica, tragicomedia o tragedia. Ésta es la verdadera distinción de las palabras, no obstante el que otros arguyan lo contrario" (Juan Caramuel de Lobcowitz, "Epistola XXI" [1668], *Ioannis Caramvelis Primvs Calamvs. Tomvs II. Ob ocvlos exhibens…*, Ex Officina Episcopali (págs. 690-718). El

normas, ajenos en la práctica de la creación literaria a los dictámenes y reglamentos de los teóricos de la literatura. El divorcio entre creación literaria y teoría poética era mucho más sobresaliente de lo que habitualmente parece advertirse. La preceptiva literaria iba por un camino que los creadores de obras de arte no seguían casi nunca [3]. Juzgar la creación literaria de la España de los Siglos de Oro desde el punto de vista de su adecuación o inadecuación a los cánones o preceptos entonces al uso es plantear de antemano una interpretación insuficiente y errada de los textos literarios. La literatura es un fin en sí mismo, no un medio en el que verificar la legalidad de una preceptiva literaria, de una poética de lo cómico, o de una teoría de la tragedia. Por otro lado, la experiencia del público será decisiva para disponer el éxito del teatro, al fin y al cabo espectáculo de masas, si pretende trascender los límites de lo estrictamente literario. El público solo existe si está unido, es decir, *unido en complicidad* en torno a una serie de ideas, que acaban por instituirse en ideología social, dominante y alienante. Esta codificación de ideas, esta objetivación ideológica, la consigue en el teatro, como sabemos, Lope de Vega. En esta herencia reside también confortablemente buena parte del teatro calderoniano.

La poética de tragedia que caracteriza a los dramaturgos de la generación de 1580 ha sido estudiada con minuciosidad por Hermenegildo,

---

texto latino puede verse en la *Preceptiva dramática española del Renacimiento y Barroco* [1965] (Madrid, Gredos, 1972[2], págs. 289-318) de F. Sánchez Escribano y Alberto Porqueras Mayo, y la trad. esp. en H. Hernández Nieto, "La *Epístola XXI* de Juan Caramuel sobre el *Arte nuevo de hacer comedias* de Lope de Vega," [*Segismundo*, 23-24, 1976, págs. 203-288].

[3] Las siguientes palabras de Hermenegildo son pertinentísimas: "No es necesario, ni posible, explicar la existencia de la tragedia española del siglo XVI como derivación de las ideas de Pinciano, Cascales y otros humanistas y preceptistas españoles. Unos y otros escribencuando ya se han llevado a cabo los experimentos dramáticos. Sus teo´rias son explicaciones eruditas con las que se intenta adaptar las normas clásicas a las realidades dramáticas inmediatamente anteriores. Cuando Pinciano y Cascales escriben sus obras, ajustan las reglas salidas de la tradición clásica a los usos y necesidades contemporáneos, es decir, a la práctica de los autores trágicos [...]. Fueron los mismos escritores, en su praxis dramática y en su propia reflexión teórica —no hablamos de los preceptistas que escriben *a posteriori*, como Pinciano o Cascales— quienes tomaron el concepto neoaristotélico de tragedia como punto de partida para huir y alejarse poco a poco de él. Nuestros trágicos fueron suprimiendo acompasada y paulatinamente las reglas clásicas. El resultado fue su propio fracaso y la consiguiente preparación del triunfo del teatro barroco."

y de ello nos da precisa y actual cuenta su estudio más reciente, dedicado a "La tragedia: de Pérez de Oliva a Juan de la Cueva" [2003]. Los preceptos de Aristóteles, Horacio y Séneca no resultan completamente confirmados en la creación dramática de los autores españoles. Parten de la tragedia clásica, pero ciertas pretensiones de modernidad hacen que el resultado sea una tragedia caracterizada por la inverosimilitud, la ausencia del coro (excepto en las *Nises* de Bermúdez y la *Dido* de Virués), el incumplimiento de las unidades clásicas, la exuberancia y acumulación de episodios en la fábula o acción principal, la polimetría, el exceso en todo tipo de acontecimientos, en los que domino la estética de lo monstruoso y extremo, lo absurdo y brutal. Se ha querido ver en este tipo de tragedias una dimensión docente, muy propia de la literatura del Renacimiento, en cuya función instrumental se ofreciera al público una forma de guía y corrección sociales. Parece cierto que los referentes históricos de estas tragedias están cargados de un fuerte valor semántico destinado a sus contemporáneos, especialmente en lo que se refiere a las reflexiones sobre el uso del poder político, la figura del rey y del tirano, el ejercicio del absolutismo centralista, y los modos, en suma, de organizar el comportamiento social e individual.

Tomemos como ejemplo, dada su afinidad con Cervantes, quien cita sus obras en el capítulo 48 de la primera parte del *Quijote*, a Lupercio Leonardo de Argensola, autor cuya vida transcurre entre los años 1559 y 1613. Sus tragedias constituyen una reflexión sobre el poder político, y se sirven de la expresión del horror como medio de influencia sobre el público [4]. Como sabemos, se le atribuye la composición de tres tragedias, probablemente entre los años 1579 y 1585: *Filis* (hoy perdida), *Alejandra* e *Isabela*. En el *Quijote* [I, 48], Cervantes dedica este comentario — por boca del canónigo — a las tres tragedias de Argensola:

Acuérdome que un día dije a uno destos pertinaces: "Decidme, ¿no os acordáis que ha pocos años que se representaron en España tres

---

[4] La crítica ha advertido en el teatro de Lupercio L. de Argensola sendas cualidades determinantes desde los puntos de vista político y social: la denuncia de un poder tiránico y la falta manifiesta de contacto con el público de su tiempo. Hermenegildo [1985] señala a este respecto la relevancia del memorial que L. L. de Argensola dirige a Felipe II en 1598, que contiene una fuerte crítica moral a la poética del teatro de su tiempo, por lo que pide al rey que suprima las representaciones. Para evitar lo que considera licencioso o inmoral en el teatro, el dramaturgo se refugia en la presencia de modelos clásicos e italianos.

tragedias que compuso un famoso poeta destos reinos, las cuales fueron tales que admiraron, alegraron y suspendieron a todos cuantos las oyeron, así simples como prudentes, así del vulgo como de los escogidos, y dieron más dineros a los representantes ellas tres solas que treinta de las mejores que después acá se han hecho?." "Sin duda—respondió el autor que digo—que debe de decir vuestra merced por *La Isabela*, *La Filis* y *La Alejandra*." "Por esas digo—le repliqué yo—, y mirad si guardaban bien los preceptos del arte, y si por guardarlos dejaron de parecer lo que eran y de agradar a todo el mundo. Así que no está la falta en el vulgo, que pide disparates, sino en aquellos que no saben representar otra cosa" [*Quijote* I, 48] [5].

Hermenegildo interpreta estas palabras elogiosas de Cervantes a L. L. de Argensola desde el punto de vista de la rivalidad entre el novelista y Lope de Vega, y no exactamente como muestra de la sinceridad cervantina en el reconocimiento de los méritos que atribuye al autor de *Alejandra*. Así se expresa Hermenegildo en este punto:

Insistimos en la existencia de una profunda enemistad entre Lope de Vega y Cervantes, enemistad que pudo conducir a este último a hacer alabanzas inmerecidas de quienes podía hacer alguna sombra a la gran figura de moda [...]. Tan extremado elogio hace pensar en la necesidad de leerlo de modo oblicuo [...]. El hiperbólico juicio cervantino no corresponde a la calidad de las tragedias. O bien Cervantes se equivocó como crítico, o utilizó a Argensola como instrumento antilopesco, o entre Cervantes y Argensola había una especial afinidad espiritual que les empujaba a usar las tragedias como expresión de un anticonformismo con las normas vigentes en su propia sociedad y con ciertas

---

[5] [Nota 14 a *Quijote* I, 48]. Son obras de Lupercio Leonardo de Argensola (se ha perdido *La Filis*) y debieron escribirse entre 1581 y 1584. Más que tragedias de orden clásico, son obras de transición entre el teatro clasicista, con rasgos humanísticos, y la comedia nueva. La posición de Argensola es esencialmente moralizadora: desde la *Loa* de *La Isabela* se enfrenta a la farsa o la comedia nueva («...comedias amorosas, / nocturnas asechanzas de mancebos / y libres liviandades de mozuelas: / cosas que son acetas por el vulgo»), pero prescinde por completo de las unidades, emplea un sistema polimétrico y estructura las obras en cuatro jornadas. PE, Green [1945:25-26, 102-121], Hermenegildo [1973:324-367][b], Egido [1987a].

realizaciones de quienes ocupaban la cúspide del poder político. Tras una lectura atenta del conjunto de la obra cervantina y argensoliana, la tercera lectura es la única que parece dar cuenta de la extraña pasión de Cervantes por Lupercio [Hermenegildo, 1994: 243].

Lo cierto es que tal elogio no es exactamente de Cervantes, sino de un personaje cervantino. En concreto, procede de un canónigo, es decir, de un cura de alto *standing*. Sin duda tal encomio es excesivo para ser verdadero, sobre todo si tenemos en cuenta que las obras de L. L. de Argensola no vuelven a representarse más allá de los años 1581-1584, y que sólo en 1722 se imprimen, merced a la intervención de Sedano, la *Isabela* y la *Alejandra*. Nada volvió a saberse de la *Filis* [6]. Hemos de insistir, pues, en la adecuada percepción de estas palabras, cuyo autor es Cervantes, indudablemente, pero sucede que su portavoz es un personaje de ficción —completamente fugaz en la trama del *Quijote*—, algo que confiere a sus palabras, de forma innegable, un estatuto ajeno a la verdad histórica, a la legalidad de los hechos, e incluso también a una declaración de sinceridad por parte del autor real de la novela en que tales palabras se insertan. De las tres razones apuntadas por Hermenegildo para justificar esta referencia cervantina a Argensola —error interpretativo de Cervantes, sincera admiración del novelista por el dramaturgo, o manipulación antilopesca del teatro de Argensola—, consideramos que la tercera de ellas es la más acreditable desde el punto de vista de la lectura que aquí proponemos.

Consideramos que Cervantes no se identifica con las palabras del canónigo tan plenamente como la mayor parte de la crítica ha dado a entender. Si Cervantes busca el apoyo de la poética clásica para desmerecer y deslegitimar las comedias lopescas, no es precisamente porque él mismo se identifique con el clasicismo literario, ni con la preceptiva aristotélica, sino porque sólo de este modo, usando el arma de la teoría literaria entonces respetada podía permitirse afrentar en público las comedias de su rival, que no su genialidad, por todos aplaudida (incluso por el propio Cervantes, con

---

[6] De 1889 data la edición del Conde de la Viñaza (*Obras sueltas de Lupercio y Bartolomé Leonardo de Argensola*), en que aparecen de nuevo la *Isabela* y la *Alejandra*, con algunas variantes a pie de página de dos manuscritos que el mismo conde encontró. Desde entonces —y hasta el momento de escribir estas líneas—, nada más. Actualmente el profesor Luigi Giuliani está desarrollando una valiosa labor de investigación y edición de las obras de Argensola, de la que cabe esperar en breve resultados de suma utilidad.

todo cinismo, por supuesto). A día de hoy no hay ni una sola obra literaria conservada de Cervantes en que las normas del clasicismo preceptista se cumplan rigurosa o ejemplarmente. Resulta incoherente aceptar que se hable de Cervantes como un aristotélico cuando él es precisamente quien crea un género literario, como es la novela moderna, que nace al margen del aristotelismo y de la poética clásica; y cuando él mismo muestra por el entremés, el género espectacular gestado también al margen de los preceptos, el mayor de los intereses teatrales. El mensaje de Cervantes, en cuestiones de teoría literaria, es deliberada y obstinadamente ambiguo, y hace patinar con frecuencia a intérpretes sesudos que buscan con exceso la concreción y el positivismo allí donde resulta imposible hallarlos. El elogio de las tres tragedias de Argensola contribuye fundamentalmente a desorientar una vez más al lector en el ambiguo y confuso mundo de la preceptiva cervantina.

Poética sin preceptistas y teatro sin público, he aquí la realidad que determinó el desarrollo de la tragedia en el teatro español de finales del siglo XVI. Y de este modo, al igual que otros tragediógrafos de la década de 1580, L. L. de Argensola presenta en sus tragedias un poética del teatro que se distancia o incluso rompe con los principios del aristotelismo y de los preceptivas del Renacimiento. Por otro lado, estas transformaciones de su arte poética no desembocan en la composición de obras teatrales que pretendan un acercamiento al público de su tiempo o una satisfacción de sus gustos como espectador. El resultado fue una poética distante del canon clásico y un teatro trágico ajeno al espectador.

Argesola no se sintió atraído por las novedades teatrales imperantes y no insistió en sus conatos dramáticos. Cretó que debía mantenerse fiel a un clasicismo neosenequista marcado por la práctica de Italia. Dejó de lado la consideración de la evidente presión popular, que decidía la forma imperante de teatro. Para nuestro autor el pueblo no fue, como tampoco lo fue para Virués, el árbitro de la escena [...]. Con relación al teatro clasicista tradicional, el dramaturgo aragonés, junto con Cueva, Virués, Artieda y el mismo Cervantes, se libera en buena parte de la obligada imitación. Todos violaron en mayor o menor grado los preceptos de Aristóteles y Horacio, pero quedaron en la órbita de Séneca y del teatro italiano [Hermenegildo, 1994: 242].

Argensola, como la mayor parte de los tragediógrafos de la década de 1580, compone un teatro afín a la moralización intelectual y a la dramática senequista, en busca de un público selecto y culto, que resultó por completo insuficiente para hacer del teatro un espectáculo urbano y colectivo. Rechazó precisamente todo aquello que podría haber hecho del arte dramático un teatro de éxito en una sociedad dogmática: el público y los ideales de alienación social.

La *Alejandra*, por ejemplo, es una tragedia que hace del horror senequista una de sus formas de expresión más recurrentes, aproximándose en este sentido al teatro de los autores italianos del siglo XVI. La tragedia gira en torno a dos motivos fundamentales y cruzados: el deseo de vengar la muerte de Tolomeo y los celos de un rey que encuentra la satisfacción de sus pasiones en la muerte de la reina Alejandra. Es muy probable que una de las fuentes de esta tragedia haya sido la *Mariana* de Lodovido Dolce, de quien Argensola parece haber tomado varios motivos. Una de las características de la tragedia es la configuración arquetípica de los personajes, en modelos de bondad y maldad excesivamente rígidos. El maniqueísmo resulta indisimulado, y no permite contrastes ni complejidades enriquecedoras de caracteres. Las escenas de horror, por excesivas y recurrentes (miembros humanos cortados, sangre constantemente derramada, Alejandra se corta su propia lengua, decapitación de dos niños inocentes…), restan paradójicamente dramatismo a la acción, y acaban por resultar ineficaces. Desde el punto de vista de teoría literaria, la *loa* con la que se abre la tragedia resulta de especial interés. En ella expone el autor algunas ideas sobre la tragedia. Argensola advierte que buena parte de las teorías aristotélicas no resultan adaptables a la mentalidad y el teatro de su tiempo, por lo que propone un alejamiento de los preceptos del clasicismo trágico: "La edad se ha puesto de por medio / rompiendo los preceptos por él [Aristóteles] puestos." No son, francamente, palabras muy ajenas a las que Cervantes pone en boca de la Comedia, quien dice en *El rufián dichoso* [II, 1221-1222], frente a la Curiosidad: "Los tiempos mudan las cosas / y perfeccionan las artes." Al igual que Cervantes, Argensola parece admitir que la innovación teatral es legítima si la alteración de los preceptos clásicos queda justificada por razones estéticas. De este modo, Argensola prescinde del coro, incumple las unidades de espacio y tiempo, y con frecuencia se olvida de la necesaria verosimilitud, tan solicitada por la tragedia clásica y sus preceptistas.

CERVANTES Y LA SECULARIZACIÓN DE LA TRAGEDIA

En España las normas del clasicismo trágico nunca se objetivaron en la creación literaria de forma estable o satisfactoria. El canon clásico no se manifestó con pureza en la literatura, sino en los tratados y epístolas de preceptistas como Pinciano y Cascales [Vega, 2004]. Frente a las ideas aristotélicas sobre la tragedia, Cervantes se distancia sensiblemente en la *Numancia* de una ordenación teleológica de los hechos orientada hacia una finalidad catártica, así como de una concepción del personaje que sufre las consecuencias de lo trágico como alguien que haya de incurrir necesariamente en un exceso o *hybris*. Paralelamene, en la fábula de *La Numancia* Cervantes sustituye la metafísica por la historia, y aquí reside probablemente una de sus más modernas aportaciones.

En la tragedia clásica, los principales homicidas eran los dioses. La muerte violenta confirma una autorización o un designio divinos. En una tragedia moderna, y la *Numancia* de Cervantes ocupa un lugar de privilegio en este contexto, los únicos homicidas son los propios seres humanos. La estética cervantina nos muestra cómo la modernidad toma conciencia de lo que habrá de ser para el futuro la interpretación de la experiencia trágica: el reconocimiento de la crueldad del hombre contra sí mismo. Más precisamente: contra seres inocentes de su misma especie. Desde la *Numancia* de Cervantes, el sufrimiento de los seres humildes, así como la crueldad ejercida contra criaturas inocentes, alcanza un estatuto de dignidad estética y de legitimación laica que conservará para siempre. La poética de la Edad Contemporánea encuentra aquí una de sus dimensiones más fundamentales: Büchner, Valle, Pirandello, Lorca, Brecht, Beckett, Dürrenmatt... En la poética cervantina lo cómico se disocia por completo de la humildad social, que ocupa ahora un lugar nuclear en la tragedia, subrogando el hombre común a los antiguos atridas y a los modernos aristócratas, antaño protagonistas exclusivos de la *fábula* trágica. Simultáneamente, la religión no desempeña en *La Numancia* ningún valor funcional. Pese a la apoteosis contrarreformista, todo transcurre en un mundo pagano. Un mundo gentil que habrá de ser sacrificado por completo, y por la mano del hombre. Sin dioses. Sin profetas. Sin ministros de religiones normativas. *Numancia* es una tragedia deicida. Los numantinos fueron capaces de profanar, con su incredulidad en los númenes y su convicción ante el suicidio, todo el dogmatismo de la Contrarreforma. *Numancia* es ante todo una profanación. Es la secularización de la tragedia. Es la modernidad. Conciencia de libertad contra corriente.

El valor del destino y de las fuerzas supranaturales se encuentra en la *Numancia* formalmente referido, pero funcionalmente muy atenuado. Las invocaciones al mundo metafísico y suprasensible desempeñan en la tragedia un valor emotivo, formal o retórico, antes que discursivo o funcional; el resultado de las experiencias agoreras y adivinatorias no influye decisivamente en el curso de los acontecimientos ni en las decisiones de sus protagonistas. Más tienen a veces de escenas costumbristas que de hechos auténticamente reveladores de las secuencias funcionales de la acción. Son numerosos los momentos en los que, a lo largo de la *Numancia*, se alude a una realidad trascendente en la que no se identifica ni reconoce de forma explícita un poder superior, capaz de intervenir funcionalmente en el curso de los acontecimientos y acciones humanas. El propio Escipión, en su arenga a los soldados romanos, advierte, con claridad sorprendente para la época, que la fortuna nada tiene que ver con el desenlace del enfrentamiento que mantienen contra los numantinos, sino que es más bien el poder de la voluntad humana, la diligencia frente a la pereza, lo que ha de determinar, en el cerco de Numancia, el triunfo o la derrota de las tropas romanas. Sin duda la imagen de Marte a la que aquí alude Escipión preludia la pintura de Velázquez, en la que el dios de la guerra desmiente, con tu actitud distendida y abandonada, la expresión de cualquier acto heroico: "La blanda Venus con el duro Marte / jamás hacen durable ayuntamiento / [...] hállase mal el trabajoso marte" [I, 89-90 y 154]. Cervantes llega a afirmar que algo semejante a que cada ser humano es en cierto modo dueño de su propio destino, desterrando así la influencia de una realidad metafísica en el desarrollo de los asuntos humanos: "Cada cual se fabrica su destino, / no tiene aquí Fortuna alguna parte" [I, 157-158].

Desde el punto de vista de la poética, la *Numancia* cervantina se distancia de una exigencia fundamental para la tragedia antigua. Los dioses son ahora simplemente divinidades a las que se atribuyen agüeros en los que creen—o no creen, diríamos mejor—los personajes de la tragedia, pero en ningún momento los númenes intervienen directa o individualmente en el poema, ni de obra ni de palabra. La secuencia protagonizada por Leoncio y Morandro, que sucede a la comprobación oficial de los augurios que acaba de llevar a cabo la comunidad del pueblo numantino, confirma, desde el ámbito de la experiencia humana individual, la intención cervantina de contraponer al poder de los dioses y la superstición metafísica la solvencia de la razón y la voluntad del hombre. Las palabras de Leoncio se encuentran, en cierto modo, muy próximas a las de la arenga de Escipión a sus soldados: la fortuna y los agüeros nada tienen que ver con la voluntad y el "ánimo esforzado" del buen militar. Una vez más la acción de una realidad trascendente queda excluida del ámbito de la acción del hombre. Sólo una voluntad humana puede vencer el poder de la voluntad humana. Una interpretación radical de estas palabras podría llegar a identificar en el discurso de Leoncio un fondo nihilista inadecuado a la época en que escribe Cervantes; sin embargo, resulta imposible leer los enunciados de este personaje, concretamente en su diálogo con Morandro, sin percibir una declarada negación de la presencia del destino en la vida existencial del ser humano. El discurso de Leoncio enfrenta la voluntad humana con la metafísica, y niega el valor del destino y sus imperativos sobre las facultades volitivas del hombre, presididas siempre, desde el punto de vista cervantino, por el ejercicio de la libertad. Ni Edipo, ni Electra, ni Orestes, se atreverían jamás a repetir estas palabras sobre la existencia y el poder del orden moral trascendente que guiaba sus vidas.

Sin duda el silencio de los dioses es, en la concepción cervantina de un mundo trágico, mucho más expresivo que su verbo. En la modernidad es central el problema de la secularización: es época de dioses huidos. Aquí radica, sin duda, una más de las cualidades que hacen de la *Numancia* una de las primeras tragedias de la modernidad, al proponer una concepción del hecho trágico profundamente secular, por completo diferente a la exigida por la poética antigua. Cervantes es el primer dramaturgo de la historia de la literatura occidental que sustituye la Metafísica por la Historia: el *ananké* trágico no reside en los imperativos de los dioses, sino en el *fatum* de realidades históricas consumadas. La existencia humana no está ya determinada por una realidad metafísica. En adelante, los protagonistas de la tragedia serán seres humildes, no aristócratas elegidos por los dioses. Por último, la teleología de la experiencia trágica no será la confirmación de una realidad trascendente, numinosa y metafísica, sino que se verá sustituida por un referente nihilista en el que la historia deposita y disuelve a todo aquello que en alguna ocasión ha formado parte de ella. Büchner, Brecht, Beckett, Dürrenmatt... son algunos de los continuadores de la poética de *La Numancia*.

UNIVERSIDAD DE VIGO

Obras citadas

Blüher, Karl Alfred. *Seneca in Spanien. Untersuchungen zur Geschichte der Seneca Rezeption in Spanien vom 13. bis 17. Jahrhundert.* München: Francke, 1969. Trad. esp.: *Séneca en España. Investigaciones sobre la recepción de Séneca en España desde el siglo XIII hasta el siglo XVIII.* Madrid: Gredos, 1983.

Cervantes, Miguel, *La Numancia.* Ed. de F. Sevilla y A. Rey. Madrid: Alianza Editorial, 1996.

Carroll, Johnson B. *"Voces clamantes in deserto*: Cervantismo y materialismo en el contexto norteamericano." *Ínsula* 697-698 [2005]: 17-19.

Hermenegildo, Alfredo. *Los trágicos españoles del siglo XVI.* Madrid: Fundación Universitaria Española, 1961.

Hermenegildo, Alfredo. *La tragedia en el Renacimiento español.* Barcelona: Planeta, 1973.

Hermenegildo, Alfredo. "Hacia una descripción del modelo trágico vigente en la práctica dramática del Renacimiento español." *Crítica Hispánica* 7 [1985]: 43-45.

Hermenegildo, Alfredo. "Norma moral y conveniencia política. La controversia sobre la licitud de la comedia." *Revista de Literatura* 47 [1985]: 5-21.

Hermenegildo, Alfredo. *El teatro del siglo XVI.* Madrid & Gijón: Júcar, 1994.

Hermenegildo, Alfredo. "La tragedia: de Pérez de Oliva a Juan de la Cueva." *Historia del Teatro Español. De la Edad Media a los Siglos de Oro (I). Del siglo XVIII a la época actual (II).* Ed. Javier Huerta Calvo. Madrid: Gredos, 2003. 475-499.

Hermenegildo, Alfredo, ed. *El tirano en escena. Tragedias del siglo XVI.* Madrid: Biblioteca Nueva, 2002.

Hermenegildo, Alfredo, ed. *Teatro español del siglo XVI.* Madrid: Biblioteca Nueva, 1998.

Maestro, Jesús G. "Poética de lo trágico en el teatro de Miguel de Cevantes y de Georg Büchner." *Volver a Cervantes. Actas del IV Congreso Internacional de la Asociación de Cervantistas.* Ed. A. Bernat Vistarini. Palma de Mallorca: Universitat de les Illes Balears, 2001. 965-982.

Maestro, Jesús G. "Los límites de una interpretación trágica y contemporánea del teatro de Calderón: *El príncipe constante." Teatro calderoniano sobre el tablado. Calderón y su puesta en escena a través de los siglos. XIII Coloquio Anglogermano sobre Calderón. Archivum Calderonianum X.* Ed. Manfred Tietz. Stuttgart: Franz Steiner Verlag, 2003. 285-327.

Maestro, Jesús G. "El teatro de Cervantes y la literatura europea. El triunfo de la heterodoxia." *El teatro de Miguel de Cervantes ante el IV Centenario.* Ed. Jesús G. Maestro. Pontevedra: Mirabel Editorial, 2003. 15-45.

Maestro, Jesús G. *La secularización de la tragedia. Cervantes y 'La Numancia'.* Madrid: Ediciones Clásicas & University of Minnesota, 2004.

Ruiz Ramón, Francisco. *Calderón, nuestro contemporáneo.* Madrid: Castalia, 2000.

Vega Ramos, María José, ed. *Idea de la lírica en el Renacimiento. (Entre Italia y España).* Pontevedra: Mirabel Editorial, 2004.

The Poetic Unity of *Don Quixote* and Cervantes' Other Narrative Works

ERIC MAYER

I WOULD LIKE TO DISCUSS what I perceive to be a type of poetic unity existing among *Don Quixote* and Cervantes' other narrative works. Poetic unity, in the context of this discussion, refers to the presence in various Cervantine narratives of a certain narrative configuration that tends to elicit a specific type of reader response. This discussion's point of departure will be the general concept of perspectivism. This concept is general given that perspective can be discussed in a variety of ways in relation to Cevantes' work. We have for example, Américo Castro's framing of perspective based on the *ser-parecer* opposition, where a multiplicity of individual perspectives renders problematic the relationship between object and essence, something emblematized in the *baciyelmo* incident (*Pensamiento* 83). This example concerns character perspective without complicating reader perspective in any way, given that the object in question is known to be a barber's basin and not Mambrino's helmet. Otherwise, those studying the narratology of *Don Quixote*—most notably John J. Allen (1969) and James Parr (1988)— would illuminate the ways in which various textual sources and narrative voices and presences serve to complicate reader perspective by requiring him to navigate a labyrinth of discourse separating him from the highly elusive truth of things. David Castillo (2001) returned to the question of perspective via the concept of anamorphosis, a theoretical vehicle for studying the split in ideological perspectives observable in *Don Quixote* and other Golden Age texts. In trying to illustrate what I perceive to be a type of poetic unity among Cervantes' works, I will be dealing exclusively with reader perspective. Specifically, I'd like to describe some of the ways that Cervantine texts resist the coherent and unequivocal communication of their own content to the reader, with interpretative uncertainty being the result. In other words, a common trait of *Don Quixote* and other Cervantine narratives is that they often confront the reader with puzzling, incomplete, or contradictory information concerning such essential things as plot parameters and character motivation. Consequently, these textual phenomena have the potential to thwart the reader's comprehension of the story's most basic truth concerning who, what, where, and why. To illustrate this, I would like to provide examples from *La Galatea*, *Los trabajos de Perisles y Sigismunda*, and the *Novelas ejemplares*. By viewing *Don Quixote* within this context it will be possible to understand how some of the narrative innovations so often celebrated in the 1605 work are also characteristic of Cervantes' other works.

In Cervantes, reader perspective is made problematic owing to a certain narrative configuration which can be described as the conscious cultivation of a disparity between text and story. The "text" is, of course, the book the reader holds in his hands, with all of the print contained therein, and all the information that is made available to the reader via that printed matter. The "story" is simply the subject matter which the author [via narrator(s) and character] proposes to transmit to the reader in the text. When reading *Don Quixote* for the first time a reader may have certain expectations about the depth and breadth of information he will receive as to the life and exploits of the knight-errant, Don Quixote de La Mancha. Whatever those expectations might be, it is a fact that every reader of this book will forever be left wondering about the precise town of origin of our knight, just as he will never receive solid clarification of the protagonist's name in *Don Quixote* I.[1] As these two simple examples illustrate, the disparity exisiting between text and story — or how the text fails to transmit basic information implied in or even essential to the story — encompasses the various narratological issues arising in *Don Quixote*, concerning the multiple, unreliable, and incomplete sources and treatments of the protagonist's biographical data, all of which are reminders of the text's ultimate inability to transmit the whole "truth" of the story. Thus, my purpose here is simply to call attention to the tension inhering in these texts (and experienced by the reader) arising from the author's paradoxical literary project of telling stories whose fascination often lies in their own resistance to be told.

The examples given so far have touched on the narratology of *Don Quixote* and I am certainly not saying anything new by indicating how that

---

[1] I would add that the name "Alonso Quijano el Bueno" is just as uncertain as the other possibilities, given the established fallibility of the various "histories" comprising the book.

narrative is structured as a disparity between text and story. Yet, it seems to me that this slippage and the problems of interpretation that this might pose for the reader are not unique to *Don Quixote* and turn up fairly frequently in Cervantes' other narratives, especially the *Novelas ejemplares*, although *La Galatea* and the *Persiles* each have at least one major sub-plot structured along these same lines. The first example is the episode of Teolinda and Artidoro from *La Galatea*. The interpretative uncertainty arising from this episode is a function of a narrator prone to strategic silences, as he fails to relay the underlying truth of certain events which the reader does not "witness" for himself and which are otherwise ambiguously or incompletely relayed via the characters themselves. The result is that the reader is forced to make a number of assumptions over the course of the story, the latent truth of which is never made manifest by story's end. One could say that this episode from *La Galatea* exemplifies the narratological "elusiveness" that Américo Castro identified in *Don Quixote* (*Hacia Cervantes* 300-01).

Teolinda's retrospective narration becomes one of various lengthy stories within the story of *La Galatea*. It happens that her narration contains an anecdote—the story within a story within a story, so common to Cervantes—with which she prefaces her narration. The intertextual relevance of this anecdote merits a brief summary. Lidia, who is in love with Eugenio, comes crying to Teolinda, telling her that a "cinta encarnada" she had given Eugenio had recently been spotted in the possession of Leocadia, another girl from the same village (216-17). [2] Furthermore, Eugenio had disappeared from the environs "sin decir[l]e nada" to Lidia. For Lidia, the ribbon and Eugenio's absence become signs indicating a love affair existing between Eugenio and Loecadia: "por donde se me ha confirmado la sospecha que yo tenía de los amores que el traidor con ella trataba" (216). Teolinda laughs and tells her to not "hacer caso de semejantes niñerías" and that she would do better to tend to her *honra* and her flock (217). Teolinda's cavalier attitude toward Lidia's woes will now be subject to ironic treatment. For, unbeknownst to Teolinda, her own misadventures in love begin in a fashion exactly like those of Lidia, from mere suspicions based on circumstantial evidence: an absent boyfriend and an anonymously authored poem. And, as with Lidia, the underlying truth of Teolinda's suspicions will never receive clarification in the text.

---

[2] All citations are from *La Galatea*, eds., Francisco López Estrada and María Teresa López García-Berdoy, (Madrid: Cátedra, 1995).

Teolinda falls in love with Artidoro, a "pastor forastero" who visits her village (216). Having decided to marry, they arrange that he will depart and in three day's time will send "alguna honrosa tercería" to ask Teolinda's parents for her hand in marriage (241). Here, we learn that Teolinda has a twin sister named Leonarda. The following day, Leonarda returns from grazing her sheep and tells Teolinda of a strange encounter befalling her: an unnamed man approached her and began treating her in a very familiar manner, calling her Teolinda. Leonarda's frigid reception of the man left him "llamándo[la] ingrata, desagradecida y de poco conocimiento" (243). Teolinda, shocked at this news, believing this man to have been Artidoro, dissimulates in order to keep her engagement a secret. The following morning, unable to locate Artidoro to "desengañarle del error en que había caído," suddenly sees some verse etched into a tree (244-45). It is unsigned and describe's a suitor's failed love. The poem ends with what could be an allusion to suicide: "tendré por dulce partido / si fui vivo aborrecido / ser muerto y por ti llorado" (248). Teolinda believes the verse to be Artidoro's and, concerned that he might "poner en ejecución lo que en los últimos versos dejó escrito," she abandons her home and flock to search for him.

Before continuing, we must take stock of what has transpired. Teolinda's decision to leave home springs from two events. The first is Leonarda's fateful and deceptive encounter with an unnamed shepherd whom Teolinda assumes to be Artidoro (the reader, like Teolinda, can only assume the man confronting Leonarda was Artidoro, for he is never named with certainty; also it was not Artidoro who was to return to the village but rather "alguna honrosa tercería"). Second, she sees the unsigned verse carved into the tree and assumes it to be Artidoro's: "claramente entendí que los versos que había leído eran de mi querido Artidoro" (248). Thus, the recognitions about which Teolinda's narration is structured are — like Lidia's — peculiar in that they are tenuously circumstantial. The omniscient narrator, ever silent, is of no help to the reader in deciphering the authenticity of the signs being read: was the man encountered by Leonarda really Artidoro?; was the verse on the tree authored by Artidoro? These questions will remain unknown for the remainder of the tale. Far from gratuitously cross-examining our fiction, this inquiry into the nature of Teolinda's (and the reader's) knowledge is useful in determining just how the author sets up the final recognition scene. For, if these initial recognitions are characterized by a lack of epistemological grounding, then they will culminate in a recognition scene which, for the reader, will only elicit more questions rather than bring closure.

In Book IV, Teolinda and Leonarda cross paths with a man they both recognize. Teolinda recognizes him as Artidoro, while Leonarda recognizes him as somebody else, Artidoro's twin brother, Galercio, with whom Leonarda had been romantically involved: "Leonarda creyó que el pastor era su querido Galercio, y Teolinda tuvo por verdad que era su enamorado Artidoro" (460). Thus, we have a double recognition the certainty of which is yet to be decided, given that what one character "believes" is just as uncertain as what the other "takes as true" (and the narrator has yet to set things straight). Leonarda's insistence that the man is Galercio and Teolinda's refusal to believe this invites the intercession of a third party, Rosaura, who never actually speaks with Galercio directly, but rather with his sister, Maurisa. She then informs Teolinda and Leonarda that the man in question "se llamaba Galercio y que tenía otro llamado Artidoro, que le parecía tanto que apenas se diferenciaban si no era por alguna señal de los vestidos o por el órgano de la voz, que en algo difería" (461). For his part, Artidoro "andaba en unos montes algo de allí apartados, repastando parte del ganado de Grisaldo... y que nunca había querido entrar en el aldea ni tener conversación con hombre alguno después que de las riberas de Henares había venido" (461). While this news makes Teolinda "sosegada," it leaves Leonarda "descontenta, viendo cuán descuidadas estaban las mientes de Galercio de pensar en cosas suyas" (462). That is, Galercio, still reeling from Gelasia's ill treatment of him, seems not to recognize Leonarda (whether he can even distinguish between the sisters is still another question). When his sister finally informs him of the two girls' identity, he simply "se despidió de ellas y de los pastores, y con su hermana dio la vuelta a su aldea" (463).

Thus, what begins to unfold as a simple recognition tale ends by posing questions, for reader and character alike. First, neither Teolinda nor the reader ever learns if Artidoro was indeed the man deceived by Leonarda; Maurisa's reference to her brother's desire to never return to "las riberas de Henares" allows only inference that Teolinda's suspicions were actually well founded. Thus, the reality underlying of Teolinda's life-transforming recognition and flight from home is never made concrete. Oppositely, whether Artidoro has truly abandoned his plans to marry Teolinda is never clarified in the text; one is left assuming along with Teolinda. Secondly, we have two sisters recognizing the same man each taking him to be somebody different. Only after circuitous questioning of his sister by Rosaura do we learn his identity. Not only does he never speak to the sisters, but he also never indicates that he recognizes either of them. Thus, we are left with what can only be called unrequited recognition: the recognized never reciprocates recognition, and final recognition among all parties, including Artidoro, never occurs within what remains of the book. Far from a satisfying Aristotelian "move from ignorance to knowledge," all that this scene yields up is the information that this man is Galercio, while the reader, and especially the characters themselves, have yet to fully clarify the underlying causes of the girls' problematic relationships, something which is never resolved within what remains of the book.

The second example is an episode from *Persiles* and tells the story of Feliciana de la Voz. Feliciana, pregnant by her lover Rosanio, one day goes into premature labor. The baby is delivered just as her father enters her room. The father recognizes the presence of the crying baby, unsheathes his sword, and hunts for the child of his disgraced daughter. Feliciana escapes, but knows not the whereabouts of the baby, who was spirited away by a servant. Later, when presented an infant that appears likely to be hers, she fails to recognize it as hers. She admits that never having really examined the child, she has no way of telling which child might be hers: "Y si yo la viese, si no por el rostro, pues nunca le he visto..." (295).[3] She then realizes that she might recognize the infant by its swaddling clothes, but that attempt also fails. Finally, the infant in question had been left with a gold chain belonging to the biological father; yet, Feliciana states that she has never seen such a chain in the father's possession. Finally, all hope of this being Feliciana's child seems lost when she is described as not feeling any instinctive or biological bond to the child: "[l]leváronsela, miróla y remiróla, quitóle las fajas; pero en ninguna cosa pudo conocer ser la que había parido, ni aun, lo que más es de considerar, el natural cariño no le movía los pensamientos a reconocer el niño" (297). Throughout this examination the reader has been left in the dark, uncertain as to the child's true identity owing to the suppression of the narrative voice. Feliciana then decides to leave for Rome, a move that threatens completion of the recognition process.

Having made their way to Guadalupe, the pilgrims enter a church. Feliciana begins to sing and her voice is recognized by her father, who tries to stab her. At that moment a group of noblemen arrives, including Rosanio, the father of Feliciana's child. Rosanio defends Feliciana from her angry father and brothers. Don Juan de Orellana, Rosanio's friend and present guardian of the infant, pleads with her brother, Don Sancho, to desist from

---

[3] All citations are from *Los trabajos de Persiles y Sigismunda*, ed., Juan Bautista Avalle Arce (Madrid: Castalia, 1992).

revenge, informing him that he has a newborn nephew who looks just like him: "Mirad, señor Don Sancho, que tengo una prenda vuestra en mi casa, un sobrino os tengo, que no le podréis negar si no os negais a vos mismo: tanto es lo que os parece" (308). Don Sancho, stunned by this revelation, offers no resistance as his father takes the dagger from his son's hand. Subsequently, amends are made and violence averted.

Ultimately, recognition is achieved, but under the most bizarre and epistemologically tenuous circumstances. First, the recognition is not of a child by a parent, but of an absent child by his grandfather and uncle solely on the basis of a verbal assertion of a physical family resemblance ("tanto es lo que os parece"); that is, the child is not even present in this scene. Secondly, the recognition that truly matters is the one between mother and child. Not only was this once denied by Feliciana, but it never does occur as the episode comes to a close. The multiple disconnects in this recognition scene are not left unresolved by the narrator, who, given the general lack of epistemological grounding, is finally forced to set the record straight: "y en este tiempo, que fue el de tres días, envió Don Francisco [Feliciana's father] por el niño que le había llevado la labradora, que era el mismo que Rosanio dio a Periandro la noche que le dio la cadena..." (309). Here, the reader arrives at the truth of things, but not without having to once again review the details of prior events, reconstructing the circumstances of recognition, which have come to assume the form of a narrative puzzle. Thus, a recognition does occur, yet it is oddly incomplete, as the tale ends without Feliciana recognizing her own child, as far as the reader knows.[4]

Just as in the example from *La Galatea*, the episode of Feliciana de la Voz elicits interpretive uncertainty owing to the text's resistance to clearly and coherently communicate the underlying truth of its own story. As Todorov would say, "the essence has not made itself clear" (902). What differenciates the two episodes is that "what really happens" is never manifested in the example of Teolinda, while in the case of Feliciana the narrator suddenly intervenes at the last moment in order to confirm the heretofore inaccessible truth of the child's identity. Yet, this does not resolve all complications. That Feliciana never did and never does recognize her child is a looming question that the reader must deal with on his own with no assistance from the narrator. Thus, again we have a disparity between text and story, given that both stories continue to hold latent content that is never made manifest, and

---

[4] See Sacchetti (2001) and Mayer (2004).

hence resolved, in the text.[5] Furthermore, the fact that both of these are recognition tales, or tales structured on *anagnorisis*, is significant in that both stories have been configured in a way that plays creatively on the neo-Aristotelian preoccupation with epistemological rigor in the composition of recognition tales.[6] Rather differently, Cervantes appears to have recognized the artistic potentialities in writing stories not along the lines of systematic and clear revelation of concealed truths – as so revered by neo-Aristotelians in Sophocles' *Œdipus Tyrannus* – but rather by the nearly reverse process of cultivating mystery in the text and uncertainty in the reader precisely where clarification and closure would be expected. This cultivation of mystery which we just observed in two works emerges, of course, in Don Quixote in a variety of ways, some subtle (Don Quixote's underlying and tantalizingly underarticulated orientation toward women, so thoughtfully analyzed by Carroll B. Johnson [1983]) and some not so subtle (the obfuscation of Don Quixote's "true" identity). In all cases a mystery exists as an underlying reality in the story that achieves only fragmentary, yet deliberate articulation in the text. Perhaps the *Novelas ejemplares* go the farthest to illustrate this point..

In light of the idea that much of *Don Quixote* and certain parts of *La Galatea* and the *Persiles* are configured as a disparity between the content of the story and the incomplete articulation of this content in the text, then a number of examples to illustrate this point are found in the *Novelas ejemplares*. *La ilustre fregona* offers various examples of which we will cite three. The most obvious is found in the final scene, in which Costanza's identity is finally revealed, as her biological father comes to take custody of

---

[5] Normand Holland first used the terminology "latent content" and "manifest content." In making use of Holland's terminology for its descriptive value, I have modified its theoretical application, namely that Holland's application of "latent content" is psychoanalytical, while I merely use it to describe what is left un- or underarticulated in the text.

[6] Castelvetro believed that recognition should unfold with a logically rigorous presentation of the signs and unfolding of events ("cose") of recognition: "per successione di cose dipendenti l'una dall'altra" (I, 474). Likewise he insists that recognition should arise logically from the story's action, or "per la constituzione delle cose" (I, 460). *Œdipus Tyrannus*, with its carefully crafted piecemeal recognition, became a paradigm for this technique of systematic, logical, and irrefutable revelation of underlying truth. Logic and certainty are also factors in the neo-Aristotelian interest in a particular example of *anagnorisis* cited by Aristotle from the *Odyssey* having to do with paralogism, or false logic. See Cave 75-78.

her. What is odd about this scene is that the reader learns the identity of the father, yet the father, for reasons left unclear, suppresses the name of the mother, describing her in the vaguest of terms.[7] Thus, we never learn the complete truth of Costanza's identity, the newly revealed truth of which is fundamentally incomplete.[8] Tzvetan Todorov would describe this strategic suppression of information as being like so many unknowable "secrets" found in Henry James' short stories (901).

A second example is when Don Diego sees Costanza at the inn for the first time. R.M. Price has observed (1989) the curious anachronism in the fact that Don Diego has never before seen Costanza, yet seems to recognize her when seeing her for the first time. As Costanza approaches the two men, Don Diego remarks, "Yo creo, señor, don Juan, que hemos hallado todo aquello que venimos a buscar" (II, 191). Just as puzzling as this comment is a question he poses a Gallegan maid. After the girl informs him as to Costanza's duties at the inn, he asks: "Luego esta niña, a esa cuenta [. . .] debe de dejarse manosear y requebrar de los huéspedes" (II, 192). Very deliberately, Carriazo has just inquired about Costanza's chastity, but in an oblique way. Only after verifying this, does he seek out the innkeeper to effect the recognition test: "Contentísimo quedó el caballero de lo que había oído a la Gallega, sin esperar a que se le quitasen las espuelas, llamó al huésped... ." (II, 192). The point here is that Don Diego, having come to identify his daughter, has begun by ascertaining her chastity. On one level, this could be a parody of the test of female chastity found, for example, in the final recognition scene in the *Aethiopica*.[9] On another level, it has the effect of shattering the idealism of the tale by introducing an element from the "real" world, in which determining Costanza's worth as a woman in seventeenth-century Spain is now the issue, rather than simply determining

---

[7] "El padre--respondió Don Diego--yo lo soy; la madre ya no vive: basta saber que fue tan principal, que pudiese yo ser su criado. Y porque como se encubre su nombre no se encubra su fama, ni se culpe lo que en ella parece manifiesto error y culpa conocida, se ha de saber que la madre desta prenda, siendo viuda de un gran caballero, se retiró a vivir a una aldea suya, y allí, con recato y con honestidad grandísima, pasaba con sus criados y vasallos una vida sosegada y quieta" (I, 194). All citations are from *Novelas ejemplares*, Harry Sieber, ed. (Madrid: Cátedra, 1997).

[8] A related mystery involves just how the *mayordomo* would know to contact Don Diego upon the death of Costanza's mother, given that both rapist and rape victim remained anonymous to eachother.

[9] In Book X, 382, Chariklea's chastity is proven to her parents and others as she emerges unscathed from a sacrificial fire.

her consanguinity, which is the usual function of recognition and the ostensible purpose of Don Diego's visit to the inn. Nevertheless, how her chastity becomes a factor in Don Diego's decision to claim her is a perplexing question, about which the narrator offers no clarification. The fact that he soon thereafter arranges for her to marry Tomás would appear to indicate Don Diego's foreknowledge of events to later unfold at the moment he posed the question (chastity could become a factor if marriage were imminent) thus creating one of many "secrets" embedded in this text.

La Gitanilla and *El amante liberal*, while different in various ways, conlcude by posing a similar problem of interpretation for the reader. Both tales conclude with radical and seemingly inexplicable character transformations. Many readers have commented on the silence held by Preciosa after learning of her true identity. This silence not only contrasts with her previous character development, it also contrasts with what a reader might expect of a character after being reunited with her parents. Preciosa displays little if any affection for her newfound family. More strangely, within the remainder of the tale, she never again speaks with her *abuela*, the woman who cared for her for the past sixteen years. Much is left undescribed and hence is left unresolved in this final scene, namely Preciosa's underlying motivation. In addition to the traditional symbolical or allegorical interpretation her behavior, one would be justified in interpreting Preciosa's uncharacteristic behavior as simply one more example of a Cervantine text that cultivates mystery by creating a disparity between the content of the story (what motivates Preciosa) and the incomplete articulation of this content in the text.

The ending of *El amante liberal* similarly confronts the reader with a sudden and radical transformation of character, which gives rise to various interpretative dilemmas. First, the reader is asked to believe that Ricardo is now, by offering Leonisa to Cornelio, abandoning his only goal in the story: marriage to Leonisa. This strikes one as implausible from any angle. Second, this change in behavior is traditionally attributed to Ricardo now being a spiritually transformed man, yet this transformation is nowhere described in the text. Third, if he has undergone a spiritual transformation, then one might expect him to recognize the truly serious error he committed in attacking Leonisa, Cornelio, and the latter's family. To be sure, Ricaredo mentions that violent encounter in the garden. However, when doing so, he rhetorically transforms himself into the victim and eliminates all mention of his violence: "Bien se os debe acordar… de la desgracia que algunos meses ha en el jardín de las Salinas me sucedió con la pérdida de Leonisa...." (I, 185). Fourth, Ricardo does finally experience a recognition, but it is not the recognition of this truly egregious error. Rather the error he now recognizes is that of having tried to give what is not his, a recognition of his own "liberalidad." Thus, if Ricardo is now a transformed man capable of recognizing the error of his ways, then, as he frames it, his only error now appears to be no error at all, or at least an error beyond reproach: the paradoxical "error" of excessive generosity.[10] In any case, one can observe how the traditional allegorical interpretation of Ricardo's transformation is a response to a text in which articulation of "what really happens" in these final scenes is left conspicuously incomplete.

   La española inglesa is a story fraught with such moments in which a lack of description of "what really happens" in the story leaves the reader with various unanswerable questions. These moments of interpretative impasse are often subtle, yet can also be quite overt. A more overtly problematic example is Ricaredo's delayed arrival in Spain after leaving his family home. He concocts a plan to escape from home to flee to Spain and marry Isabela. His ruse is simply to tell his parents that he must visit Rome to "assure his conscience" before being married to Clisterna: "no se casaría ni daría la mano a su esposa la escocesa sin haber primero ido a Roma a asegurar su conciencia" (I, 271). That is, as far as the reader knows, the idea of travel abroad is smoke and mirrors meant to fool his parents so as to be able delay the arranged marriage and flee to Spain. Yet, it happens that Ricaredo does travel abroad for some two years before arriving in Spain. Why he simply does not go to Spain on leaving his home is not justified in the text and is a mystery which Isabela herself (via the narrator) invites the reader to ponder: "Luego imaginó Isabela, que el haber dejado Ricaredo a Inglater[r]a sería para venirla a buscar a España... " (I, 274).[11] Again, one experiences the

---

   [10] Gonzalo Díaz-Migoyo offers an insightful look into the logic of Ricardo's "giving what is not his": "En vez de liberalidad es un simulacro de liberalidad; en vez de dar, Ricardo hace como si diera. No sólo porque no pueda dar lo que no tiene, como él dice---cuestión práctica concebiblemente contraria---, sino porque, le falta por decir, no es posible que nadie pueda demostrarse liberal de aquello que sigue deseando--imposibilidad, esta vez, lógica; situación inconcebible cuya existencia sólo puede ser verbal" (71).

   [11] It happens that Ricaredo had also told Isabela to be prepared to wait for him in Spain for a period of no more than two years, by which time he would arrive (I, 271). More interpretative problems ensue when ones tries to comprehend this request of his, given that the proposed pilgrimage is, again, simply a ruse, as far as

text's failure to communicate the whole story and, in this case, the text will go so far as to call attention to the story's inaccessibility, an example of self-reflexivity rather reminiscent of *Don Quixote*. A subtler example would be the mystery surrounding the disparity in information contained in a letter received by Isabela versus what Ricaredo later tells us.[12]

In conclusion, in celebrating 400 years of *Don Quixote*, there is something to be gained by reconsidering this monumental work within the context of Cervantes' other narratives. There is a discernible similarity in the way Cervantes configured his texts to elicit interpretative uncertainty in the reader by carefully controlling reader access to information in the story. One could say that the poetic unity of Cervantes' narrative works rests on what might be called a poetics of uncertainty, a narrative configuration based on the deliberate underarticulation in the text of information that is essential to a coherent telling and basic comprehension of the "true" story. Whatever one makes of the many mysteries found in these texts, they are a part of what makes Cervantes' work a literary universe that continues to fill with wonder and delight those deciding to journey into its seemingly limitless expanses.

Works Cited

Allen, John. J. *Don Quixote: Hero or Fool? A Study in Narrative Technique*. University of Florida Press, Gainsville: 1969.

Castelvetro, Ludovico. *Poetica d'Aristotele vulgarizzata e sposta*. 1576. 2 vols. Ed. Werther Romani. Roma: Laterza, 1978.

Castillo, David. *(A)wry Views: Anamorphosis, Cervantes, and The Early Picaresque*. Purdue University Press, 2001.

Castro, Américo. *Hacia Cervantes*. Madrid: Taurus, 1960.

---

the reader and Isabela know. That fact that a number of events beyond his control later befall him during the next two years (to the day, incidentally) only show his request for two years time to be one of various mysteries in this tale that obscure a clear understanding of this character's motivation and of the exact parameters of the plot itself.

[12] Isabela receives a letter falsely stating that Ricaredo had been killed killed in France (I, 275). Then, in Ricaredo's own narration he says he was attacked (but obviously not killed) in Aquapendente, Italy (I, 280). This along with Isabela's brief meditation on whether somebody might "fingir" Ricaredo's death inspires questions as to the letter's origin and its inaccuracies, the most egregious being the false report of Ricaredo's death.

————. *El pensamiento de Cervantes.* 1925. Barcelona: Noguer, 1972.

Cave, Terence. *Recognitions: A Study in Poetics.* Oxford: Clarendon, 1988.

Cervantes, Miguel de. *Don Quixote de la Mancha.* 2 vols. Ed. Luis Andrés Murillo. Madrid, Castalia: 1978

Díaz-Migoyo, Gonzalo. *La Diferencia novelesca: lectura irónica de la ficción* (Madrid: Visor, 1990).

————. *Historia etiópica de los amores de Teágenes y Cariclea.* Trans. Fernando de Mena. Heliodorus Ed. Francisco López Estrada. Madrid: RAE, Bibioteca selecta de clásicos españoles, 1954.

Holland, Norman N. *The Dynamics of Literary Response.* New York: Oxford UP, 1968.

Johnson, Carroll B. *Madness and Lust: A Psychoanalytical Approach to Don Quixote.* University of California Press: Berkeley and Los Angeles, 1983.

Mayer, Eric D. "Homer, Heliodous, and Cervantes: Some Observations on Anagnorisis in *Los trabajos de Persiles y Segismunda.*" *Comitatus* 35 (2004): 108-23.

Parr, James. *Don Quixote: An Anatomy of Subversive Discourse.* Newark, DE: Juan de la Cuesta, 1991.

Price, R.M. "Cervantes and the Topic of The Lost Child Found.'" *Anales Cervantinos* XXVII (1989): 203-214.

Sacchetti, Maria Alberta. *Cervantes' "Los trabajos de Persiles y Sigismunda": A Study of Genre.* London: Tamesis, 2001.

Todorov, Tzvetan. "The Structural Analysis of Literature: The Tales of Henry James" ["Le secret du récit"]. Trans. David Robey. In *The Critical Tradition: Classic texts and Contemporary Trends.* Ed. David H. Richter. New York: St. Martin's, 1989.

Scientific and Technological Imagery in *Don Quijote*

CORY REED

WHEN DON QUIJOTE ATTACKS the windmills he is, both literally and figuratively, thrown for a loop. Cervantes writes that the *ersatz* knight "embistió con el primero molino que estaba delante; y dándole una lanzada en el aspa, la volvió el viento con tanta furia, que hizo la lanza pedazos, llevándose tras sí al caballo y al caballero, que fue rodando muy maltrecho por el campo."(I, 8: 82) Instantly creating for posterity the most widely recognized iconographic image associated with the ingenious *hidalgo*, Don Quijote's topsy-turvy encounter with the revolving mechanical arms of the windmill encapsulates the essence of the quixotic impulse. The episode demonstrates the hero's obsession with the chivalric literature on which he has modeled his life, it concisely expresses the thematic preoccupation with the illusory nature of worldly appearances, and it establishes the conflicting worlds of knight and squire, which sets the stage for the dramatic tension that drives their relationship as the story progresses.

The encounter with the windmills also shows us a protagonist who is so consumed with the way of life of a bygone era (and, more specifically, a fictionalized representation of that era) that he cannot comprehend the changing world around him, at least not at first. The episode contrasts an outmoded, scholastic world view that localizes truth in the written word with another that understands an empirical basis for the realities of existence. Don Quijote, who lives in and through the books he reads, quite expectedly relies on their textual authority for his interpretation and comprehension of reality. But the real world of seventeenth-century Spain is a world of windmills, artillery, fulling mills, printing presses, mechanical contraptions, modern judicial processes, and political and economic realities that have neither precedence nor explanation in chivalric literature. Lost in a fantasy world that never existed in an era long gone, the doubly-anachronistic knight cannot come to terms with these trappings of early modern

167

existence, a reality which, at every turn, throws obstacles in his path and thwarts his noble project of reviving the long-lost "ciencia de la caballería" and the pre-industrial, utopian Golden Age.

Whether considered a reference to capitalist agrarian production, a *costumbrista* reminder of daily rural existence, or a symbol of Spanish decadence throwing off the personified figure of a Spain that refuses to modernize, the windmills need to be recognized for what they are in the simplest of terms: machines. Windmills were a ubiquitous presence in the Castilian countryside, indicative of mankind's successful mechanization of nature in an era of tremendous scientific and philosophical change. Consequently, windmills, perhaps more than any other machine available to Cervantes, effectively proclaim the widely recognized advent of technological progress. Appearing in Castile only a century before Cervantes's birth and having undergone a design improvement that increased their proliferation during the author's lifetime, windmills were an ever-present high-tech symbol of the sixteenth century and were acknowledged contemporaneously as such. In other words, the windmill may be understood as representing metaphorically the modern world that is at odds with Don Quijote and with which the protagonist engages in a continuous struggle.

The turn of the seventeenth century was a period of transition not only in what we would now call the scientific realm, but also in the social, political, philosophical, and artistic arenas. The new Copernican cosmology, which began circulating throughout Europe in the second half of the sixteenth century, proposed a heliocentric universe, departing from the Ptolomaic-Aristotelian model that had been embraced by the medieval scholastic tradition, and significantly influencing the curriculum in Spanish universities before such views were judged heretical. The rise of humanism as an intellectual endeavor sought a reconciliation of classical authority with Christian doctrine by recuperating original texts and abandoning the medieval interpretations written by the schoolmen or Muslim commentators. The development of mechanics promised greater efficiency in labor while increasing human domination of the natural environment. In politics, the era witnessed the advent of the modern nation-state, the further consolidation of political power in the monarchs and their bureaucracies, and the development of a citizenry whose sense of national identity was participatory by way of taxation and election of local officials.

Cervantes comments in his novel on these and many other transformations that characterized the period in which he lived and wrote. In the figure of Don Quijote, he creates an individualized protagonist who confronts these changes, who cannot comprehend them at first, and then who gradually accedes to the modern world, learning to "tocar las apariencias con la mano para dar lugar al desengaño" (II,11: 613) as he loses his hold on the medieval episteme he had fought to revive. Don Quijote's confrontations with machinery and with the burgeoning empiricist thought of his age come to serve as a metaphor for this brave new world of social and scientific change.

Someone once asked me how Cervantes could know anything about scientific issues; after all, he was only a novelist. (This person, by the way, was a tenured mathematics professor.) But it's important to remember that in the seventeenth century, "science" as a unique academic discipline or methodology, as we now know it, did not exist. Investigating the nature of the world was called natural philosophy, and the related field of technological inquiry was known as mechanical philosophy. The classical division of the trivium and quadrivium, further elaborated upon by Muslim scholars and Christian scholastics during the Middle Ages, implied a theoretical divisibility of knowledge into units, but all areas of intellectual inquiry were considered equally "sciences" in the time. Cervantes uses the term in this way on several occasions, including during the dialogue between Don Quijote and Don Lorenzo, the son of Don Diego de Miranda, in Part Two. In their discussion of liberal education, Don Lorenzo asks the knight:

—Paréceme que vuesa merced ha cursado las escuelas: ¿qué ciencias ha oído?

—La de la caballería andante—respondió don Quijote—, que es tan buena como la de la poesía, y aun dos deditos más.

—No sé qué ciencia sea ésa—replicó don Lorenzo—, y hasta ahora no ha llegado a mi noticia.

—Es una ciencia—replicó don Quijote—que encierra en sí todas o las más ciencias del mundo. (II, 18: 664-65)

In addition to the aforementioned science of poetry, Don Quijote then goes on to provide a long catalogue of sciences of use to the knight errant, including jurisprudence, theology, medicine, astrology, and mathematics.

The term "science" in Cervantes's day commonly denoted any quantifiable field of knowledge. Natural philosophy, like other "sciences," was the domain of all intellectuals, including writers, and it was firmly grounded in the observation of the material world. What we now term "science," then, was not understood as separate from other philosophical questions, particularly in the context of the changing face of cosmology, for example, which had theological, metaphysical, political, and even artistic ramifications.

Steven Shapin describes a fundamental reordering of thinking that occurred in Europe during the sixteenth and seventeenth centuries (Shapin 2). He identifies four principal aspects of this reordering: the mechanization of nature (through the development of useful technology), the depersonalization of knowledge (the growing separation of subject and object and the rise of "objectivity"), the mechanization of knowledge itself (through the creation of rules and methods to regulate the production of knowledge), and the use of the resulting knowledge to achieve moral, social, and political ends (Shapin 13), what Jessica Wolfe also refers to as "instrumentality" or the application of mechanized knowledge and methods to social and political realms (Wolfe 1). The so-called Scientific Revolution witnessed the development of machinery to dominate and control nature, such as the windmill and, perhaps even more significantly, the clock, which radically transformed human management of time and came to symbolize the perceived inherent order of nature itself and a model for social and political stability.[1] The new emphasis on empiricism and direct observation challenged the traditions of scholasticism and its reliance upon textual authority and precedence, although Spain self-consciously would embrace a return to scholasticism in the face of what it eventually came to define as heresy.

The transitional period in which Cervantes lived and wrote was epistemologically fluid, fraught with inconsistencies, and characterized by fundamental changes that could not entirely be appreciated in their own time. Wolfe accurately describes the sixteenth century rise of mechanical philosophy as heterogeneous, characterized by simultaneous "competing doctrines and attitudes." (Wolfe 1). There was no singular, unified belief system that guided the development of scientific and technological ideas in the late sixteenth century. A rich diversity in approaches to knowledge and

---

[1] See, for example, Antonio de Guevara's *Reloj de Príncipes* (1529).

to its practical uses percolated throughout Europe in the early modern period, with its forward-looking embrace of human potential even reaching Counter-Reformation Spain while the Spanish outlook still remained open to European influence. Science, as we now call it, at the turn of the seventeenth century, was a changing, unstable system of ideas, concepts, and inventions, rather than the systematic or codified methodology to be conferred upon scientific thought a century later by Newton and Descartes.

José María López Piñero understands the last three decades of the sixteenth century in Spain as a period of tension between receptivity to new ideas and self-conscious closure, culminating in the triumph of a regressive Counter-Reformation mentality, rendering Spanish thought "completamente de espaldas a los nuevos plantamientos" while Europe forged ahead with its Scientific Revolution (López Piñero 19). By the century's end, Counter-Reformation scholasticism would transform several decades of aperture into closure. The turn of the seventeenth century marks in Spain what Carlos Valverde Mucientes calls "la *Segunda Escolástica* o ... la *Escolástica española*" (Valverde 170) and consists of a simultaneous withdrawal from new ideas considered threatening to old hierarchies and a deliberate return to the methodology and teachings of the schoolmen. The dictum of the age, "todo lo nuevo aplace," which seems to reflect a societal preoccupation with novelty, is thus not without its dark side. New ideas were fine, as long as they did not constitute a challenge to the Hapsburg dynasty's increasingly dogmatic Catholicism. Like Don Quijote, then, Spanish scientific development took a deliberate and self-conscious step backward in the face of the forward march of modernity, a regression to be challenged only a century later when the pace of the Enlightenment was so great that Spain had no choice but to become integrated.

To be sure, the late sixteenth century represents scientific change in its infancy, brought about in an *ad hoc* fashion by various sectors of society, each idea conceived of within its own contexts, without full knowledge of the cross-disciplinary impact it would later have. What these disparate methods and technologies had in common was a rising belief in empiricism and the power of direct observation, a positive conception of mechanization that characterized not only machines but also method, technique, and outlook in practical applications as well as in the realms of politics and social productivity, and a sense of playfulness and excitement about the wonders of the natural world and man's ability to harness, manipulate, and control it with increasing ease.[2]

Thomas S. Kuhn describes this kind of epistemological change as a "paradigm shift." According to Kuhn, a paradigm is a system of accepted theories and practices designated as normative in a given era (Kuhn 10). Paradigms change or shift when the tenets of normative science no longer are sufficient to explain observable phenomena. This insufficiency precipitates a crisis, which can be resolved by either the amplification of the normal science or the emergence of a new paradigm and a battle over its acceptance (Kuhn 84). The Scientific Revolution represents one such paradigm shift. It is a reordering of thinking, characterized by the mechanization of nature and knowledge, the rise of empiricism to replace scholasticism, the destruction of Aristotelian cosmology, and the application of method to nearly all fields of human endeavor. These developments, and the philosophical, political, and spiritual ramifications thereof, contributed to the climate of intellectual change that was hotly and openly debated in Cervantes's time as the forces of Counter-Reformation conservatism threatened to squelch this incipient progress.

We also must remember that change in this period had practical concerns beyond philosophical, cosmological, or theoretical implications. Spain, in particular, maintained throughout this time of increasing closure an avid interest in mechanics and technology, those aspects of the emergent Scientific Revolution less likely to be viewed as heretical and more likely to produce useful, practical applications. Spain remained in the foreground of technologies it found useful, including navigation, artillery, and other practices necessary for maintaining its political and commercial interests at home and abroad. Many of these same technologies, artillery in particular, would serve Cervantes as the bane of Don Quijote's chivalric existence. In juxtaposition with the anachronistic knight's values of a pre-technological Golden Age and the pastoral ideal, these machines would come to represent the "edad de hierro" so detested by the protagonist.

A particularly fascinating example of the interest in mechanics is the pictorial genre of machine books known as the *theatrum mechanorum*, which circulated widely throughout Europe and Spain in the late sixteenth and early seventeenth centuries. In the most basic of terms, a *theatrum mechano-*

---

[2] For further discussion of the playful dimension of Renaissance science and its capacity to reveal illusion in the *Quijote*, see my article, "Ludic Revelations in the Enchanted Head Episode in *Don Quijote*," *Cervantes* 24.1 (2004): 189-216.

rum is a compendium of descriptions and illustrations of machines and ingenious devices whose purpose was as much to celebrate human ingenuity as to catalogue practical inventions and their applications. Throughout Europe, the *theatrum mechanorum* enjoyed popularity evidenced by multiple reprints, multilingual editions, and translations that suggest widespread circulation. The genre flourished at the end of the sixteenth century with the work of Jacques Besson and Agostino Ramelli in France, Vittorio Zonca in Italy, and Juanelo Turriano in Spain. Besson's *Théâtre des instrumens mathematiques et mechaniques* (1569, with reprints in 1578, 1579, and 1594) gave the *theatrum mechanorum* its name. The 1578 and later editions included illustrations depicting existing instruments as well as designs for original devices, such as an improved lathe, and what may be the first workable screw-cutting machine for woodworking (Bunch 133). A Spanish translation, published in 1602 with the original illustrations, establishes Besson's circulation in Spain. Figure 1 illustrates Besson's ingenious screw-cutting device, demonstrating his inventiveness in conceiving of unique and original devices through the application of mechanics. A descriptive prose commentary corresponding to details on the pictures establishes the conventions of this pictorial genre and its delight in the artistry of machines as well as their technological achievements.

Ramelli's *Diverse e artificiose macchine* (Paris, 1588) described simple and complex machines from mills and hydraulic devices to ingenious automata. His detailed diagram of a windmill and its working parts is considered the earliest complete illustration of this ubiquitous machine (Bunch 134). He also includes instructions for building speaking statues, reminiscent of Don Antonio's enchanted head in Part Two of the *Quijote*, and a fanciful book-wheel, or reading machine with multiple lecterns revolving around a gear shaft, similar in structure to a water wheel. Figure 2, one in a series of plates elaborating upon the horizontal waterwheel, shows Ramelli's improvement of existing designs, with an emphasis on innovation and greater efficiency. The horizontal waterwheel (in which the wheel itself is horizontal, respective to a vertical shaft) represented a design improvement for milling technology in areas with limited water resources. A number of Ramelli's machines improve further upon this design by submerging the waterwheel in order to reduce shock and turbulence. Figure 3 illustrates Ramelli's book-wheel, another testament to Renaissance ingenuity, drawing associations between mechanics and the creative imagination in conceiving of such original instrumentation. In this case, Ramelli fancifully applies technology to make privatized reading more accessible and pleasurable. In both figures, Ramelli's inventions strive to accomplish difficult tasks with ease, inspiring a sense of wonder in the reader, and presenting technology as a visual, artistic spectacle to be viewed and appreciated.

In Spain, the *theatrum mechanorum* culminates in *Los veintiún libros de los ingenios y máquinas* of Juanelo Turriano, evidently commissioned by Philip II in the 1580s or sometime thereafter. True to the *theatrum* genre, Juanelo's work is an exceptionally detailed catalogue of known technologies, with emphasis on hydraulic machines and their functions, as well as more imaginative devices that display the Renaissance playfulness of scientific and technological inquiry. Juanelo lists fifteen separate mill designs, apparently based on empirical observation, and includes the most detailed schematic drawing of a functioning windmill found in sixteenth century Spain. Figure 4 shows Juanelo's windmill, documenting the technical aspects of its construction and use, although the description is not nearly as complete as in the corresponding sections of Ramelli. Figure 5, possibly derivative of Ramelli, illustrates Juanelo's improved technology for the horizontal waterwheel, turning multiple wheels with the same water source to maximize efficiency.

A related genre of illustrated military treatises complements the development of the *teatrum mechanorum*. Among them, Roberto Valturio's *De re militari* was published in Verona in 1472, but enjoyed renewed popularity through multiple reprints in the sixteenth century. Valturio's work, dealing specifically with military technology and war machines, details a wide array of practical and imaginative inventions, including tower fortifications, hoists and levers, cannon improvements, and armored ships. He also includes fanciful designs, such as an armored tank in the shape of a fierce animal and a multiple cannon-laden war machine in the form of a dragon. In figure 6, we see an early precedent for the association of war machinery with diabolical influences, a Renaissance commonplace found in Milton, for example, as well as Cervantes. Valturio's machine expresses a clear consciousness of technology being caught between eras. It not only celebrates the modern era and the ingenuity of its new war machines, but also contemplates the past in the form of the dragon, associated with fantastic chivalric lore from the story of St. George through medieval tradition. In a sense, Valturio's mechanical dragon prefigures Don Quijote's comments in his discourse on arms and letters about the "endemoniados

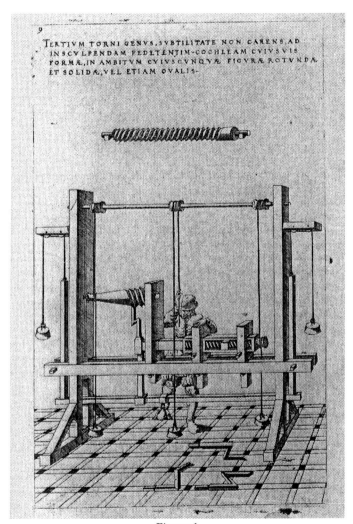

Figure 1

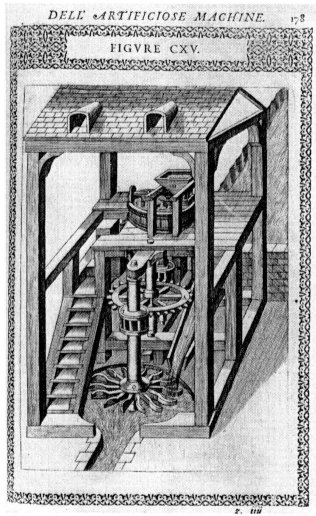

Figure 2

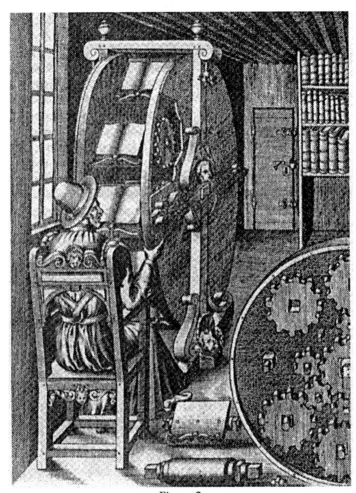

Figure 3

instrumentos" of artillery being a "diabólica invención" (I, 38: 393) and his consciousness of being caught between two incompatible eras.

As we can appreciate in Valturio, Ramelli, Besson, and Turriano, technological imagery in the early modern period suggests an underlying self-consciousness, an awareness of modernity's definition in opposition to the past that is intrinsically nostalgic. There is a tension in the very instability of Renaissance mechanics, nervously reflected in its disparate, inconsistent, and experimental technological practices prior to the emergence of coherent scientific method. By virtue of their very newness, early modern machines reflect a kind of nostalgia for the pre-industrial period, which Don Quijote would call "la edad de oro."

The *theatrum mechanorum* is, in effect, the aesthetic manifestation of a theoretical and practical interest in machines and the effects of mechanization. Renaissance treatises on mechanics displayed a high level of technical proficiency balanced by an intellectual curiosity and artistic inventiveness bordering on the playful. As Wolfe asserts, "Designed for the printed page, Renaissance machines are born out of the demands and concerns of a humanistic culture, contrived to pose and answer intellectual, aesthetic, and moral questions even at the expense of their own effectiveness."(Wolfe 238) The *theatrum mechanorum* evidences a conception of the machine as a metaphor for modernity, the new, the improved, and the innovative, cast in aesthetic terms as well as technical ones. These treatises have in common a celebration of human ingenuity, of mankind's triumph over the natural world through mechanization, and of accomplishing difficult tasks with ease (a concept closely related to the Renaissance court culture of *sprezzatura*). They reflect a consciousness of becoming, of participating in a process of advancement, creating, as Wolfe says, a sort of aesthetic of instrumentality that propels Renaissance society forward, embracing human ingenuity and reveling in the creation of artful illusions.

Cervantes's literary use of technological imagery likewise views machines as avatars of progress, mechanization as an emblem of modern existence, and instrumentality as a testament to the power of artifice through the mediation of *industria* and *ingenio* (two concepts which Cervantes routinely praises in numerous episodes of his novel) Here it is interesting to reflect momentarily on the multiple meanings of the terms *industria* and *ingenio*: the former, *industria*, which implies a mechanization and organization of human creativity as a process or method, speaking to Wolfe's concept of instrumentality; and the latter, *ingenio*, which not only

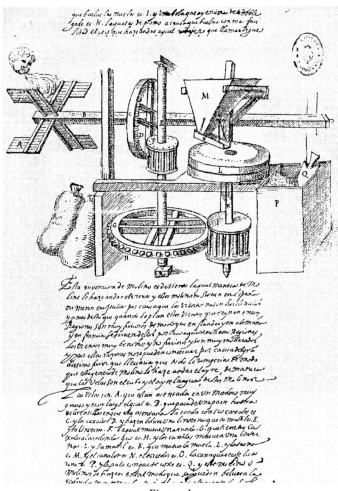

Figure 4

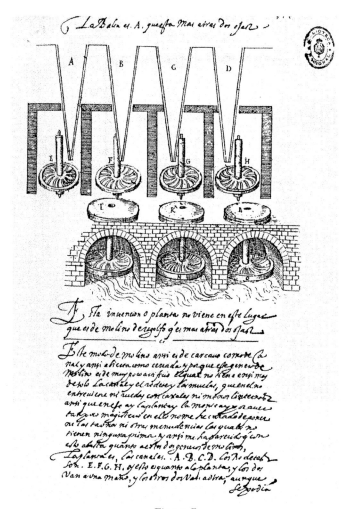

Figure 5

Figure 6

refers to human ingenuity but also in technical language means "engine" or "machine," and in rhetorical terms means "wit," associated with aesthetic concepts of *agudeza*.[3]

I have tried herein to articulate briefly a theoretical framework for the analysis of technological imagery in the *Quijote*, focusing on machines as metaphors of modernity and instrumentality as Don Quijote struggles to come to terms with a modern world he does not fully understand, at first rejecting it but eventually acceding to it as empiricism and observation replace his scholastic reliance upon textual authority as a basis for the determination of reality. Time does not allow for a detailed consideration of each of the many episodes in the *Quijote* involving technology, but perhaps a brief overview will hint at some of the possibilities inherent in such an analysis.

The windmills adventure (I, 8), as mentioned earlier, represents Don Quijote's first confrontation with the machinery of the modern world. Here we see technology defeating the knight, as the passive machine, with no connection to either providence or heroism, literally turns the knight and his medieval world-view upside-down and demonstrates the violent consequences of his reliance upon the written word when that model inevitably breaks under the weight of empirical reality. As Don Quijote moves toward his ultimate *desengaño*, his character evolves, and he continues to confront technology at significant points in his formative journey of self-discovery.

In direct contrast with this adventure, in which Don Quijote fails at first to recognize technology that he is familiar with, the episode of the *batanes* (I, 20) shows how the protagonist recognizes another kind of innovative milling technology (fulling mills, or water wheels retrofitted with hammers to flatten textiles) despite his never having seen one. This episode, which also evokes comparisons to giants ("seis jayanes," I, 20: 188) and lofty claims of chivalric destiny, dialogues implicitly with the windmills adventure, showing the beginnings of a change in Don Quijote's engagement with the modern world. For the first time, experience raises a crisis in his fantastical episteme and the knight is forced to recognize what his senses report to him. Don Quijote talks about the importance of experience, calling it in his own words, "la madre de las ciencias todas," (I, 21: 191) and beginning the initial stages of a paradigm shift. The knight begins to recognize the challenges that the modern world presents to his revival of the pre-industrial Golden

---

[3] I elaborate in more detail on these dualities in my forthcoming book on scientific and technological imagery in the *Quijote*.

Age, a project which Sancho mocks derisively at the end of this chapter. In Part Two of the novel, Don Quijote further develops this recognition of the importance of experience, concluding, as mentioned above, "que es menester tocar las apariencias con la mano para dar lugar al desengaño." (II, 11: 613)

A third episode involving milling technology, of course, is the adventure of the enchanted boat, a significant step in Don Quijote's overall movement toward *desengaño* in that he resigns himself to defeat at the hands of modernity. Don Quijote articulates his awareness of the complexity of the changing world around him and his inability to understand it, saying, in effect, "I give up," when he utters: "Dios lo remedie: que todo este mundo es máquinas y trazas, contrarias unas de otras. Yo no puedo más." (II, 29: 755) As the windmills episode establishes the parameters of Don Quijote's madness, this episode, involving mills of another type, begins the final breakdown of Don Quijote's fantasy world. From this point, we see a pensive, introspective Don Quijote who is repeatedly abused and defeated by those around him, leading to the eventual renouncement of chivalry on his deathbed. We also see how Don Quijote gradually acknowledges the world around him, and speaks quite eloquently about contemporary issues such as education, ethics, law, governance, and marriage.

Don Quijote's additional encounters with technology include his ongoing diatribe against the evils of artillery in which he adopts a common view in an age when technological advancement outpaces the rest of society: that machines and technology are evil and can bring about the downfall of civilized existence. The question raised here is the role of technology when it surpasses our own moral capacity to evaluate it. The ersatz knight also has numerous adventures with ingenious mechanical contraptions including Clavileño (a mechanical horse whose imaginary flight helps Sancho challenge Don Quijote's medieval conception of cosmology), and a speaking automaton in the adventure of the enchanted head, which deconstructs Don Quijote's belief in enchantment for Cervantes's reader, reducing it to technological innovation and *ingenio*. Don Quijote's final encounter with a printing press in the urban center of Barcelona reveals that books, the authoritative sources of truth in his chivalric world, are commercial products mass-produced for a modern consumer market in which the printed word is now dependent upon technology for its existence.

By the end of Part Two, Don Quijote recognizes, and is sometimes forced to recognize, that experience and observation are keys to understanding the world. By coming to this realization, Don Quijote also must admit that there is no place for his anachronistic existence in such a world. In his novel, Cervantes articulates an epistemological contrast between conflicting eras through the use of technological imagery and related metaphors of change. The protagonist's confrontations with various machines depict a time of technological modernization in which Spain itself, like Don Quijote, was struggling with the inconsistencies of a text-based, scholastic understanding of the world and fighting the inevitable embrace of empiricism and modernity as symbolized by technological advancement.[4]

Works Cited

Besson, Jacques. *Théâtre des instrumens mathématiques et méchaniques*. Lyon, 1578.

Bunch, Bryan and Alexander Hellmemans. *The Timetables of Technology. A Chronology of the Most Important People and Events in the History of Technology*. New York: Simon and Schuster, 1993.

Cervantes, Miguel de. *Don Quijote de la Mancha*. Ed. Martín de Riquer. Barcelona: Juventud, 1979. 2 vols.

Kuhn, Thomas. *The Structure of Scientific Revolutions*. Second Edition. Chicago: U Chicago P, 1970.

López Piñero, José María. *La introducción de la ciencia moderna a España*. Barcelona: Ariel, 1969.

Ramelli, Agostino. *La Diverse et artificiose machine*. Paris, 1588.

Shapin, Steven. *The Scientific Revolution*. Chicago: U of Chicago P, 1996.

Turriano, Juanelo. *Los veintiún libros de los ingenios y máquinas de Juanelo Turriano*. Ed. Fundación Juanelo Turriano. 7 vols. Madrid: Doce Calles, 1996.

Valturio, Roberto. *De re militari*. Paris, 1532.

Valverde Mucientes, Carlos. "La filosofía." *El siglo del* Quijote *(1580-1680). Religión, Filosofía, Ciencia*. Vol. 1. Madrid: Espasa Calpe, 1996. 161-247.

Wolfe, Jessica. *Humanism, Machinery, and Renaissance Literature*. Cambridge: Cambridge UP, 2004.

[4] I am grateful to the Program for Cultural Cooperation Between Spain's Ministry of Culture and United States Universities for its generous support for research related to this paper.

Reading Male Pregnancy in *Don Quijote* in its Early Modern Context

SHERRY VELASCO

MUCH HAS BEEN WRITTEN about Cervantes' use of male maternity as metaphor for intellectual fertility in the prologue to *Don Quixote*. Scholars tend to agree that the reproductive imagery was consistent with similar metaphors used by Juan Huarte de San Juan in his 1575 scientific treatise on humors and aptitude (*Examen de ingenios para las ciencias*), which describes men's intellect and creativity in terms of fertility and childbirth. Just as Huarte uses the language of procreation to explain what makes men *ingeniosos*: ("Se empeña y pare y tiene hijos y nietos... se llaman genios por ser fecundos en producir y engendrar conceptos tocantes a ciencia y sabiduría" [188-89]), Cervantes follows Huarte's lead when he explains to his "desocupado lector": ¿qué podrá engendrar el estéril y mal cultivado ingenio mío sino la historia de un hijo seco, avellanado, antojadizo y lleno de pensamientos varios y nunca imaginados de otro alguno" (50).

While many critics have analyzed Cervantes' novelistic prologue in Part One, less has been written on the masculine reproduction theme in chapter 47 of *Don Quixote*, when the topic of male pregnancy resurfaces during a conversation between the Barber and Sancho. When the Barber accuses Sancho of being of the same humor or wit as Don Quixote, his comments reengage the interconnections among reproduction, creativity, and delusion: "¡...Por lo que os toca de su humor y de su caballería! En mal punto os empreñastes de sus promesas, y en mal hora se os entró en los cascos la ínsula que tanto deseáis" (563) (see also Ziomek 115 and Río Parra 149). Of course Sancho is unable to recognize the other usage of *empreñarse* intended by the Barber (which is defined by Covarrubias as "El que fácilmente cree lo que le dizen parece empreñarse de palabras, porque las aprehende y

185

concibe de manera que totalmente excluye lo contrario" [509]). Sancho's defensive response reveals his literal understanding of the reproductive imagery, thereby implying a perceived insult in terms of "procreative sodomy": "—Yo no estoy preñado de nadie—respondió Sancho—, ni soy hombre que me dejaría empreñar, del rey que fuese" (563).[1]

Given the Barber's reference to Sancho becoming "impregnated" with his master's promises and the consequent fixation on the *ínsula*, it may be more than a coincidence that the male pregnancy theme resurfaces in Part Two when Sancho actually does become governor of Barataria. In chapter 43 of Part Two, while Don Quixote continues to give advice to the first-time politician, it is the narrator who describes Sancho metaphorically as a pregnant leader who expectantly awaits the birth of his new government: "Atentísimamente le escuchaba Sancho, y procuraba conservar en la memoria sus consejos, como quien pensaba guardarlos y salir por ellos a buen parto de la preñez de su gobierno" (360). In other words, Sancho becomes impregnated by the promises of an *ínsula* in Part One, and in Part Two he finally gives birth to his long-awaited dream. In fact, if we follow Mauricio Molho's theory of the femininization of Sancho and the folkloric origins of his suggestive *panza*, the next step would logically imply male pregnancy.

Perhaps worth noting for our discussion here, in Avellaneda's continuation of Cervantes' best-seller, the knight's new squire at the end of the apocryphal novel literally *does* give birth, as Don Quixote looks on in amazement at what initially appears to be a miraculous male delivery. Of course the reader knows that the squire is actually a pregnant woman disguised in men's clothing:

> Llevando por escudero a una moza de soldada … vestida de hombre, la cual iba huyendo de su amo porque en su casa se hizo o la hicieron preñada, sin pensarlo ella, si bien no sin dar cumplida causa para ello; y con el temor se iba por el mundo. Llevóla el buen caballero sin saber que fuese mujer, hasta que vino a parir en medio de un camino, en presencia suya, dejándole sumamente maravillado el parto. (462)

Despite its comical intent as well as the narrator's judgment of the young servant, the passage allows us a possible glimpse into the fear and

---

[1] For more on "procreative sodomy," see Knight.

isolation that an unmarried pregnant woman with limited economic and social resources might have experienced during that time.

When considering the possible significance of the male matrix in Cervantes' *Don Quixote*, we might first examine how this imagery surfaced in other popular texts during the early modern period in Spain. The concept of male reproduction was not new in the seventeenth century and as a result Cervantes' prologue and other references to male pregnancy in *Don Quixote* participated in a well-established tradition of male autogenesis, dating back Greek philosophers and scientists, who believed that "the male alone was the true parent" (Zoja 115). Likewise, examples of childbirth as metaphor for the "labor" of literary invention abound throughout the early modern period. Many critics, in fact, have noted the connection between the embryological debate during the seventeenth century and how male writers expressed their creative literary processes in terms of pregnancy and reproduction. Raymond Stephanson, for example, argues that "Just as preformationist theories gave way to more complex embryological views of fetal development and sequential growth from apparently unorganized material, tropes of the pregnant male brain turned increasingly to ideas of enigmatic but purposeful growth within the creative mind" (109-110). In her study on male births and the scientific imagination in early modern England, Ruth Gilbert describes how men appropriated images of birth in their intellectual and technological aspirations while attempting to avoid the abject connection to women and the "messier" aspects of reproduction. When discussing this practice in early modern France, Kirk Read similarly concludes that canonical male writers masculinize maternity in order to empower their writing.

Along similar lines, in European folklore, legends of male pregnancy have persisted in numerous versions and adaptations for centuries. The pregnant man motif is present in texts such as Boccaccio's *Decameron* and numerous variations of Aesopic fables. In his review of some of the Spanish versions of male pregnancy (as well as the figure of the couvade), François Delpech demonstrates that this figure has been utilized since the Middle Ages for varying purposes that include both serious and ennobling as well as comical or grotesque.

When we review some of the cultural references to male deliveries with which readers of *Don Quixote* might have been familiar, we discover a variety of literary, theatrical, scientific, and tabloid-style texts that could easily have inspired connections with Cervantes' novel. For example, a fascinating news item published in Barcelona just one year after the publication of the first part of *Don Quixote*, narrates the strange tale of a man from Granada named Hernando de la Haba, who became pregnant and gave birth to a monstrous creature. The description of Hernando's delivery demonizes the birthing experience with details that shock and entertain the reader. In this *relación* (attributed to Pedro Manchego) we first find Hernando in labor, seated on a chair or birthing stool, as a midwife coaches him through the painful delivery. The newborn not only emerges from the man's anus, but the demonic imagery is reinforced by the fact that the creature had no sooner been born when it violently scratches the midwife's face. The reader later discovers that Hernando's pregnancy was caused by the actions of a vindictive ex-lover with whom he broke an engagement before marrying another woman. After the jilted lover sought the help of a sorceress (who convinced the man to ingest her special "medicine"), the husband soon finds his belly swollen and confesses his condition to his wife: "Vive Dios que estoy preñado,/ porque en la barriga siento/ que me dan brincos y saltos." When his wife touches his belly she concurs: "Por Dios hermano,/ que teneys razón, no ay duda,/ que el diablo os ha empreñado" (Manchego, n.p.).

Later (under torture) the old witch confesses the contents of her evil potion but the narrator will only state that "por ser tan suzio y feo,/ le dexo passar en blanco" (Manchego, n.p.). Given the anal imagery, demonic involvement, and the need for silence, Pierre Cordoba supposes the presence of sperm in the concoction (325). Not surprisingly, the narrative of this creature's birth has been compared to other accounts of the birth of the Antichrist, thus tracing its paternity to the Devil (Cordoba 320-327 and Delpech 563). After the shocking delivery, the authorities investigate the case and discover that an old sorceress was to blame, and once she is paraded, ridiculed, and executed in public the text reveals its misogynistic message to the male readers: "Abrid los ojos señores/ no os fiéys de malas hembras/ ... Mirad que son gusanillos/... que os van chupando la sangre/... Son víboras ponçoñosas/... Guardad no os hagan parir/ como hizo esta alcahueta/ a este hombre" (Manchego, n.p.).

As José González Alcantud argues, it is not by chance that this fantastic tale takes place among a community of *moriscos* during a conflictive period in Granada, not long before their expulsion. And whether the news pamphlet was intended to further criminalize this marginalized group through its details of monstrosities and sorcery, the narrative reveals a much bigger fear: women's power to alter or manipulate reproductive issues that can impact men in dangerous and terrifying ways.

Not unlike the reception of the American tabloid *Weekly World News*'s July 7, 1992 issue ("Man Gives Birth to a Healthy Baby Boy!") it is difficult to know exactly how these sensationalist *relaciones* were interpreted by seventeenth-century consumers.[2] We do know, however, that Lope de Vega refers to the 1606 news pamphlet in his 1609 play *La octava maravilla*. The playwright apparently takes advantage of the tabloid-style *relación* to show the naïve nature of "uncivilized" Spaniards (perhaps not unlike Sancho) who are inclined to believe such tales (Morley and Bruerton 40). When Motril praises the verses that narrate the story of a man who gives birth in Granada, Don Juan laments the gullibility of people like Motril: "¡Qué se sufre tanto error!/ mas concreto se confirma/ la barbaridad de España" (Vega, *Octava* 255) (Cordoba 308 and Caro Baroja 51-53). Of course the author of the news pamphlet (using the penname Pedro Manchego) addresses both the unbelievability of the story as well as the topic of barbarous nations to confirm the veracity of his news item.

Interestingly, Lope de Vega had already incorporated the idea of male pregnancy (around the time that Cervantes was drafting the first part of *Don Quixote*) in the plot of another play that contrasts the "civilized" urban protagonists with barbarous Spaniards from an isolated region of Extremadura in *Las batuecas del Duque de Alba* (written between 1598 and 1600 and was published in 1638) (Morley and Bruerton 173, 362 and Delpech 579). When Brianda (disguised as a man named Celio) gives birth and is found nursing the newborn, "he" is able to convince some of the gullible inhabitants of the remote mountain village that men from the city are capable of getting pregnant and giving birth.

Surely the readers of *Don Quixote* had been exposed to these popular representations of male pregnancy on stage in Lope's *comedias* and through the news pamphlet of 1606. Likewise, mid-century readers may have seen the enormously popular actor Juan Rana perform a carnivalesque male delivery in Lanini y Sagredo's *entremés El parto de Juan Rana*. Two-thirds into the one-act play the (in)famous cross-dressed and pregnant celebrity (who years earlier had been arrested for sodomy) appears on stage, bemoaning his plight in song. When his water breaks, he quickly goes into labor, screeching in pain as two other men come to his aid by holding him up while he

---

[2] See "A Gallery of Pregnant Men" http://www.sscnet.ucla.edu/ioa/arnold/arnoldwebpages/pregmen.htm

narrates the delivery. Suddenly his newborn son (who is played by a young actress) pops out from under his long skirt. The *entremés* ends with the lively song and dance by father and son, as the other officials soon join in the festivities. Interestingly, Juan Rana has the final word, answering the "what if men could give birth" question by confirming the long-held fear that men can never really be sure of their children's identity as long as women are the ones who give birth.

Like the prologue to *Don Quixote*, this *entremés* begins by highlighting the relationship between biological procreation and men's intellectual fertility. As the interlude opens and the local officials are discussing Juan Rana's crime of being a pregnant mayor, their dialogue reflects Huarte's scientific theories of "ingenios." Since brain power is tantamount to social power, in *El parto de Juan Rana* the dilemma created by an individual who (as a man) should not have the biological capacity to bear children but who (as a political leader) should possess the intellect to give birth to new concepts and solutions, is carried to farcical proportions. In a conversation between the mayor Berrueco and the notary, the two men play with sexual and political meanings of sterility and fertility: The Escribano asks: "¿Necedad es bien rara/ fecundo quereis que sea?" while Berrueco replies: "Pues la vara/ a un alcalde absoluto/ ¿de que provecho le es,/ si no da fruto?" (220). The Escribano then questions the comparison: "¿La vara comparáis agora al sexo?" (220). Berrueco answers: "Vos, escribano, no entendéis bien de eso;/ una vara concibe dos mil cosas/ luego puede parirlas prodigiosas" (220).

Of course in the *entremés* the *vara* or rod of patriarchal power and authority also serves as a phallic symbol of the protagonist's sexual behavior that led to the present scandal. Conversely, just as Sancho adamantly denies any suggestion of procreative sodomy in chapter 47 of Part One, when he becomes a local political leader in Part Two, he does not possess a *vara* but does prove to be surprisingly *fecundo* in terms of giving birth to new solutions while on the job.

Interestingly, Cervantes returns to the pregnant man motif in chapter 8 of book three of *Los trabajos de Persiles y Sigismunda*. Tozuelo, as we remember, cross-dresses in a country dance wearing the clothing of his pregnant girlfriend in order to protect her from the possible dangers of miscarriage: "Ella está encinta, y no está para danzar ni bailar" (329). Tozuelo's interesting solution to the risk of miscarriage complies (in spirit, at least) with the recurrent recommendations for pregnant women and their husbands during the early modern period. In his 1529 *Relox de príncipes*, for example, Antonio de Guevara urges husbands not to allow their pregnant wives to be too active, as pregnant women should avoid running, dancing, or jumping; reminding them also that women who "bounce around" acquire a bad reputation (393). While the author assigns blame for the miscarriage to the woman ("this all happens because of women's actions, they become the author of their own homicides... It is their own fault that they miscarry,") he also includes a specific section on the role that men can play to ensure the successful pregnancy of their wives: "The husband should keep his wife from doing a lot of work ... since it is a rule for pregnant women that too much work makes them miscarry" (402).

While Diana de Armas Wilson describes Tozuelo's cross-dressing as a "rare literary act of male nurturing" (47), she also acknowledges the more problematic association with male transvestism: "An ad hoc 'pregnant male,' Tozuelo's liminality seems pointedly daring in [the] light of... how transvestism was used, in Cervantes's Spain, as part of the death sentence for homosexuality" (47), referring to the practice of parading convicted sodomites in women's clothing and curled hair as they walk to their death (see also Garza and Donnell).

Of course, popular theater, *relaciones*, and fictional narratives were not the only cultural spaces to explore the topics interconnected to the male matrix. The medical community had long been debating possibilities for mutations in sex assignment. Fray Antonio de Fuentelapeña's seventeenth-century treatise on monstrosities, for example, reveals fascinating analyses of men who transmuted into women and of men who gave birth (229-248). Fuentelapeña confirms the existence of men who were known to have given birth but explains this phenomenon through a "hidden hermaphrodite" argument. In other words, the men who became pregnant and gave birth without the participation of a woman actually had female reproductive organs hidden inside their bodies. Although the author does not explain how these previously unidentified androgynes were impregnated, his argument implies that potentially any man could have the capacity to procreate, given a hermaphroditic condition unbeknownst to him and to others.

In light of the context in which Cervantes' novel was created and interpreted, we might assume that the references to the male matrix in both parts of *Don Quixote* as well as in the *Persiles* participated in a cultural dialogue involving issues inherent in male pregnancy: namely an enduring preoccupation with paternity, power, and the control over reproduction as well as the fear of sexual activity between men. Moreover, since the veracity of the *relaciones* is not questioned in the narratives, the image of a pregnant man may become less implausible in the minds of certain early modern consumers, perhaps those who, like Sancho, easily allow themselves to become impregnated by the ideas conceived by other men's *ingenio*.

UNIVERSITY OF KENTUCKY

Works Cited

Avellaneda, Alonso Fernández de. *El ingenioso hidalgo don Quijote de la Mancha, que contiene su tercera salida y es la quinta parte de sus aventuras*. Ed. Fernando García Salinero. Madrid: Castalia, 1987.

Caro Baroja, Julio. *Ensayo sobre la literatura de cordel*. Madrid: Revista de Occidente, 1969.

Cervantes, Miguel de. *El ingenioso hidalgo don Quijote de la Mancha*. Ed. Luis Andrés Murillo. Madrid: Castalia, 1982.

Cordoba, Pierre. "L'homme enceint de Grenade. Contribution a un dossier d'histoire culturelle." *Mélanges de la Casa de Velázquez* 23 (1987): 307-330.

Covarrubias, Sebastián de. *Tesoro de la Lengua Castellana o Española*. Barcelona: Editorial Alta Fulla, 1989.

Delpech, François. "La patraña del hombre preñado: algunas versiones hispánicas." *Nueva Revista de Filología Hispánica* 34.2 (1985-86): 548-98).

Donnell, Sidney. *Feminizing the Enemy. Imperial Spain, Transvestite Drama, and the Crisis of Masculinity*. Lewisburg: Bucknell UP, 2003.

Fuentelapeña, Fray Antonio de, *El ente dilucidado: Discurso único, novísimo que muestra hay en la naturaleza animales irracionales invisible, y cuáles sean*. Ed. J. Ruiz. Madrid: Editora Nacional, Biblioteca de visionaries, heterodoxos y marginados, 4, 1978.

Garza Carvajal, Federico. *Butterflies Will Burn. Prosecuting Sodomite in Early Modern Spain and Mexico*. Austin: U of Texas P, 2003.

Gilbert, Ruth. "Masculine Matrix: Male Births and the Scientific Imagination in Early-Modern England" in *The Arts of 17th-Century Science. Representations of the Natural World in European and North American Culture*. Ed. Clair Jowitt and Diane Watt. Aldershot and Burlington: Ashgate, 2002: 160-176.

González Alcantud, José A. "Monstruos, imaginación e historia. A propósito de un romance." http://www.alyamiah.com/cema/modules.php? name= News&file=article&sid= 32

Guevara, Fray Antonio de. *Obras completas, II. Relox de príncipes*. Madrid: Biblioteca Castro, 1994.

Huarte de San Juan, Juan. *Examen de ingenios para las ciencias*. Ed. Guillermo Serés. Madrid: Cátedra, 1989.

Knight, Rhonda. "Procreative Sodomy: Textuality and the Construction of Ethnicities in Gerald of Wales's *Descriptio Kambriæ*." *Exemplaria: A Journal of Theory in Medieval and Renaissance Studies* 14.1 (2002): 47-77.

Lanini y Sagredo, Francisco Pedro. *Entremés de El parto de Juan Rana*. Transcription by Peter Thompson. Comedia Performance 1.1 (2004) 219-237.

Manchego, Pedro. *Retrato de un monstruo, que se engendró en un cuerpo de un hombre, que se dize Hernando de la Haba, vezino del lugar de Fereyra, Marquesado de Cenete, de unos hechizos que le dieron. Parteole Francisca de León, comadre de parir, en veynte y uno de Junio, de 1606, por la parte tras ordinaria.* Compuestas por Pedro Manchego, vezino de Granada. Barcelona: Sabastian de Cormellas al Call, 1606.

Molho, Mauricio. "Doña Sancho (*Quijote*, II, 60)." *Homenaje a José Manuel Blecua*. Madrid: Gredos, 1983, 443-448.

Morley, S. Griswold and Courtney Bruerton. *The Chronology of Lope de Vega's Comedias*. New York: Modern Language Association and London: Oxford UP, 1940.

Río Parra, Elena del. *Una era de monstruos: Representaciones de lo deforme en el Siglo de Oro español*. Madrid: Iberoamericana, 2003.

Stephanson, Raymond. *The Yard of Wit. Male Creativity and Sexuality, 1650-1750*. Philadelphia: U of Pennsylvania P, 2004.

Vega, Lope de. "Las batuecas del Duque de Alba." *Obras de Lope de Vega*. Ed. Marcelino Menéndez Pelayo. Madrid: Atlas, 1968. 351-403.

———. "La octava maravilla." *Obras dramáticas*. Madrid: Sucesores de Rivadeneyra, 1930. 247-285.

Zoja, Luigi. *The Father. Historical, Psychological and Cultural Perspectives*. Trans. Henry Martin. New York: Brunner-Routledge, 2002.

Ziomek, Henryk. *Lo grotesco en la literatura española del Siglo de Oro*. Madrid: Ediciones Alcala, 1983.

Debate: Did Cervantes Make Mistakes?

THE FINAL EVENT OF the symposium was a debate between Dan Eisenberg and Tom Lathrop with the title above. Both debaters agreed that Cervantes did make mistakes. It was Dan's contention that the mistakes were more or less careless, and it was Tom's contention that the mistakes were more or less planned. A good time was had by all. The debaters were undeniably eloquent and passionate in their arguments.

The event was ably refereed by Mike McGaha. Rules were made up as the debate developed.

The winner was determined by audience applause. Dan was declared the winner. The loser was to buy the winner a nice dinner. This festive repast has not yet taken place.

Tom, Mike, and Dan after the debate.
Photograph made wth a cell phone.

OT 7 / X 229

Printed in the United States
48019LVS00006B/260

9 781588 710888